C000128601

Cryptocurrency Mining

2nd Edition

by Peter Kent and Tyler Bain

for
dummies®
A Wiley Brand

Cryptocurrency Mining For Dummies®, 2nd Edition

Table of Contents

Introduction

Welcome to *Cryptocurrency Mining For Dummies.* We're here to help you enter the wonderful world of cryptocurrency mining. Of course, you don't need our help. You can just go to Google or some other major search engine, search, and jump right in. You'll find plenty of information to help you!

Hah! Try it and see. It'll be like drinking from the proverbial firehose — you'll drown in a flood of confusing blog posts, conflicting "news" articles, unintelligible wiki articles, misleading YouTube videos. . . .

So that's where we come in. Our job is to break it all down into intelligible, easy-to-digest, bite-sized pieces that ordinary folk like yourself can read and understand.

About This Book

This book explains, simplifies, and demystifies the world of cryptocurrency mining. You find out what you need to know and do in order to decide if and how you're going to begin cryptocurrency mining.

In this book, we explain

>> How cryptocurrency mining works, and what it's *for* (it can't *just* be a way for you to make money, right?)

>> The different algorithms and how they function — Proof of Work, Proof of Stake, Delegated Proof of Stake, and more — and what hashing is all about

>> The different types of mines: pool mining, solo mining, cloud mining

>> The different types of hardware: CPU mining, GPU mining, FGPA mining, and ASIC mining

>> How to pick the right cryptocurrency to mine

>> How to find and work with a pool mining service

>> How to set up your mining hardware and software

>> How to calculate your potential earnings (or losses!), taking into account network hash rate, your mining rig's hash rate, currency exchange rate, the price of electricity, and so on

>> Where to find a plethora of helpful resources to guide you on your cryptocurrency mining journey

>> And plenty more!

Foolish Assumptions

We don't want to assume anything, but we have to believe that if you're reading this book, you already know a few things about the Internet and cryptocurrency. We assume that you understand how to work online and work with personal computing equipment. We also assume that you know how to buy and sell cryptocurrency, how to work with exchanges and wallets, and how to keep it safe.

This alone is a complicated subject, which would take an entire book to explain. It is essential that you understand these basics; this book focuses on a more advanced subject, cryptocurrency mining, and we just don't have room to cover these basics. We recommend you check out Peter's 8-hour online video course, which you can find at CryptoOfCourse.com; but one way or another, it's essential that you learn how to work with cryptocurrency safely, in a way that protects you from theft and loss.

Icons Used in This Book

This book, like all *For Dummies* books, uses icons to highlight certain paragraphs and to alert you to particularly useful information. Here's a rundown of what those icons mean:

A Tip icon means we're giving you an extra snippet of information that may help you on your way or provide additional insight into the concepts being discussed.

The Remember icon points out information that is worth committing to memory.

TECHNICAL STUFF

The Technical Stuff icon indicates geeky stuff that you can skip if you really want to, although you may want to read it if you're the kind of person who likes to have the background info.

WARNING

The Warning icon helps you stay out of trouble. It's intended to grab your attention to help you avoid a pitfall that may harm your website or business.

Beyond the Book

In addition to what you're reading right now, this product also comes with a free access-anywhere Cheat Sheet that covers a variety of useful facts, such as background information on commonly mined cryptocurrencies, coin divisibility, popular pool mining services, and so on. To get this Cheat Sheet, simply go to www. dummies.com and enter **Cryptocurrency Mining For Dummies Cheat Sheet** in the Search box.

For information on Peter's *Crypto Clear: Blockchain & Cryptocurrency Made Simple* video course, visit www.CryptoOfCourse.com.

Where to Go from Here

As are all good reference tools, this book is designed to be read when needed. It's divided into several parts: cryptocurrency background and basics; mining-related foundational information; how to get started in cryptocurrency mining; the economics of mining; and the Part of Tens. We recommend that you start at the beginning and read through sequentially, but if you just want to know how to find pool mining services, read Chapter 7. If you need to understand how to calculate what equipment you would need to mine a particular cryptocurrency, read Chapter 11. If all you need is to understand the different forms of mining, Chapter 4 is for you.

However, cryptocurrency is a complex subject, and cryptocurrency mining more so. All the topics covered in this book are interrelated. We strongly recommend that you read everything in this book before you begin mining; it's essential that you have a strong understanding of everything involved before you begin. After all, your money is at stake!

1

Getting Started with Cryptocurrency Mining

Chapter **1**

Cryptocurrency Explained

You may be eager to get your mining operation started, but before you can create cryptocurrency, we want to make sure you understand what cryptocurrency actually is.

The cryptocurrency thing is so new — or at least, most of the interest in cryptocurrency has occurred recently, even though cryptocurrencies of various forms have been around since the 1980s — that most people involved have a rather shaky understanding of what cryptocurrency is and how it works. The average cryptocurrency owner, for example, may not know what they own.

In this chapter, we review the history of cryptocurrency and how the different components function together. You'll have a better foundation to understand how to mine cryptocurrencies if you understand what it is.

A Short History of Digital Dollars

Cryptocurrency is just one type of digital currency . . . a special type. At the end of the day cryptocurrency may be thought of as a form of digital currency.

So, what's *digital currency,* then? Well, digital currency is a very broad term that covers a variety of different things. But in a general sense, it's money that exists in a digital form rather than tangible form (think coins and banknotes). You can transfer digital currency over an electronic network of some kind, whether the Internet or a private banking network.

TIP

In fact, even credit card transactions may be thought of as digital currency transactions. After all, when you use your credit or debit card at a store (online or off), the money is being transferred electronically; the network doesn't package up dollar bills or pound notes and mail them to the merchant.

First, take the Internet

The cryptocurrency story really all begins with the Internet. Digital currencies existed before the Internet was in broad use, but for a digital currency to be useful, you need, well, some kind of digital transportation method for that currency. If almost nobody is using a digital communications network — and until 1994 very few people did — then what's the use of a digital currency?

But after 1994, millions of people were using a global, digital communications network — the Internet — and a problem arose: How can you spend money online? Okay, today the answer is pretty simple: You use your credit cards, debit cards, or PayPal account. But back in the mid-90s, it was more complicated.

Add credit card confusion

Back in the mid-90s, some of you may recall (and many of you were too young back then to remember this, I realize), people were wary of using credit cards on the Internet. When I had my own publishing company and was selling books through my website in 1997, I (Peter — Tyler's too young to remember 1997) would often receive printouts of my website product pages in the mail, along with a check to pay for the book being purchased. I was taking credit cards online, but many people simply didn't want to use them; they didn't trust the Interwebs to keep their plastic safe.

In addition, setting up a payment gateway for credit cards was difficult and expensive for the merchant. These days, it's a pretty simple process to add credit card processing to a website — it's built into virtually all ecommerce software, and with services like Stripe and Square lowering the barriers of entry, getting a *merchant account* is no longer the huge hassle and expense it used to be.

Of course, we're talking commercial transactions here, but what about personal transactions? How can someone send a friend the money they owe, or how can a parent send beer money to their child away at college? (I'm talking PPP . . . pre-PayPal and web-based transfers between bank accounts.) If we were going to live in a digital world, surely we needed digital money.

REMEMBER

One important characteristic of cash is that cash transactions are essentially anonymous — there's no paper trail or electronic record of the transaction taking place. Plenty of people thought an equivalent form of anonymous or pseudonymous digital currency would be a vast improvement over traditional settlement methods.

So, many people thought there had to be a better way. We needed a digital currency for a digital world. These days, perhaps that viewpoint seems naïve; looking back it was obvious that the credit companies weren't going to see trillions of dollars of transactions shifting online and just wave goodbye! They wanted a piece of the action, unwilling to give up their monopoly, and so today, the primary transaction methods in the United States and most of Europe are bank cards of various kinds.

Add a dash of David Chaum

In the mid-1990s, people were streaming online and for various reasons many didn't want to, or couldn't, use credit cards (see preceding section). Checks were even more difficult (unless you wanted to mail it), and cash was out of the question. (Though — and here's a joke for the older geeks among you — I do recall a friend telling me to UUENCODE the $10 I owed him and email it to him. Again, this is Peter talking; I'm betting Tyler is too young to know what UUENCODE is.)

But back in 1983, a guy called David Chaum had written a paper called "Blind Signatures for Untraceable Transactions." Chaum was a cryptographer (someone who works with cryptography) and professor of computer science. His paper described a way to use cryptography to create a digital-cash system that could enable anonymous transactions, just like cash. (Modern cryptography is the science of securing online communications; we'll come back to this later.) In fact, Chaum is often referred to as the Father of Digital Currency as well as the Father of Online Anonymity.

Result? DigiCash, E-Gold, Millicent, CyberCash, and More

Bring together the Internet, complicated online transactions, a fear of using credit cards online, a desire for cash-like anonymous online transactions, and David Chaum's work in the '80s (see preceding section), and what do you end up with?

You get DigiCash, for a start, David Chaum's 1990 digital-cash system. Unfortunately, Mr. Chaum seems to be early for the party too often, and DigiCash was out of business by 1998. There was also E-Gold, a digital cash system supposedly backed by gold, DEC's Millicent (yes, yes, most of you are too young to remember DEC, too. . . . I'm starting to feel old writing this "historical" section), First Virtual, CyberCash, b-money, Hashcash, eCash, Bit Gold, Cybercoin, and many more. There was also Beenz, with $100 million in investment capital; Flooz, endorsed by Whoopi Goldberg (no, really!); Liberty Reserve (shut down after being accused of money laundering); and China's QQ Coins.

With the exception of QQ Coins, still in use on Tencent's QQ Messaging service, all these digital currencies are gone. Notably, many of these early digital currencies were in one way or another centralized with a trusted third-party intermediary.

Digital currency was not over, though. It got off to a rough start, with much trial and error, but plenty of people still thought that the world needed cash-like (in other words, anonymous) online transactions. A new era was about to begin: The cryptocurrency era.

The earlier digital currencies also depended on cryptography, it's true, but they were never known as cryptocurrencies. It wasn't until cryptocurrency was combined with a blockchain in 2008 that the term cryptocurrency started to gain usage, and the term really didn't begin to appear widely until around 2012. (Blockchain? It's a special form of database, but we'll describe in more detail later in this chapter.)

The Bitcoin white paper

In 2008 Satoshi Nakamoto published and posted in a cryptography forum known as the "Cypherpunk Mailing List" a document titled "Bitcoin: A Peer-to-Peer Electronic Cash System," saying, "I've been working on a new electronic cash system that's fully peer-to-peer, with no trusted third party," he said.

The following list of attributes, Nakamoto stated, were key to Bitcoin:

>> Double-spending is prevented with a peer-to-peer network.

>> No mint or other trusted parties.

>> Participants can be anonymous.

>> New coins are made from Hashcash style proof of work.

>> The proof of work for new coin generation also powers the network to prevent double spending.

The document is a fairly dry read, but it's worth spending a few minutes checking it out. You can easily find it by navigating to https://bitcoin.org/bitcoin.pdf. The abstract for the Bitcoin white paper begins with the following statement: "A purely peer-to-peer version of electronic cash would allow online payments to be sent directly from one party to another without going through a financial institution," Nakamoto wrote. He explains that his method has solved the "double-spending" problem, an issue plaguing earlier digital currencies: the challenge was to make sure that a digital currency couldn't be spent twice.

Nakamoto also describes using blockchain functionality, although the term block-chain appears nowhere in the white paper:

> We propose . . . using a peer-to-peer network. The network timestamps transactions by hashing them into an ongoing chain of hash-based proof-of-work, forming a record that cannot be changed without redoing the proof-of-work.

Bitcoin: The first blockchain app

Early in January 2009, Nakamoto launched the Bitcoin network into action, using blockchain (a concept that had been around since the early 1990s, though this was the first time it had been correctly implemented), and created the first block in the blockchain, known as the *genesis* block.

This block contained 50 Bitcoin, as well as the text *"The Times 03/Jan/2009 Chancellor on brink of second bailout for banks"* as a justification and explanation as to why a system like Bitcoin was so important. Nakamoto continued coding updates into the protocol, running a node, and potentially mined around a million Bitcoin, a number that would make him one of the richest people in the world by the end of 2017 (at least "on paper").

By the end of 2010, Satoshi Nakamoto published his last forum post and officially signed off from the project, but by this time many other cryptocurrency enthusiasts had joined in, began mining, supporting open source code development, and the rest is history.

Who (or what) is Satoshi Nakamoto?

So, who was this Satoshi Nakamoto guy . . . or gal . . . or organization? Nobody knows. Satoshi Nakamoto doesn't seem to be a real name; it's most likely a pseudonym. And if anyone knows for sure who Nakamoto really is, they're not saying. It's the great mystery of cryptocurrency.

There is a Japanese American man named Dorian Prentice Satoshi Nakamoto, born Satoshi Nakamoto apparently. This person was a trained physicist, systems engineer, and a computer engineer for financial companies — perhaps he was the Satoshi Nakamoto. However, he's denied it several times.

How about Hal Finney, who lived just a few blocks from Dorian Prentice Satoshi Nakamoto's home? He was a pre-Bitcoin cryptographer and one of the first people to use Bitcoin and claims to have communicated via email with the founder of Bitcoin. Some people have suggested he "borrowed" Satoshi Nakamoto's name and used it as a pseudonym.

Then there's Nick Szabo, who has long been involved in digital currency and even published a white paper on bit gold, before Nakamoto's Bitcoin white paper. Or what about Craig White, who at one point claimed to be Nakamoto, but was later accused of fraud? Or Dr. Vili Lehdonvirta, a Finnish economic sociologist, or Michael Clear, an Irish graduate student in cryptography, or the three guys who filed a patent that included an obscure phrase ("computationally impractical to reverse") also used in the Nakamoto Bitcoin white paper, or Japanese mathematician Shinichi Mochizuki, or Jed McCaleb, or some type of government agency, or some other kind of team of people, or Elon Musk, or, well, nobody knows, but theories abound.

The second biggest Bitcoin mystery? Nakamoto owned around a million Bitcoin, which in December 2017, was worth about 19 or 20 billion dollars. The entirety of Nakamoto's estimated Bitcoin fortune has not been moved or spent; why hasn't he touched this money?

What's the Blockchain?

In order to understand cryptocurrency, you need to understand a little about blockchains. Blockchain technology is complicated, but that's okay — you don't need to understand everything. You just need to know the basics.

Blockchains are types of databases. A *database* is simply a collection of structured data. Say that you gather together a bunch of names, street addresses, email addresses, and phone numbers and type them into a word processor. That's not a database. That's just a jumble of text.

But say that you enter that data into a spreadsheet. The first column is the first name, the second is the person's last name, and then you have columns for the email address, phone number, street address, city name, zip code, country, and so on — that's structured data. That's a database.

Most people use databases all the time. If you use some kind of financial management program, such as QuickBooks, Quicken, or Mint, your data is stored in a database. If you use a contact management program to store contact information, it's stored in a database. Databases, behind the scenes, are an integral part of modern digital life.

Blockchain around the world — the blockchain network

The blockchain is a database; it stores information in a structured form. You can use blockchains for many different purposes: for example, for *property rights registries* (who owns this piece of land, and how did they come to own it?), or *supply chain tracking* (where did your wine or fish come from, and how did it get to you?). Blockchains can store any kind of data. In the case of cryptocurrencies, though, blockchains store transaction data: who owns what amount of cryptocurrency, who gave it to them, and who have they given it to (how have they spent it)?

Of course, blockchains have several special characteristics. Firstly, they are networked. There is a Bitcoin network, a Litecoin network, an Ethereum network, just like there's an email network or a World Wide Web network.

Bitcoin, for example, is a network of thousands of nodes or servers, spread across the entire planet.

These nodes each contain a copy of the Bitcoin blockchain, and they communicate with each other and stay in sync. They use a system of *consensus* to come to an agreement regarding what the current, valid blockchain database looks like. That is, they all contain a matching copy of the blockchain.

Hashing: "Fingerprinting" blocks

Having the blockchain duplicated across many different computers is powerful, making it much harder to hack or manipulate. But there's something else that's also powerful: *hashing*. A *hash* is a long number that is a kind of fingerprint for data. The blockchain uses it as follows:

1. **A computer running a node gathers and validates Bitcoin transactions (records of Bitcoin sent between addresses within the blockchain) that are going to be added to the blockchain.**

2. **When the computer has collected enough transactions, it creates a block of data and *hashes* the data — that is, it passes the data to a special hashing algorithm, which passes back the hash.**

   Here's an example of a real-life hash, from a block in the Bitcoin blockchain:

   ```
   0000000000000000000297f87446dc8b8855ae4ee2b35260dc4af61e1f5eec579Th
   ```

   A *hash* is a fingerprint for the data, and thanks to the magic of complex mathematics, it can't possibly match any other set of data. If the hashed data is changed even slightly — a 0 changes to a 5, or an A is changed to a B — the hash fingerprint will no longer match the original data.

3. **The hash is added to the block of transactions.**

4. **The block is added to the blockchain.**

5. **More transactions are collected for the next block.**

6. **After a full block of transactions is ready, the hash of the previous block is added to the current block.**

7. **The block — the transactions and previous-block's hash — are hashed again.**

8. **The process repeats, creating a timestamped chain of blocks.**

So, every block contains two hashes: the previous block's hash and the current block's hash, which is created by hashing the combination of all the Bitcoin transactions and the previous block's hash.

That's how blocks are chained together into the blockchain (see Figure 1-1). Each block contains the previous block's hash — in effect, a copy of the previous block's unique fingerprint. Each block is also, in effect, identifying its position in the blockchain; the hash from the previous block identifies the order in which the current block sits.

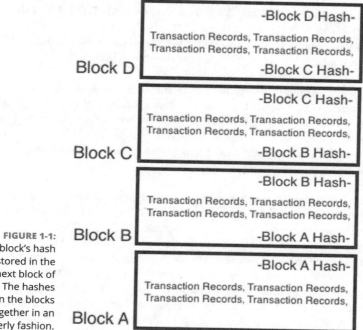

Blockchain is "immutable"

You may have heard that the blockchain is virtually *immutable*, which simply means that it can't easily be changed. If the Bitcoin blockchain says you own x Bitcoin, then you do own x Bitcoin, and there can be no disagreement . . . and nobody can go into the blockchain and hack it or somehow change or mutate it.

Imagine what would happen if someone went into a block (we'll call it Block A) and changed a little bit of data — for example, they go in and show that instead of sending someone 1 Bitcoin you sent 9 Bitcoin.

Well, the hash in Block A would no longer match its data. Remember, a hash is a fingerprint that identifies the data, so if you change the data, the hash no longer matches.

Okay, so the hacker could rehash Block A's data and then save the "corrected" hash. But wait, now the next block (Block B) would not match because Block B is carrying Block A's hash. So now say the hacker changes the Block A hash stored in Block B.

But now Block B's hash doesn't match Block B's data, because that hash was created from a combination of Block B's transaction data and Block A's hash!

So, Block B would have to be re-hashed, and the hash updated. But wait! That means Block B's hash stored in Block C now doesn't match!

See where we're going? This would ripple through the entire blockchain. The entire blockchain is now broken, by just modifying one single character in a block lower down. In order to fix the problem, the entire blockchain has to be recalculated. From the hacked block onwards, it must be "re-mined." What may look like a simple hack and database edit now turns into a major computational headache that cannot be easily completed.

So, this hashing function, combined with the fact that thousands of other nodes must be in sync with identical copies of the blockchain, makes the blockchain virtually immutable; it simply can't be easily hacked.

Nobody can change it or destroy it. Hackers can't get into the peer-to-peer node network and create transactions in order to steal crypto, governments can't close it down (China, for example, could attempt to shut down Bitcoin within its borders, but the blockchain would continue to exist in many other countries), a terrorist group can't destroy it, one nation can't attack another and destroy its blockchain, and so on. Because there are so many copies of the blockchain, and as long as enough people want to continue working with the blockchain, it's practically immutable and indestructible.

Where's the Money?

You may be wondering, "So where is the cryptocurrency? Where's the money?" Or perhaps you've heard of cryptocurrency wallets and think that's where the money is stored. Wrong. There's no money in a cryptocurrency wallet. In fact, there is no cryptocurrency.

Cryptocurrency blockchains are often described as ledgers. A *ledger* is described by Google Dictionary as "a book or other collection of financial accounts of a particular type." Ledgers have been around for hundreds of years, used to record transactions for individuals, businesses, government departments, and so on. The statement you get from your bank account or credit card is a form of ledger, showing you your individual transactions; money you pay to others, and money you receive from others.

FINDING THE BALANCE IN THE BLOCKCHAIN

Well, okay, the blockchain doesn't actually store a balance for each address. Nowhere in the blockchain does it state how much of the cryptocurrency any particular owner owns or how much any particular address has associated with it. Rather, you can use a blockchain explorer to follow all your transactions, incoming and outgoing, and the blockchain explorer can figure out your balance based on those transactions.

In the context of cryptocurrency, the blockchain is a digital ledger recording cryptocurrency you send to others, and cryptocurrency you receive from others.

Think of it this way. Say that you're a little compulsive and like to keep a record of the cash in your pocket. You carry a notepad, to record every time you put money into your pocket and every time you spend it, and you calculate the current balance. That notepad is a kind of transaction ledger, right?

Cryptocurrency is very similar to this ledger of cash transactions . . . except there's no pocket. The blockchain is the ledger; it stores a record of every transaction (when you first purchased or were sent the cryptocurrency, when you spent it or sold it, and the balance you own).

But there's no pocket and no cryptocurrency sitting in storage somewhere. The blockchain is simply a series of "mythical" (or virtual) transactions stored in the ledger. No currency is being physically transferred; we simply update the record to state that currency has been transferred.

The ledger says you own cryptocurrency, so everyone can validate and accept that you own it. And remember, that ledger can't be edited after being solidified into the chain — it can't be hacked. (See the preceding section for more on this topic.) So if the ledger says you own, say, half a Bitcoin, then you absolutely do, and you can sell that half Bitcoin to someone else by modifying the ledger to say that they own it!

But what about the wallet? The wallet must store money, right? No, cryptocurrency wallets do not store cryptocurrency. They store private keys, public keys, and addresses. Private keys are the most important because they control the addresses with which your cryptocurrency is associated in the blockchain.

What's the Crypto in Cryptocurrency?

The *crypto* in cryptocurrency refers to cryptography. So, what exactly is cryptography?

According to The Oxford English Dictionary, cryptography is "the art of writing or solving codes." Wikipedia's explanation is more complicated and more digital: "The practice and study of techniques for secure communication . . . cryptography is about constructing and analyzing protocols that prevent third parties or the public from reading private messages."

The history of cryptography goes back at least 4,000 years. People have always needed to send secret messages now and then, and that's what cryptography is all about.

Today's cryptography, with the help of computers, is far more complicated than the ancient ciphers of the classical world, and it's used more extensively. In fact, cryptography is an integral part of the Internet; without it, the Internet just wouldn't work in the way we need it to work.

Almost every time you use your web browser, you're employing cryptography. Remember the little lock icon, shown in Figure 1-2, in your browser's Location bar?

FIGURE 1-2:
Your browser's lock icon means that data submitted back to the web server will be encrypted with cryptography.

The lock icon means the page is secured. When you send information to and from the browser to the web server and back, that information is going to be *encrypted* — scrambled — so that if it's intercepted on the hundreds or thousands of miles of Internet transmission between the two, it can't be read. When your credit card number is transmitted to an ecommerce site, for example, it's scrambled by your browser, sent to the Web server, and then unscrambled by the receiving server.

Ah, so, the blockchain is encrypted, right? Well, no. Cryptocurrency uses cryptography, but not to scramble the data in the blockchain. The blockchain is open, public, and auditable. Figure 1-3 shows you an example of a blockchain explorer designed for Bitcoin. Using a blockchain explorer, anyone can investigate the blockchain and see every transaction that has occurred since the genesis block (the first block of Bitcoin created).

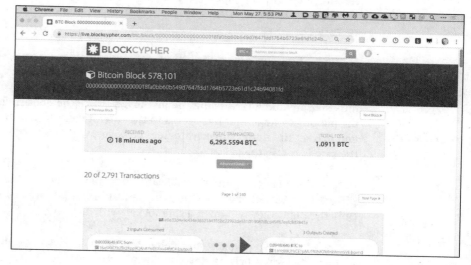

FIGURE 1-3:
An example of a blockchain explorer tool, found at `https://live.blockcypher.com/btc`.

ENCRYPTED BLOCKCHAINS

You can build encrypted blockchains and encrypt data within a blockchain. For example, while the Bitcoin blockchain is unencrypted and open to inspection by anyone (see the blockchain explorer in Figure 1-3), it is still possible to create encrypted blockchains that obscure the transaction data, such as Zcash, but, in general, cryptocurrency blockchains are not encrypted, so anyone can read the transactions stored within them.

No, cryptocurrency isn't used to encrypt the data in the blockchain. It's used to sign messages that you send to the blockchain. These messages are the ones that trigger transactions and updates to the blockchain ledger.

Public Key Encryption Magic

Public key encryption is a clever little trick created using digital cryptography. And, by the way, this type of encryption is all accomplished using hugely complicated mathematics — the sort of mathematics that even most people with degrees in mathematics don't understand, the sort of mathematics that has names like *Carmichael numbers* and *Goppa codes*, the sort of mathematics that we certainly don't understand, and you don't either (well, most of you, dear readers, don't). But that's fine: Gravity isn't well understood either, but we all use it every day.

So, forget how this amazing stuff works, and consider instead what it is actually accomplishing. Now, imagine a safe, with two keyholes and two associated keys. One is a public key, and one is a private key. Now imagine that you put something into the safe and lock it using the public key. Once the door is closed and locked, the public key no longer has access to the safe; it can't be used to unlock the safe and extract the item. The private key, however, will work. The only way to open the safe is to use the private key.

In fact, this magical mathematical safe works both ways. You can lock it with the private key, but after you lock it, you can't use the private key to open the safe. Only the public key will open a safe locked with a private key.

Oh, and these two keys are magically associated. They work only with each other and no other keys. Private Key X will work only with Public Key X, and vice versa. You can't lock the safe with Public Key X and then unlock the safe with Private Key W or Private Key K, for example.

Okay, same principle, but now think of electronic messages. You can lock an electronic message with a public key — that is, you can use a key to scramble, or encrypt, the message. That message may be an email or information being sent from your browser to a web server.

After that locked (encrypted) message is received at the other end (the email recipient or the web server), only the private key can unlock it; the public key is useless at this point. And it must be the magically associated (okay, mathematically associated) key, and no other.

Encryption is a handy tool. It means I can give you a public key, and you can write me a message and encrypt it using the public key, and once encrypted nobody in the world can read it unless they have the private key. So, if I'm carefully protecting my keys, I'm the only person in the world who can read it.

The names of these keys aren't arbitrary. The private key should be truly private — only you, and nobody else in the world, should have access to it. The public key can be truly public. You can give it away. For example, if you want to have people email their messages to you, you can publish your public key — on your website, in the footer of your emails, on your business card, or whatever — so that anybody who wants to send a message to you can encrypt it with your public key knowing that you are the only person in the world who can read it (because you keep the private key secret).

TIP

How do you encrypt emails? Email encryption has been around for decades, but it simply never caught on with the public at large. Still, you can encrypt email from most email systems, such as Outlook, Gmail, and Yahoo! Mail, and there are systems, such as ProtonMail, that encrypt it by default.

This process is essentially what your web browser uses when you send your credit card information online; the browser uses the web server's public key to scramble the data so that only the web browser, with the associated private key, can decrypt and read the credit card information. (Okay, that's a simplification. Browser-to-server communication is more complicated than this description, involving temporary session keys, and so on; but the basic principle still applies.)

Messages to the blockchain

You use public-key encryption when you send transactions to the blockchain. When you want to send, say, Bitcoin, to someone else, you send an encrypted message to the blockchain saying "send *x.xx* of my Bitcoin to this address."

But wait. I just told you the blockchain isn't encrypted, and now I'm telling you the messages to the blockchain are encrypted! So why do you care if the message going to the blockchain is encrypted if you're just going to decrypt it anyway?

Well, remember I told you this lock/unlock thing works both ways. You can lock with the public key and unlock with the private key or lock with the private key and unlock with the public key. Either way, the data is scrambled. The difference is who has the ability to unscramble it. If you scramble something with the public key, the only person in the world who can unscramble it is the person with the private key. But if you scramble it with the private key, the only person in the world who can open it is . . . everybody! Anybody and everybody can get to the public key. It's public, remember!

So, what's the purpose of encrypting a message with the private key? Not to secure it, obviously, because anybody can decrypt it. No, the purpose is to *sign* the message (transaction) and prove ownership of the associated public key.

Signing messages with the private key

Say that I publish my public key on my website, in my emails, and on my business cards. Now, one day you get a message that seems to come from me. But how can you be sure it's from me? Well, I encrypted the message using my private key. So, you take my public key (which is publicly available) and use it to decrypt the message. If the message really is from me, my public key will decrypt it, and you'll be able to read it. If it isn't, the decryption won't work, because it came from someone else.

So, by encrypting the message with the private key, I have in effect signed the message, proving that it came from me. The recipient knows that the message was created by the person holding the private key that is associated with the public key that opened the message up and made it readable.

The blockchain address — your money's home

All the cryptocurrency in the blockchain is associated with addresses. Here's one I just grabbed from the Bitcoin blockchain using the blockchain explorer at `blockchain.com`, for example:

```
1L7hHWfJL1dd7ZhQFgRv8ke1PTKAHoc9Tq
```

Trillions of different address combinations are possible, so this address is fundamentally unique. Now, where did this address come from? It came from a wallet that generated it from the private key. That wallet contains a public key and a private key.

The public key is associated with the private key; in fact, it's created from the private key. The address is associated with the public key; in fact, it's created from the public key. So, all three are mathematically, and uniquely, associated with each other.

Sending a transaction message

So, here's how cryptography is used when you want to send a transaction to the blockchain, to transfer a cryptocurrency balance to another person. Say there's an address in the blockchain with Bitcoin associated with it. When I checked, 1L7hHWfJL1dd7ZhQFgRv8ke1PTKAHoc9Tq had a balance of 0.10701382 Bitcoin. Now, say this is your Bitcoin, and you want to send, perhaps, 0.05 Bitcoin to a friend, an exchange, or a merchant from whom you are buying a good or service.

The address I use in this example is a real address; you can see it for yourself in a blockchain explorer. (Use this link to get to it: https://blockstream.info/addr ess/1L7hHWfJL1dd7ZhQFgRv8ke1PTKAHoc9Tq.) At the time of writing, it had 0.10701382 Bitcoin. By the time you see it, the number may be different, of course.

You send a message to the blockchain saying, essentially, "I own address 1L7hHWfJL1dd7ZhQFgRv8ke1PTKAHoc9Tq, and I want to send 0.05 Bitcoin to address 1NdaT7URGyG67L9nkP2TuBZjYV6yL7XepS."

If I just sent a plaintext (unencrypted) message to the blockchain, there would be a huge problem of verification and validity. How would the Bitcoin node receiving this message know that I do indeed own this address and the money associated with it? I could just be spoofing this information and making this up, right?

What we do is use the wallet to sign the message using the private key associated with the address. In other words, we use the private key to encrypt the message. Then we take the public key, add it to the encrypted message, and send it all out across the cryptocurrency network.

MESSAGE TO THE BLOCKCHAIN

How do you send a message to the blockchain? That's what your wallet software does. In fact, wallet software is less like a wallet — your wallet contains no cryptocurrency — and more like an email program. Your email program sends messages across the email network. Your wallet sends messages (about transactions) across the cryptocurrency network.

Unraveling the message

So, the node — a computer containing a copy of the cryptocurrency blockchain — receives the message. It takes the public key that has been attached and decrypts the message. The node learns something: "This message must have been encrypted — signed — by the private key associated with the public key." Of course, that's not really saying much. It's virtually a tautology! By definition, if the public key can decrypt a message, the message must have been encrypted with the matching private key. Whoop-de-doo.

But remember, the public key is mathematically associated with the address 1L7hHWfJL1dd7ZhQFgRv8ke1PTKAHoc9Tq. So now the node can examine the two, asking in effect "Is the public key associated with the address?" If the answer is yes, then the node also knows that the private key is associated with the address (all three are uniquely associated with each other). So, what does the node tell itself?

"This message, sending money from 1L7hHWfJL1dd7ZhQFgRv8ke1PTKAHoc9Tq, was sent by the private key that was used to create this address . . . so the address must have been sent by the person who owns the address and therefore owns the money associated with the address."

TIP

I know this concept can be confusing; it's hard to "get your head around." So here's another way to think about it: The only person who could have sent an encrypted message with transaction instructions for this address along with the public key that originally created the address is the person controlling the associated private key — that is, the owner of the address and the money associated with it, thus verifying ownership and validating the transaction.

WHOEVER OWNS THE PRIVATE KEYS OWNS THE MONEY

Okay, so maybe there are more people with access to the key. But as far as the technology is concerned, it doesn't matter. Whoever has access to the private key has the cryptographic right to control the money assigned to the blockchain address associated with the key. You may hear the phrase "whoever has the private key owns the money" or "not your private key, not your Bitcoin." They may not have acquired it legitimately or legally own it, but they can control it nonetheless. So, protect your private keys!

PSEUDONYMOUS CRYPTOCURRENCIES

Some cryptocurrencies are more anonymous than others. Bitcoin, for example, is often termed *pseudonymous* because it's only partially anonymous. Imagine that someone subpoenas transaction records from an exchange and discovers that you purchased a couple of Bitcoin on the exchange and your identity was tied to those transactions via AML (anti-money laundering) and KYC (know your customer) data collection procedures required by law in the United States (and other countries). They'll have the address that the exchange used to store those Bitcoin, right? Well, now they can trace the transactions from that address through the blockchain using a blockchain explorer. And different addresses can be associated with each other in certain ways, so it would be possible for someone with the information — a tax authority, for example, or police agency — from a single starting point, to create a picture of a person's Bitcoin transactions. So, Bitcoin as it is commonly used today is not fully anonymous. Other currencies, such as Monero or Zcash, claim to get much closer to true anonymity. However, improvements to Bitcoin, such as conjoin and Layer 2, are likely to make Bitcoin more anonymous in the future.

So that's the crypto in cryptocurrency! You can control money in the blockchain anonymously through the use of cryptography, using public and private key pairs and associated addresses, by cryptographically signing messages.

The Basic Components of Cryptocurrency

The following sections take a look at how the basic components of cryptocurrency fit together.

What's in a wallet?

The *wallet* is where everything begins as far as your cryptocurrency is concerned. When you create a wallet file, the wallet software will create a private key. That private key is used to create a public key, and the public key is used to create an address. The address has never before existed in the blockchain and still doesn't exist in the blockchain yet.

After you have an address, you have a way to store cryptocurrency. You can give the address to someone from whom you're buying cryptocurrency or an exchange, for example, and they can send the cryptocurrency to that address — in other words, they send a message to the blockchain saying "Send x amount of crypto to address *x*." Now the address exists in the blockchain, and it has cryptocurrency associated with it.

A *wallet program* is a messaging program that stores your keys and addresses in a wallet file. The wallet program does these primary things:

>> It retrieves data from the blockchain about your transactions and balance.

>> It sends messages to the blockchain transferring your crypto from your addresses to other addresses, such as when you make a purchase using your cryptocurrency.

>> It creates addresses you can give to other people when they need to send cryptocurrency to you.

Private keys create public keys

The private key in your wallet is used to create the public key that is used to unencrypt your messages sent to the blockchain. Private keys must be kept private; anyone with access to the private key has access to your money in the blockchain.

Public keys create blockchain addresses

Public keys are also used to create addresses. The first time an address is used, someone's wallet software sends a message to the blockchain saying "Send *x* amount of cryptocurrency to address *x* from address *y*." Until this point, the address did not exist in the blockchain. After the wallet software has sent the message, though, the address is in the blockchain, and money is associated with it.

The private key controls the address

The private key controlling the address is a hugely critical concept in cryptocurrency, and people who lose access to their cryptocurrency, or have their cryptocurrency stolen, don't understand this (see Figure 1-4). In this book, we won't be going into detail about protecting private keys, but make sure you protect your private keys! Don't lose them and don't let other people discover them!

FIGURE 1-4: The cryptocurrency is associated with an address in the blockchain; the address is derived from the public key, which is associated with a private key . . . which is kept safe in a wallet.

Where Does Crypto Come From? The Crypto Mines (Sometimes)

So where does cryptocurrency come from? Cryptocurrency can be *mined* – the least common form, though the one you're evidently most interested in based on your interest in this book — or it can be *pre-mined*.

To say that a cryptocurrency has been *pre-mined*, or is *nonmineable*, simply means that the cryptocurrency already exists. The blockchain is a ledger containing information about transactions. When the blockchain was first created, the ledger already contained a record of all the cryptocurrency that the founders planned for. No more will be added; it's all there in the blockchain already.

In fact, although we hear a lot about cryptocurrency mining, the majority of cryptocurrencies (at the time of writing, more than 2,000 different flavors) are pre-mined: 74 or so of the top 100 cryptocurrencies are nonmineable, and overall, around 70 percent of all cryptocurrencies cannot be mined.

An example of a pre-mined currency is XRP, often known as Ripple, which is currently the second biggest cryptocurrency (in terms of *market capitalization* — that is, the value of all the cryptocurrency in circulation). XRP is stored within the RippleNet blockchain.

When the Ripple blockchain was created, 100 billion XRP were already recorded in the blockchain, although most had not been distributed. The founders of Ripple held 20 percent, and even now almost 60 percent of the currency is not in circulation.

Another example is Stellar, a payment network originally funded by the Stripe payment service, which at the time of writing was the fourth largest cryptocurrency. Stellar has a total supply of more than 100 billion lumens, 2 percent of which were assigned to Stripe for its investment.

So, no, not all cryptocurrencies can be mined (in fact, most can't). But that's not why you're reading this book, now, is it?

The good news, though, is that you can mine around 600 cryptocurrencies (though you'll never want to mine the vast majority). To decide which ones to mine, see Chapter 8.

Chapter **2**

Understanding Cryptocurrency Mining

lthough not all cryptocurrencies require mining, Bitcoin and other mineable cryptocurrencies rely on miners to maintain their network. By solving computationally difficult puzzles and providing consent on the validity of transactions, miners support the blockchain network, which would otherwise collapse. For their service to the network, miners are rewarded with newly created cryptocurrencies (such as Bitcoin) and transaction fees.

When a miner sends a transaction message across the cryptocurrency network, another miner's computer picks it up and adds the transaction to the pool of transactions waiting to be placed into a block and the blockchain ledger. (You can find the details about cryptocurrency and blockchain ledgers in Chapter 1.) In this chapter, we explore how cryptocurrencies use mining to create trust and make the cryptocurrency usable, stable, and viable.

Understanding Decentralized Currencies

Cryptocurrencies are *decentralized* — that is, no central bank, no central database, and no single, central authority manages the currency network. Conversely, the United States has the Federal Reserve in Washington, D.C., the organization that manages the U.S. dollar, the European Central Bank in Frankfurt manages the euro, and all other fiat currencies also have centralized oversight bodies. (A *fiat* currency is legal tender supported by governments via a central bank.)

However, cryptocurrencies don't have a central authority; rather, the cryptocurrency community and, in particular, cryptocurrency miners and network nodes manage them. For this reason, cryptocurrencies are often referred to as *trustless*. Because no single party or entity controls how a cryptocurrency is issued, spent, or balanced, you don't have to put your trust in a single authority.

REMEMBER

Trustless is a bit of a misnomer. Trust is baked into the system. You don't have to trust a single authority, but your trust in the system and fully auditable codebase is still essential. In fact, no form of currency can work without some form of trust or belief. (If nobody trusts the currency, then nobody will accept it or work to maintain it!)

SO WHY IS THE PROCESS CALLED MINING?

When you compare cryptocurrency mining to gold mining, why the process is referred to as mining becomes clear. In both forms of mining, the miners put in work and are rewarded with an uncirculated asset. In gold mining, naturally occurring gold that was outside the economy is dug up and becomes part of the gold circulating within the economy. In cryptocurrency mining, work is performed, and the process ends with new cryptocurrency being created and added to the blockchain ledger. In both cases, miners, after receiving their reward — the mined gold or the newly created cryptocurrency — usually sell it to the public to recoup their operating costs and get their profit, placing the new currency into circulation.

The cryptocurrency miner's work is different from that of a gold miner, of course, but the result is much the same: Both bring a new money supply to the market. For cryptocurrency mining, all of the work happens on a mining computer or *rig* connected to the cryptocurrency network — no burro riding or gap-toothed gold panners required!

In the trustless cryptocurrency world, you can still trust the cryptocurrency community and its mechanisms to ensure that the blockchain contains an accurate and *immutable* — unchangeable — record of cryptocurrency transactions. Cryptocurrencies are established using a set of software rules that ensure that the system can be trusted, and the mining process is part of this system that allows everyone to trust the blockchain.

Cryptocurrencies have no central bank printing new money. Instead, miners dig up new currency according to a preset coin-issue schedule and release it into circulation in a process called *mining.*

Exploring the Role of the Crypto Miner

Cryptocurrency miners add transactions to the blockchain, but different cryptocurrencies use different mining methods, if the cryptocurrency uses mining at all. (Some cryptocurrencies don't use mining — see Chapter 1.) Different mining and consensus methods are used to determine who creates new blocks of data and how exactly the blocks are added to the blockchain.

REMEMBER

How you mine a particular cryptocurrency varies slightly depending on the type of cryptocurrency being mined, but the basics are still the same: Mining creates a system to build trust between parties without needing a single authority and ensures that everyone's cryptocurrency balances are up-to-date and correct in the blockchain ledger.

The work performed by miners consists of a few main actions:

>> Verifying and validating new transactions

>> Collecting those transactions and ordering them into a new block

>> Adding the block to the ledger's chain of blocks (the blockchain)

>> Broadcasting the new block to the cryptocurrency node network

The preceding mining process is essential work, necessary for the continued propagation of the blockchain and its associated transactions. Without it, the blockchain won't function. But why would someone do this work? What are the incentives for the miner?

The Bitcoin miner actually has a couple of incentives (other cryptocurrencies may work in a different manner).

>> **Transaction fees:** A small fee is paid by each person spending the cryptocurrency to have the transaction added to the new block; the miner adding the block gets the transaction fees.

>> **Block subsidy:** Newly created cryptocurrency, known as the block subsidy, is paid to the miner who successfully adds a block to the ledger.

Combined, the fees and subsidy are known as the *block reward*. In Bitcoin, the block subsidy began at 50 BTC. (BTC is the ticker symbol for Bitcoin.) The block subsidy at the time of this writing is currently 6.25 BTC. The block subsidy is halved every 210,000 blocks, or roughly every four years; sometime around spring 2024, it will halve again to 3.125 BTC per block.

Figure 2-1, from the BlockChain.com blockchain explorer (`https://www.blockchain.com/explorer`), shows a transaction with the block subsidy being paid to an address owned by the miner who added the block to the blockchain. A reward of 12.5 BTC is being paid as the subsidy because this transaction was before the most recent reward halving in 2020; the actual sum received by the miner (the full reward, 13.24251028 BTC) is larger, because it also includes the transaction fees for all the transactions in the block.

FIGURE 2-1:
The block subsidy and transaction fees being paid to a miner, from the BlockChain.com blockchain explorer.

Making Cryptocurrency Trustworthy

For a cryptocurrency to function, several conditions must be met by the protocol. We like Jan Lanksy's six-factor list (Jan is a cryptocurrency academic, teaching at a university in the Czech Republic). Mining (in the mineable cryptocurrencies; nonmineable currencies have different mechanisms) is an integral part of making sure these conditions are met:

>> **The system doesn't require a central authority and is maintained through distributed consensus.** That is, everyone agrees on the balances associated with addresses in the blockchain ledger. Mining is an integral part of adding transactions to the blockchain and maintaining consensus.

» **The system keeps track of cryptocurrency units and their ownership.** Balances can be proven at any point in time. Mining adds transactions to the blockchain in a way that becomes immutable — the blockchain can't be changed. If the blockchain shows your balance is five Bitcoin, then you absolutely do own five Bitcoin!

» **The system defines whether new cryptocurrency units can be created, and, if so, the system defines the circumstances of their origin and how to determine the ownership of these new units.** A fixed issuance or inflation rate is predefined. Mining provides a way to release new cryptocurrency into circulation at a predetermined, controlled rate, with ownership being assigned to the miner.

» **Ownership of cryptocurrency units is proved through cryptography.** The three conditions of authenticity, nonrepudiation, and immutability are met, through the use of cryptography. Miners, using cryptography, verify that transaction requests are valid before adding them to a new block. The miner verifies that the transaction request is for a sum that is available to the owner of the crypto, that the owner has correctly signed the request with their private key to prove ownership, and that the receiving address is valid and able to accept the transfer.

» **The system allows transactions to be performed in which ownership of the cryptographic units is changed.** Transactions can be submitted only by senders who can prove ownership of the cryptocurrency being transferred. Cryptocurrency owners prove ownership by signing transactions using the addresses associated with a private key. Mining is the process through which transactions are accomplished, and miners verify ownership before adding the transaction to the blockchain.

» **If two different instructions for changing the ownership of the same cryptographic units are simultaneously entered, the system performs at most one of them.** Double-spending the same unit is not possible. The problem of double-spending was one that weakened earlier digital currencies. But with modern cryptocurrencies, miners vet transactions, searching the blockchain record of transactions to determine whether the owner actually has sufficient balance at that moment. If a sufficient balance isn't accounted for within the spend address (the Input address) in the transaction request, the transaction will be rejected by the node software and never mined onto the blockchain. Also, if the same sender has two or more pending transaction requests, but doesn't own enough cryptocurrency to cover them all, miners can decide which of the requests is valid. Additional transactions will be discarded to avoid *double-spending* the same currency.

If even one of these six conditions isn't met, a cryptocurrency will fail because it can't build enough trust for people to reliably use it. The process of mining solidifies and satisfies every single one of these conditions.

Reaching Agreement through Consensus Algorithms

A mind exercise known as the *Byzantine Generals Problem* (or the *Byzantine Fault*, the *error avalanche*, and by various other names) illustrates the problem that cryptocurrency consensus algorithms seek to solve.

The overall problem? You're trying to reach consensus; in cryptocurrency, you're trying to reach agreement over the history of currency transactions. But in a cryptocurrency network, a distributed computer system of equals, you have many separate computers (nodes); the Bitcoin network, at times, has 50,000 to 200,000 nodes connected. Out of those thousands of systems, some are going to have technical problems: hardware faults, misconfiguration, out-of-date software, malfunctioning routers, and so on. Others are going to be untrustworthy; they're going to be seeking to exploit weaknesses for the financial gain of the people running the node (they are run by "traitors"). The problem is that for various reasons, some nodes may send conflicting and faulty information.

So to deal with this problem, a sort of parable or metaphor was devised, called the Byzantine Generals Problem. (Three guys — Leslie Lamport, Robert Shostak, and Marshall Pease — first told this story in 1980, in a paper related to general issues of reliability in distributed computer systems.) Originally named the *Albanian Generals Problem*, it was renamed after a long-defunct empire so as not to offend people from Albania! (Although in this interconnected world of constant social media offense, there must be at least some offended residents of Istanbul.) Apparently, distributed-computing academics like to sit around and devise these little metaphors. You may have heard of the *dining philosopher's problem*, the *reader's/ writer's problem*, and so on. In fact, the Byzantine Generals Problem was derived from the Chinese Generals Problem.

Anyway, here is the idea, as described in their original paper:

> We imagine that several divisions of the Byzantine army are camped outside an enemy city, each division commanded by its own general. The generals can communicate with one another only by messenger. After observing the enemy, they must decide upon a common plan of action. However, some of the generals may be traitors, trying to prevent the loyal generals from reaching agreement. The generals must have an algorithm to guarantee that

A. All loyal generals decide upon the same plan of action. . . .

B. A small number of traitors cannot cause the loyal generals to adopt a bad plan.

TIP

Search online for "The Byzantine Generals Problem" if you're interested in seeing the original paper.

That's the problem that cryptocurrency *consensus algorithms*, as they're known, are trying to solve: how the generals (the computer nodes) come up with consensus (all agree on the same plan of action — or transaction ledger), and avoid being led astray by a small number of traitors (faulty equipment and hackers).

Looking at the Cryptocurrency Miner

To have a chance at the mining reward, miners must set up their mining rigs (the computer equipment) and run that cryptocurrency's associated mining software. Depending on how many resources the miner is committing, they will have a proportional chance of being the lucky miner who gets to create and chain the latest block; the more resources employed, the higher the chance of winning the reward. Each block has a predetermined amount of payment, which is rewarded to the victorious miner for their hard work to spend as they wish.

So how is the winning miner chosen? That depends. In most cases, one of two basic methods is used:

» **Proof of work:** Under this method, the miner has to carry out a task, and the first miner to complete the task adds the latest block to the blockchain and wins the block reward, the block subsidy, and transaction fees. Bitcoin and other cryptocurrencies, such as ether (for now; it plans to switch to proof of stake at some point), Bitcoin Cash, Litecoin, and Dogecoin, use proof of work.

» **Proof of stake:** In this system, the software is going to choose one of the cryptocurrency nodes to add the latest block; to be in the running, nodes must have a stake, generally meaning that they must own a certain amount of the cryptocurrency. The cryptocurrency network chooses the miner who will add the next block to the chain based on a combination of random choice and amount of stake — for example, with some cryptocurrencies, the more cryptocurrency owned and the longer it has been owned, the more likely the miner is to be chosen. (It's like owning lottery tickets: the more you own, the more likely you are to win.) With other cryptocurrencies, the choice is made sequentially, one by one, from a queue of preselected miners.

When Bitcoin first started, anyone with a simple desktop computer was able to mine. The would-be miner simply downloaded the Bitcoin mining software, installed it, and let the BTC roll in! As time went on, though, competition increased. Faster and more powerful computers were built and used for mining. Eventually, specialized processing chips called Application Specific Integrated Circuits (ASICs) were developed. An ASIC, as the name implies, is a computer chip designed for a specific purpose, such as displaying high-resolution graphics quickly, running a smartphone, or carrying out a particular form of computation. Specific ASICs have been designed to be highly efficient at the forms of computation required for cryptocurrency mining — for example, for Bitcoin mining. Such a chip can be 1,000 times more efficient at Bitcoin mining than the chip in your PC, so in today's Bitcoin mining environment, it's go ASIC or go home!

For high-difficulty cryptocurrencies, such as Bitcoin, the ideal mining environment requires the following conditions.

>> **Low hardware costs:** Those mining rigs aren't free.

>> **Low temperatures:** Lower temperatures make cooling your mining rigs easier.

>> **Low electricity costs:** Mining rigs can use a lot of power.

>> **Fast, reliable Internet connections:** You need to be communicating with the cryptocurrency network rapidly with minimal downtime because you're in competition with other miners.

Fear not, though! With many different copies and mimicry of Bitcoin running rampant, Bitcoin is no longer the only game in town, and you can find lots of alternative mining choices, with varying levels of required computing power. Today, some of the most profitable cryptocurrencies to mine are lesser known and can be mined using off-the-shelf computer hardware due to less stringent difficulty levels that are associated with lower popularity and adoption.

ASIC SCHMASIC

An ASIC is, technically speaking, an *application specific integrated circuit*: an incredibly specialized computer chip that is good at doing one operation very efficiently. However, you'll likely hear cryptocurrency people refer to the specialized mining box they've purchased as an ASIC, or an *ASIC box*. An ASIC is only good for a specific mining algorithm. For example, if you've got an ASIC built to mine Bitcoin, which uses the SHA-256 algorithm, you're not going to be mining Litecoin with it because that would require an ASIC built for the Scrypt algorithm.

TECHNICAL STUFF

Historically, during the years 2013 to 2020, a large portion of global cryptocurrency mining was claimed to take place in China, at perhaps three times the rate of the next-closest nation (the United States). A combination of cheap electricity and easy access to cheap computer components for building mining rigs gave China an edge that Chinese miners have leveraged and maintained, even with their government's apparent disapproval of cryptocurrencies. Recently, China has gone as far as to outright ban the trading and mining of Bitcoin and other cryptocurrencies, but the fact that the network hardly noticed a disruption during this debacle is a testament to how resilient and difficult to shut down distributed cryptocurrency systems such as Bitcoin are.

Making the Crypto World Go 'Round

A cryptocurrency has value because a large number of people collectively believe that it does. But why do they believe cryptocurrency has value? The answer is trust. (For more on trust, see the earlier section, "Making Cryptocurrency Trustworthy.") A holder of Bitcoin can trust that their Bitcoin will be in their wallet a day from now or 10 years from now. If they want to research how the system works, they can audit the code base to understand the system on a deeper level to see how trust is maintained. However, if they do not have the skillset or the computer science knowledge to audit code, they can choose to trust that other people, more knowledgeable than them, understand and monitor the system; they can trust the overall blockchain community that is managing the particular cryptocurrency.

Without the mining functionality underpinning the distributed peer-to-peer cryptocurrency system, this collective trust (based on the proof of collective work towards the chain) would not exist. (How the pre-mined cryptocurrencies or other weak-consensus mechanisms manage to exist is another story that we're not discussing in this book; we're focusing on mined cryptocurrencies, of course.)

REMEMBER

Mining makes sure that your balances won't change without your authorization. It incentivizes everyone to behave correctly and punishes those who don't. It creates a digital form of value transfer that can be trusted by each individual user as an equal peer in the network because every part of the system is aligned for one purpose: to provide a secure way to create, verify, and transfer ownership of digitally scarce cryptographic units.

Chapter **3**

Building Blocks: The Transaction's Journey to the Blockchain

At one end, you've got your wallet or your node software. At the other, there's the blockchain. In between is the network of peer-to-peer nodes and miners creating blocks in the chain. How does a transaction that you set up on your wallet program find its way into the blockchain?

In this chapter, we look at how a transaction leaves your wallet and ends up in the blockchain and the miner's role in that process. As an example, we use Bitcoin, the first blockchain-based cryptocurrency. Other cryptocurrencies use a similar process, to varying degrees. Each has its own particulars, but understanding how Bitcoin works will give you a really good foundation.

The Cryptocurrency Network

Every cryptocurrency has its own network of nodes, operating across the Internet, and this network has both peer-to-peer and client-server aspects, depending on how you chose to interface with it and which software you utilize. (You may hear the term *blockchain network* or *Bitcoin network*, for example.)

You'll often hear a cryptocurrency network described as a peer-to-peer network, and it is — though the peer-to-peer network can also be used as a client-server network. What's the difference?

>> **Peer-to-peer networks** are networks of equal computers that work together.

>> **Client-server networks** are networks on which servers provide services to client computers.

Think about how you work with email. The Internet's email system also has two aspects. First, it has a peer-to-peer aspect comprising hundreds of thousands of email servers around the world that work together, sending emails between each other.

But the email system also has a client-server aspect, with millions of email clients. Say that you use Outlook on your computer, or perhaps you log into Gmail and use the Gmail email program in your web browser. Either way, the program you're using to write, send, receive, and read email is known as a *client*. This client program sends outgoing email to an email server and receives incoming email from a server.

Cryptocurrency networks are similar. First, there is a peer-to-peer network of *full nodes,* computers that receive and validate transactions and blocks to make sure they abide by the rules of the network and are all valid; this is the network that is doing the work of maintaining the blockchain. These nodes are peers because they're all equal and work together. (And some of these full nodes, though not all of them, are also miners.) These nodes communicate with each other across the Internet using a particular protocol (a computer language, in the case of Bitcoin using the *Bitcoin peer-to-peer protocol*), just like email servers communicate across the Internet using a protocol designed for that purpose.

Then there are client programs — software wallets that people use to send transactions to the full nodes to be added to the blockchain. When you install wallet software on your computer or smartphone or when you set up a custodial wallet by creating an account at an exchange, you're working with a client program that can communicate on your behalf with the peer-to-peer network of full nodes. (These full nodes are servers to your wallet client.)

WARNING

Custodial wallets are convenient and incredibly easy to set up; somebody else manages your keys and the wallet software for you. But they are also dangerous. You have to trust the service to protect your keys and to act in your best interests.

To eliminate third parties in their interaction with the blockchain network, users and miners often choose to run their own node as an alternative to custodial wallets and simple wallets that get all their data from full nodes on the network. These nodes receive and verify their own transactions and act as a peer in the peer-to-peer network. A typical personal computer can function as a node with the correct software.

Here are a few software tools that making running a Bitcoin node on a PC or laptop as simple as a few clicks:

>> **Bitcoin Core:** https://bitcoin.org/en/bitcoin-core

>> **BTCPay Server:** https://btcpayserver.org

>> **OpenNode:** www.opennode.com

>> **Samourai Dojo:** https://bitcoin-on-raspberry-pi-4.gitbook.io/workspace

>> **Umbrel:** https://getumbrel.com

There are also specialized hardware devices that are designed to run only a Bitcoin node. These dedicated hardware nodes often consume less electricity compared to a typical PC and can be much smaller in size. Here is a short list of providers that specialize in dedicated Bitcoin node hardware:

>> **The Bitcoin Machine:** https://thebitcoinmachines.com

>> **Lightning in a Box:** https://lightninginabox.co

>> **myNode One:** https://mynodebtc.com/products/one

>> **Nodl:** www.nodl.it

>> **RaspiBlitz:** https://shop.fulmo.org/raspiblitz

>> **Samourai Dojo:** https://samouraiwallet.com/dojo

>> **Start 9 Labs Embassy:** https://store.start9.com/products/embassy

TECHNICAL STUFF

There are actually various different kinds of nodes. In fact, nodes on the Bitcoin network have around 150 different software configuration settings, so really there's an almost infinite number of different types of nodes. We need to explain at least a few basics, though, so what follows is a bit of a simplification; understand that the following types of nodes have a lot of overlap.

Any computer connected to the network is a node, but different nodes do different things:

>> **Full nodes** — more correctly known as *fully validating nodes* — are systems that fully validate blocks and transactions. Full nodes check that the blocks and transactions being passed around the network follow the network rules. The nodes then pass the blocks and transactions on, across the network to other full nodes, and those nodes will also validate the blocks and transactions. A full node may contain a copy of the entire blockchain, but not all do; nodes may opt to *prune,* or remove, redundant data to save space. Today, the amount of disk space the Bitcoin blockchain uses is around 430GB, so pruning can be worthwhile. Most full nodes also accept incoming transaction messages from wallets. Full nodes may be *listening nodes*, often known as *super nodes*, or *nonlistening nodes*. Some full nodes are mining rigs.

>> A **listening node** or *super node* is a publicly connectable full node that allows large numbers of connections with other nodes. The node "listens" for connections from other nodes on particular ports, is generally running all the time, and is not blocked by a firewall. The Bitcoin network has around 15,000 or more of these super nodes.

>> A full **nonlistening** node is one that has had the *listen* configuration parameter turned off. Having a full listening node can require a lot of bandwidth, so most nodes have listening disabled in order to reduce communications with other nodes. They do not broadcast their presence to the network, so are not publicly connectable; rather, they have a small number of outgoing connections. Nonlistening nodes are often used by people who want to have wallets that also validate transactions and blocks, but do not want to use the resources required by a listening node. By some counts, there are around 80,000 to 100,000 nonlistening nodes on the Bitcoin network, though during Bitcoin's December 2018 peak, there were likely around 200,000.

>> A **lightweight node** is one that does not receive and verify every transaction. Most lightweight nodes are wallets; the simple wallet software on your laptop or smart phone is a form of lightweight node. Lightweight nodes communicate with full nodes to transmit transactions and receive information about transaction validation. They are completely at the mercy of the full nodes — that is, lightweight nodes don't do any transactions or block validation of their own. Most lightweight nodes use a client-server setup; the wallet (client) queries a server for information about transactions recorded to the blockchain.

>> **SPV (Simple Payment Verification) nodes** are a form of lightweight node wallets that can verify just the transactions they care about by communicating with other nodes and retrieving a copy of the block headers.

So full nodes connect to each other, they pass transactions and blocks between each other . . . but they don't trust each other. If a node receives from a wallet a transaction that the node believes is invalid, it won't pass it on to another node. But this doesn't mean a node will automatically assume that the transaction must be valid if it's being passed a transaction by another node; rather, the node will validate the transaction for itself.

In fact, if a node gets a transaction that it discovers is invalid — for example, if the transaction is spending more money than is available on the address from which the money is coming — the node throws away the transaction, but it also blocks the node that sent the bad transaction. In this way, the network "polices" itself; valid transactions and blocks are verified by thousands of different nodes, bad data is disposed of quickly, and bad actors are isolated from the network.

It's this lack of trust that builds trust. Nodes will get blocked by other nodes — depending on the infraction nodes may be blocked for a few hours, or permanently blocked for obviously intentional misbehavior — and thus the system is self-regulating. Because nodes don't trust other nodes, the overall system can be trusted.

If you'd like to get an idea of the extent and distribution of the Bitcoin full node network, take a look at `https://bitnodes.io`, shown in Figure 3-1. (This chart shows just the full listening nodes; there are likely eight or ten times this number of full nonlistening nodes.)

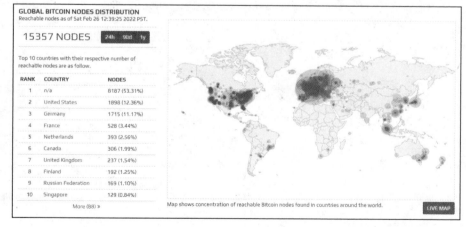

FIGURE 3-1: A live view at the time of writing of the full listening node count on the Bitcoin network as well as the distribution of these nodes across the world.

Source: `https://bitnodes.io`

Submitting Transactions

Say that you want to send someone some money, some of your Bitcoin. (Remember, we're writing this from the perspective of Bitcoin; other cryptocurrencies may function slightly differently, but the core principles are much the same.)

And say that you have a single Bitcoin associated with an address in the Bitcoin blockchain, and you want to send one tenth of that money (0.1BTC) to Joe. (It doesn't matter why — perhaps payment for a purchase, for some work Joe did for you, a charitable donation, a bribe, or whatever. All we care is that you're sending 0.1 Bitcoin to Joe.)

So, using your wallet software, you enter Joe's address, the Bitcoin address he gave you to use for the transaction. You state how much Bitcoin you're going to send him (0.1BTC). You also state how much of a fee you're willing to pay for the transaction.

Looking at transaction fees

Fees are often measured in Satoshi/byte and can range between 1 to over 2,000 Satoshi/byte (that is, the fee is based on the size of the transaction message your wallet sends to the blockchain, not the value of the transaction). The busier the network, the higher the fee required to incentivize miners to include your transaction in a block quickly. Bitcoin network fees per transaction on average fluctuate between 0.00001 BTC and 0.001 BTC, as shown in Figure 3-2.

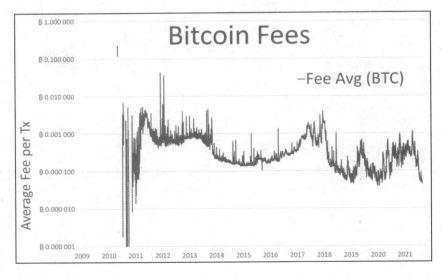

FIGURE 3-2: A view at the time of writing of the average transaction fee as measured in Bitcoin on the network.

These fees on the Bitcoin network per transaction average about to less than a few dollars to about $50 when the network is congested with high demand for transactions (see Figure 3-3).

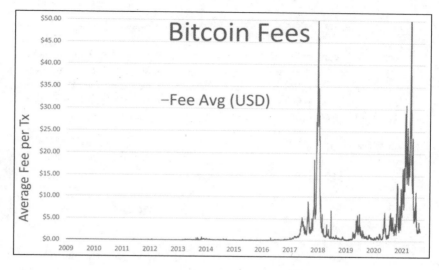

FIGURE 3-3:
A view at the time of writing of the average transaction fee as measured in dollars on the network.

A Satoshi is the smallest unit of Bitcoin — one hundred millionth of a Bitcoin. If your wallet balance is 1.00000001 BTC, the last digit denotes one Satoshi. Your wallet software will probably suggest a fee, estimated on current rates and network congestion; some wallet software will pick the fee for you, while other software lets you set that fee manually for more precision and to avoid over spending. Pay too little, and the transaction may not go through or may take a long time; pay too much, and, well, you overpaid. Transactions with higher fees will get picked up by mining software quicker than those with lower fees, of course; the more high-fee transactions in a block, the more the winning miner will earn.

For our example, say that you decide to pay a 0.0004BTC fee. Now, say this is your address:

```
1x6YnuBVeeE65dQRZztRWgUPwyBjHCA5g
```

Remember, it has a balance of 1BTC. That's what's known as the *input* for the transaction.

Here's Joe's address:

```
38DcfF4zWPi7bSPkoNxxk3hx3mCSEvDhLp
```

That's one of the *outputs* in the transaction. So far the transaction looks like this:

```
Input
1x6YnuBVeeE65dQRZztRWgUPwyBjHCA5g - 1BTC
Output
38DcfF4zWPi7bSPkoNxxk3hx3mCSEvDhLp - 0.1BTC
```

But wait, we need another output. We're putting 1BTC into the transaction, giving 0.1BTC to Joe, so we have to decide what happens to the other 0.9BTC. Actually, the other 0.8996BTC, as 0.0004BTC is being paid to the miner as a fee. So, where does the 0.8996BTC go? It goes back to you, of course, as your change. So the transaction might now look like this:

```
Input
1x6YnuBVeeE65dQRZztRWgUPwyBjHCA5g - 1BTC
Outputs
38DcfF4zWPi7bSPkoNxxk3hx3mCSEvDhLp - 0.1BTC
1x6YnuBVeeE65dQRZztRWgUPwyBjHCA5g - 0.8996BTC
```

We've shown 0.8996BTC going back to the original address. (Imagine going into a store with a ten-dollar bill, and paying $1 for something. What happens? You take $10 out of your pocket, hand it to the clerk, the clerk gives you $9 back, and you put the $9 back into your pocket.)

Change address

We've shown the change coming back to the same address used for the Input, and that's certainly possible. However, most wallet software will use a different address, or a *change address*, for the second of these outputs. Either way, you get the change back to an address owned by you, managed by your wallet software.

Note that nothing is stated in the outputs regarding the fee. That's because the transaction sent by your wallet doesn't explicitly state the fee. Rather, it says, "send 0.1BTC to the first address, send 0.89996BTC to the second address, and keep the change!" And that's just what the miner who wins the right to add this transaction to the blockchain will do: The mining rig will keep the change as a transaction fee.

TECHNICAL STUFF

This transaction information is put into a *script*, a text message that will be sent out over the crypto network. Your wallet software uses your private key to sign the transaction — that is, it encrypts the transaction information using the private key. It then adds the associated public key to the message and sends the transaction out onto the Bitcoin network. Within seconds, a node will receive the transaction; just as, when you send an email, within seconds your email will be received by a mail server. (You can think of your wallet program as a special form of messaging software, in fact.)

Verifying the transaction

The first thing the node does when receiving the transaction is to use the public key to decrypt the message so that it can read it. It must then *verify* the transaction. This process ensures that the transaction is valid, based on a number of different criteria. We won't go into all the details, but essentially the node asks itself (and answers) questions like these:

>> Is the message properly structured and not exceeding the maximum message size?

>> Does the message contain valid information — for example, does it contain valid input and output addresses and sums, within valid ranges, assigned to the addresses?

>> Does the input address exist in the blockchain with a valid balance?

>> Is a sufficient transaction fee associated with the transaction?

>> Does the wallet sending the transaction have a right to send the transaction — that is, is the public key sent with the message associated with the address from which the cryptocurrency is being sent?

What happens if the message is not valid in some way? The node throws it away because there's no point sending it on to the next node. But if it's valid, the node adds it to a pool of valid transactions (a *memory pool* or *mempool*), and sends it to other nodes on the network. These other nodes will do the same: decrypt and verify the transaction and add to their mempool if they find it valid. (That's part of the *consensus* process, ensuring that everyone agrees.) Thus the message, in a matter of seconds, *propagates* (spreads) across the crypto network, being picked up by node after node.

TECHNICAL STUFF

So the mempool is a collection of transactions waiting to be confirmed, solidified, and included into a block. The size of the mempool ebbs and flows depending on the current number of transactions hitting the network, and, of course, as the network congestion goes up, transaction fees go up. (You can find a very useful site for inspecting the current backlog of transactions in the mempool and current transaction fees at https://jochen-hoenicke.de/queue/#0,all.)

Some nodes are mining nodes. These nodes add blocks to the blockchain, in a competition to earn Bitcoin. These nodes are also creating memory pools, collections of transactions that need to be added to the blockchain.

Competing for Bitcoin, the ten-minute contest

Here's how the mining competition works. We'll begin at the point at which a miner has just won the right to add a block to the blockchain. When this happens, the winner sends the winning block out across the network, and it gets picked up by the nodes and added to their versions of the blockchain. That's when the next competition begins.

TECHNICAL STUFF

Each round of this game is designed to last around ten minutes; remember, one purpose of mining is to dribble new Bitcoin into the blockchain at a set rate; currently 12.5 Bitcoin every ten minutes. On average, a miner will succeed at the game every ten minutes, will be rewarded cryptocurrency, and the game restarts.

A miner receiving the new block first compares the block to the miner's mempool and removes transactions from the mempool that have been added to the latest block, leaving only transactions that have not yet been added to the blockchain.

The miner then gathers together transactions from the mempool into a new block, which is known as a *candidate block*. This block can be added to the blockchain, if the miner can win the competition.

HASHING?

A hash is a long number that is a kind of fingerprint for a set of data. That data, when passed through the same hashing algorithm, will always produce the same hash, and that hash cannot match any other set of data. The hash identifies the data uniquely. For more on hashing, see Chapter 2.

The miner creates a block header for the block, which includes a timestamp, a software version number, the hash of the previous block, and the hash of the block's transaction's Merkle tree root (never mind, you don't have to know about Merkle trees). The block header contains another couple of things that are related to the game that the miner has to play to compete against the other miners.

So now thousands of mining computers around the world that have created *candidate blocks* of data — records of transactions — are eager to add their own blocks to the blockchain. So the system has a choice to make: Which block, from which miner, will be added to the blockchain? That decision is based on a combination of chance and computing power. The Bitcoin network uses something called a *proof of work* task. All the miners are given the same task to undertake, and the first one to accomplish it wins, adds their block to the blockchain, and takes home the block reward: the combined transaction fees and block subsidy.

A Proof of Work task can be almost anything, as long as it is a complex task that takes a more or less predictable amount of work and results in an answer that is quickly and easily verifiable.

Primecoin, for example, has a Proof of Work task that involves finding chains of prime numbers that are then stored in the blockchain and available for use by mathematicians for, well, whatever it is they do with prime numbers. In the case of Bitcoin, the Proof of Work task has no practical use beyond securing transactions in the blockchain. Here's how Bitcoin's Proof of Work task functions.

The miner is looking for a number that matches a particular criteria; it must be a number that is below a certain target level (that target is one of the items stored in the block header).

The number is created by hashing the block header, creating in effect a digital fingerprint. (For more on hashing, see Chapter 1).

Now, the hash is a 256-digit binary number, expressed as a 64-digit hexadecimal number. Here's an example:

```
000000000000000015ecd7feb009048fb636a18b9c08197b7c7e194ce81361e9
```

Each block has a target number. The hash of the block header has to be equal to or less than the target number. Look at the preceding hash. It starts with 16 zeros and is actually a winning hash from some time ago. The more zeros at the start of the number, the smaller the number, and the harder to find, and over time difficulty typically goes up. Now, the target number is even smaller (this example, with 16 zeros at the start, is from some time ago). It begins, at the time of writing, with 19 zeroes.

The smaller the target number, the harder the task, right? Because fewer numbers are below a small number than a large number, and we need a hash that is less than the target.

So the miner hashes the block header. But every time you hash a piece of data, you're going to get the same result, right? So if the miner hashes the block header and finds that it's not less than the target, they have to change the block header. Well, the *nonce is* a piece of data in the block header. It is simply a number. The miner changes the nonce and hashes again. This time, the result of the hash will be different. Chances are, it's still not less than the target number, so the miner changes the nonce, hashes again, and checks the number, and so on.

Now, the magic of the hashing algorithm is that you can't predict which nonce will get you the result you want. The only way to find the result you want is to try, and try, and try again — thousands of times — until you get a hash that is less than the target. And if you do this before anyone else, you win!

This task is hugely difficult. A 64-digit hexadecimal number has this many possible variations (whatever this number is called!): 39,400,000,000,000,000,000,0 00,000,000,000,000,000,000,000,000,000,000,000,000,000,000,000,000,0 00,000,000,000,000,000,000,000,000,000,000,000,000,000. So the vast majority of hashes, purely based on chance, are going to exceed the target.

Say that you're the lucky miner who first finds a nonce that, when added to the block header, results in a hash that is below the target number — you win!

Winning the Bitcoin

You announce to the network that you've won. You create a block header for the block, which includes a timestamp, a software version number, the hash of the previous block, and the hash of the block's transaction's Merkle tree root. (Never mind, to successfully mine you don't have to know about Merkle trees.) You then send out your *candidate block*, with its block header and the header's hash, onto the network, so other nodes can check it. And check it they do.

A block doesn't get added to the blockchain unless it's been verified. To make sure you've won, the nodes hash the block header and check the result against the existing block header's hash. Remember, the Proof of Work task is very difficult, but easily verified, so it can be quickly seen that you have won the contest. The nodes add your block to the blockchain, and the contest resets and begins again. Oh, and you get the block reward — the transaction fees and block subsidy — assigned to your address in the new block.

That's mining!

So who typically wins these contests? It's a combination of both chance and computing power. Each time you add a nonce and hash the block header, there's a mathematically defined chance of winning. It's low, but possible. Hey, you might win on the first try! (You might, but it's just not very likely.)

How then do you increase your chances? You add a nonce and rehash over and over and over, millions of times. Each time you hash, it's like buying a lottery ticket. So the more lottery tickets you buy, the better your chances. That means the more powerful your mining rigs — the more calculations they can carry out — the more chances you have.

This process may all sound very complicated but the hard work is carried out by your mining rig and your node software. You're not going to be sitting down every ten minutes with paper and pencil hashing the block header! You set up the appropriate hardware and software and let it run.

BITCOIN PRESETS

All of these preset rules and system guidelines are baked into the software that runs the Bitcoin blockchain. A block contains around 2,000 transactions (it varies slightly depending on how much information is in each transaction). One block is added every ten minutes, more or less. In order to maintain this block emission rate, the software has to adjust its difficulty rules every now and then — every 2,016 blocks, in fact. If it's taking less than ten minutes for each block, on average — because more computing power is being used for mining, as more miners and mining rigs come online — then the target number will be proportionally reduced, to increase the difficulty. If it's taking more than ten minutes, though (as the price of Bitcoin drops, fewer people mine), then the target number is increased, reducing the difficulty. Also, every 210,000 blocks — around every four years — the block subsidy is halved. At the time of writing, the subsidy is 6.25BTC, but sometime in 2024, it will drop to 3.125BTC.

Chapter **4**

Exploring the Different Forms of Mining

I n this chapter, you find out about the different consensus algorithms used in cryptocurrency. Blockchain technology distributes data across hundreds or even thousands of computers. The challenge is to ensure that each copy of the data, on all those different computers, is correct. Different mathematical algorithms can be used to create consensus — to ensure that everyone working with any particular cryptocurrency agrees on what data should be included in the blockchain and what version of the blockchain is correct.

We explain various aspects of different consensus systems: proof of work, proof of stake, hybrid proof of stake/proof of work, and others.

Proof-of-Work Algorithms

Consensus is the process of ensuring everyone's copy of the transaction data matches — that every copy of the blockchain contains the same data. Different consensus methods can be used, but at the time of this writing, the primary method is known as *proof of work* (PoW). However, this method has less secure and trustworthy alternatives, and we touch on some of those methods in this chapter. As the cryptocurrency and blockchain space grows (it's rapidly expanding all the time), it is possible that a different system may end up becoming the "One who rules them all."

The most secure, trusted, yet energy-intensive of all the consensus systems, proof of work undeniably has the best track record. Having existed since the birth of Bitcoin, PoW has been instrumental in maintaining an unbroken chain of transactions since January 2009!

Proof of work predates cryptocurrency blockchains, though. Proof of work was originally developed as an idea for a process to counter junk mail.

The essential concept of proof of work is that in order to use a particular service — to send an e-mail for example, or to add transactions to a blockchain — one has to show that some form of work has been carried out. The goal is to inflict a modest cost (in terms of the computing power required to run the proof-of-work algorithm) on the person wanting to use the service once, but to make it very expensive for someone to use the service thousands or millions of times. This makes it cost-prohibitive to attack or disrupt proof-of-work systems.

The concept of using PoW as a countermeasure dates back to around 1993, and since then, quite a few different ideas for ways to use PoW have emerged. In the context of cryptocurrencies, proof of work prevents malicious miners from clogging up the network by submitting new blocks that can never be verified. If no work was required to submit a new block, anyone could repeatedly spam fake transactions inside new blocks and potentially grind the cryptocurrency network to a halt.

By the way, proof of work has a parallel in real-world currencies. For something to work as money, it has to be in limited supply, so either it's something that there simply isn't much of — gold, for example — or it has to be created through a process that takes significant effort.

How about sea shells, then? Sea shells have been used by various cultures as money. Consider wampum, sea shell money used by Native Americans in the eastern part of the continent well into the 18th century. "Shells," you say, "How much work does it take to pick up shells off the seashore?" Ah, but there was more to it than that. Wampum was made from very specific shells (the Channeled whelk and the quahog or poquahock clam shells), found in a very specific area (along Long Island Sound and Narragansett Bay). Furthermore, you couldn't just grab a whelk and buy dinner with it. You had to work the shells. The shells were cut down; for example, it was the inner spiral, the columella, of the Channeled whelk, that was used. Then the craftswomen (it was mostly women making wampum) drilled holes through the shells using wooden drills, and the shells were then polished on a grinding stone until they were smooth. They were finally strung together using deer hide or various other materials. This work ensured time and effort had to be put into the "currency" so that it could acquire value.

Another way to look at this concept is not that the money is "acquiring" value, but that it can't be created without a significant input of work, so the market can't be flooded with new, low-cost versions of the money, thus devaluing it.

Even the early European colonists used wampum. It wasn't until they began using more advanced manufacturing techniques to create wampum, lowering the cost of the creation of this currency and destroying its scarcity, that the value crashed, and wampum was no longer viable as a store of value and currency.

As co-author Peter relates:

> I had trouble fully getting the idea of proof of work and how it fits in when I first got involved in cryptocurrency. In case any readers are still trying to understand the purpose of PoW, I'll put it another way. The whole point of the work that the miners do (competing with each other to win the proof-of-work contest) is to ensure that adding a block to the blockchain isn't easy. If it's too easy, the blockchain is vulnerable. Bad actors could continually attack the blockchain by flooding the system with bad blocks. The idea of proof of work is to make adding a block difficult, rather like the whole idea of laboriously hand-working shells into wampum was to ensure that the wampum economy couldn't be flooded with cheap wampum.

Proof-of-work applications

A proof-of-work algorithm forces the miner to do some work — to use computational power — before submitting a block to the blockchain. The algorithm acts as security for a cryptocurrency by making unwanted actions costly and ensuring the intended outcome (the addition of only genuine, valid transactions to the blockchain) always occurs.

So what work must be performed? Essentially, the miner is required to solve a mathematical puzzle of some kind. The puzzle needs to be complicated enough to take some computational power, but not so complicated that it will take too long to validate and slow down the addition of transactions.

For example, the work being performed in Bitcoin's proof of work is just hashing the previous block of a transaction's header (along with a random number, the *nonce*) in the hope of finding a new hash that meets the required difficulty threshold.

There's a flip side to proof of work. Finding the answer to the puzzle has to be difficult, but checking and verifying the work has to be easy. That is, once the puzzle has been solved, it must be easy for other miners to check that indeed the puzzle has been solved correctly. In the case of Bitcoin, once a miner has solved the puzzle, the new hash is added to the header and the block sent to other miners and nodes to confirm. While it's hard to initially pick a nonce that will provide a good outcome — a hash number below the target level — once the nonce has been found, it is very quick and easy for other miners to run the same hashing calculation to confirm that indeed the puzzle has been solved. The work is done, and then everyone can quickly check the winning miner's block and sign off on it.

Note, by the way, that cryptocurrencies using proof of work are usually the only ones that require more efficient, specialized mining equipment. In proof of stake, described later in this chapter, almost any computer can act as a creator, verifier, and chainer of new blocks, as long as it has a significant stake in the underlying currency.

Proof-of-work examples

The use of proof of work is widely adopted in the cryptocurrency world. The largest and most successful cryptocurrency of them all, Bitcoin uses it along with a host of other popular cryptocurrencies. You may need different mining equipment for these cryptocurrencies, as each of them has a slightly different hashing algorithm, even though they all use proof of work. Here are a few examples of the more common PoW cryptocurrencies:

>> **Bitcoin** is currently the king of cryptocurrency in terms of network *hash rate* (that is, the number of hashes being processed every second), market liquidity, and overall adoption. Bitcoin has never not been the top cryptocurrency. Bitcoin pioneered proof of work and has been going strong for more than ten years on the back of this consensus system. Many other cryptocurrencies have copied the code of Bitcoin as a starting point and then modified it slightly for their own use. Most of them kept the proof-of-work component, although they may use a different hashing algorithm requiring a different mining rig setup than the one for Bitcoin.

Most capital in the cryptocurrency mining world is directed to Bitcoin, and the mining rigs used are specialized in performing the SHA-256 hashing algorithm native to Bitcoin consensus. Bitcoin-specific ASICs (Application Specific Integrated Circuits) now make up a large percentage of the system, and many are based in China, with the United States and Russia closely competing for second place.

» **Ether (on the Ethereum network**) is the second-most popular cryptocurrency, sometimes the third, depending on the day. Ethereum uses its own hashing algorithm for proof of work called *Ethash*. Don't worry too much about what Ethash is, though, as the Ethereum development team has divisive plans to leave proof of work behind and use proof of stake in the future, akin to rebuilding the aircraft engine midflight! In fact, they have a difficulty "bomb" baked into the Ethereum code. As time goes on, it becomes harder and harder to mine Ethereum via proof of work, meaning miners earn less and less. (Despite this bomb, when the price of ETH was at all-time highs, mining ether was still very lucrative.)

» **Litecoin** is generally considered the silver to Bitcoin's status as "digital gold." Litecoin focuses on fast payments (meaning quicker block times) and low transaction fees. It uses a different hashing algorithm from Bitcoin, referred to as *scrypt mining,* so no *crossover mining* (using the same mining rig for multiple cryptocurrencies) is possible between the two. Other than that, though, in general, the way Litecoin works is very comparable to Bitcoin, as it was essentially a copy of the code. Just like Bitcoin, ASICs have been designed to specifically mine Litecoin, providing the most profitable approach.

» **Monero**, one of the more private (anonymous) cryptocurrencies, was built to allow CPU or GPU mining. That is, you don't need specialized equipment; the Monero community makes a point to keep ASICs out, updating the mining algorithm slightly every few months so manufacturers can't produce ASICs. Building an ASIC designed to process a particular algorithm more efficiently is always possible; outrunning the changes is also possible. Still, designing, producing, and selling a new ASIC takes time. By switching to a different PoW algorithm every so often, Monero has effectively outrun chip manufacturers. This allows CPUs and GPUs to remain effective on that blockchain. Monero uses a very complex cryptographic mechanism called *ring signatures* to hide transaction amounts associated with addresses, making it very hard to analyze the transactions. This sets it apart from the other cryptocurrencies in this list, which have easily searchable public transaction records on the blockchain.

» **Zcash** is also a more private (anonymous) cryptocurrency. It was built using a trusted setup ceremony, as Zcash calls it, with public cryptographic parameters split between various trusted parties. (This is complicated stuff, but if you want to read more, check out the Zcash site at `https://z.cash/technology/paramgen/`.) The Zcash blockchain allows for the use of shielded cryptographic transactions (called zk-SNARKs) that are nearly impossible to track. However, these shielded transactions are computationally expensive, and many Zcash wallets available today do not fully support this feature, instead relying on publicly auditable transactions very similar to Bitcoin. The Zcash proof-of-work mechanism is referred to as *Equihash*. However, unlike Bitcoin, in which the entire block reward goes to the winning miner, Zcash shares the block reward; there's a miner's reward, but also a founder's reward and a developer's reward, to compensate the team that created and maintains the Zcash codebase and blockchain.

Upsides

The main upside to proof of work is that it works! No other system for reaching and maintaining consensus has as long and impeccable a record as proof of work. The game theory behind proof of work ensures that if all participants are rational and acting in their own economic interests, the system will function as intended, and so far, that has been the case.

Proof of work also prevents spamming of the network from malicious miners. The energy and equipment expenses required to carry out this specialized work makes attacks cost-prohibitive and unsustainable.

Another great benefit to proof of work is the balancing of power. Power is spread over a wide range of miners, potentially a million individuals in the case of Bitcoin. The amount of cryptocurrency owned by a particular miner is irrelevant; the computing power is what counts. Conversely, with proof-of-stake systems, miners *stake* currency — the more they own, the more power they have — so power over the system can become concentrated into the hands of a small number of stakers; this is especially the case for coins' initial coin offerings, also known as *premined distributions*.

This is another advantage that most proof-of-work cryptocurrencies have: fair distribution. To have found a block and gained the subsequent block reward, a miner must have provided adequate work and supported the network according to the ruleset. This, according to *cryptocurrency game theory*, provides an important incentive. Proof-of-work mechanisms, under this theory, ensure that it is much more economically beneficial to work toward consensus than against it.

**TECHNICAL
STUFF**

Game theory is a branch of study involving mathematical models that describe likely decision-making by rational decision-makers in some kind of relationship. Decisions made by these decision-makers, or actors, affect the decisions and actions of others. Thus, within cryptocurrency, the goal is to incentivize all actors to make decisions that result in a stable, trusted network.

Downsides

A big downside to proof of work is the resources required to perform the work. It's not just a single miner using the proof-of-work algorithm, and attempting to solve the hashing puzzle. Rather, it's all the miners in the world competing to solve the puzzle first! So, rather than one computer consuming electricity (and adding carbon to the atmosphere), it's thousands of computers doing it at the same time, despite the fact that only one miner gets the right to add a block!

The Bitcoin network, which has the largest number of miners, is estimated to use around 100 terawatt-hours (TWh) per year, which is roughly equivalent to the annual energy needs of a country the size of Malaysia or Sweden.

Another downside is that over time, the mining under proof of work can also become centralized. The setup cost for a mining operation is not insignificant. Miners who already have a data center and ongoing mining operations are in a much better position to add rigs. With a lower cost per mining rig, over time, those who were first movers outcompete later entrants, and centralization can occur.

Related to this centralization is the potential for *51 percent attacks*, a major concern for anyone who mines a proof-of-work cryptocurrency. A 51 percent attack can occur when a single entity gains control over 51 percent (or more) of the total active hashing power. In this scenario, it becomes possible for this majority hash controller to modify a cryptocurrency's blockchain record, destroying the trust that is fundamental to its existence. It is for this reason that decentralization of miners is promoted and encouraged in the cryptocurrency realm.

A final downside to proof of work is the wasted calculations that all the proof of work requires! While the possibility of denial-of-service attacks making a cryptocurrency unusable is very real — thus making the proof-of-work mechanism an effective protection for the blockchain — the search for a nonce provides no economic, social, or scientific benefits to anyone outside of the cryptocurrency's ecosystem. In other words, once the thousands of miners have played the game and one has solved the puzzle and added a block to the chain, all that computing power has no residual value; one may argue that the power has been wasted on a pointless game.

The short story made long is that proof of work is the most proven way we have of keeping a peer-to-peer cryptocurrency system operational. While indeed, some areas need efficiency improvements, no other solution can provide the same security benefits without different economic, consensus, and computer engineering tradeoffs, and as a result, proof of work will remain widely utilized.

Proof-of-Stake Algorithms

In the early days of cryptocurrency, PoW was the only game in town, and new cryptocurrencies primarily copied Bitcoin as the model and a starting point for their slightly different ideas and implementations.

Over time, however, some involved in cryptocurrency recognized the downsides to PoW and set out to find a better way of securing a cryptocurrency, soon settling on proof of stake (PoS).

The idea is to make miners stake their cryptocurrency as an entry ticket for adding blocks to the blockchain and earning transaction fees. The penalty for adding invalid transactions to the blockchain ledger would be loss of the coins staked. This was first proposed in 2011 by a user of the Bitcointalk.org forum. In 2012, the white paper for *Peercoin*, which expounded and solidified this idea, was published, describing a new system for securing and reaching blockchain consensus that was much less resource-intensive than pure proof of work. (While Peercoin is technically a hybrid of proof of stake/proof of work, this marked the first real-world implementation involving proof of stake.)

Today, proof of stake, along with its hybrid use (hybrid proof of stake/proof of work), helps secure and maintain trust for a few somewhat successful cryptocurrencies. While still considered the more unproven of the two main consensus systems, proof of stake has some benefits over proof of work. Proof of stake should be understood by any cryptocurrency miner worth their salt. (And you can potentially profit it from it, too!)

Proof of stake explained

Proof of stake is similar to proof of work — it's used to maintain consensus and keep the cryptocurrency ledger secure — but with one major difference: There's way less *work*! Instead of using a specialized mining rig to calculate a targeted hash, a miner who wants to create a new block chooses to stake an amount of the cryptocurrency they want to mine. Staking can be thought of as making a refundable deposit, and the purpose behind its requirement is to prove that you have a vested interest in the welfare of whatever cryptocurrency you're mining. In other words, before you can mine the cryptocurrency, you must prove that you own some of it, and you must stake it during the mining process; that is, you can't just show you own it, sell it, and continue mining. The stake is locked during the mining process.

A miner has to be selected to add transactions to the blockchain; one miner wins the contest. Different cryptocurrencies use different methods for making that

CHAIN TIP

The term *chain tip* is often used to describe the highest block number on a particular blockchain. The *chain tip* would be the block that has the most accumulated proof of work hashed toward its chain of blocks.

The second problem with pure proof of stake is called "nothing at stake." This theory states that in PoS systems, validators (miners) are not interested in consensus, because it may be in their financial interest to add invalid blocks to the blockchain, leading to forks in the blockchain creating multiple chains. That is, if one validator adds an invalid block, other miners may accept it and build on it, because they will earn transaction fees on whatever chain wins. (And because it's a PoS system, it doesn't take much computational power to do so.) This leaves open the possibility of the blockchain being manipulated by those who hold the largest stake in that system, which is the opposite of the very purpose of cryptocurrency, which was to eliminate the idea of the traditional banking system and its centralized and manipulatable ledger system.

Under proof of work, this issue would be resolved quickly, as the miners are incentivized to quickly resolve which fork of the blockchain to follow so precious mining rig resources are not wasted. The invalid block is *orphaned*, meaning that no new blocks will be built on top of it, and business continues as usual with only a single blockchain. Under proof of stake, however, it is very easy to continue building new blocks on each chain, and in theory, the blockchain could easily fork. There's a negligible cost to validating multiple chains, and if that occurs, the decentralized consensus mechanism has failed. With proof of work, chain reorganizations occur naturally as orphaned blocks, also known as *uncles*; they have their transactions placed back into the mempool and, regardless of which *chain tip* eventually becomes confirmed, the transactions and blockchain maintain validity.

Hybrid Proof of Stake/Proof of Work

In light of the disadvantages from PoW's energy consumption and PoS's "nothing at stake" problem, savvy crypto-entrepreneurs thought of a different solution: hybrid proof of stake/proof of work. This helps alleviate the issues of distribution and "nothing at stake" while also slightly reducing the cost to validate transactions from proof of work.

So how do you know if a cryptocurrency is a hybrid? Unfortunately, you may see it referred to as proof of stake, hybrid proof of stake, or hybrid proof of work, all of which are confusing. To figure out what a cryptocurrency is actually using, a quick search engine query will find you the answer. For example, "consensus algorithm for Bitcoin" will yield an explanation for Bitcoin's proof-of-work consensus system, and a search of "consensus algorithm for DASH" will show you that DASH uses proof of work and proof of stake.

Because a growing number of cryptocurrency projects are using both proof of stake and proof of work, understanding what this means for mining is a must.

Hybrids explained

Earlier in this chapter, we discuss how proof of work (PoW) and proof of stake (PoS) function; the question now is how these two components work together in a hybrid proof-of-stake/proof-of-work system. A caveat, though: The variations for different hybrid consensus systems are vast, so if you decide to mine or stake a hybrid cryptocurrency, put some effort into researching exactly how that chain's specific approach is applied to determining blockchain consensus.

In a hybrid system, both PoS and PoW are used. A particular node may carry out both PoS and PoW processes, or it may do just PoS or just PoW.

Here's an example flow for a hybrid consensus system. The miner starts by staking an amount of cryptocurrency *to themself* — that's the proof of stake — and then uses the data from this transaction and combines it with the current time (represented as the number of seconds since some fixed date).

The miner then takes this combined information (transaction information and seconds value) and calculates a hash (that's the proof of work). This scenario doesn't have a nonce, but the integer for the current time has the same effect of changing the hash output as additional calculations are computed.

Because this nonce substitute changes once every second, as time elapses, a new hash can be calculated only every second, and thus the resources required to mine are much lower than with a true PoW system, in which modern ASIC miners can calculate trillions of hashes per second. Rather than calculating numerous hashes every second, only *one* hash calculation is made every second per node. This means that most off-the-shelf computers can function as mining rigs. All you need is a computer with a wallet holding the chain's predetermined staking threshold of the hybrid cryptocurrency.

Once the hybrid miner has this hash, it is checked against a target difficulty. There is a major difference, though. This target difficulty is different for every single miner! This is because the difficulty is lowered (easier to meet) or raised (harder to meet) based on the coin age of the cryptocurrency used in the transaction that was sent at the beginning of this process, giving an edge to existing coin holders and adding barriers to entry for new miners. (*Coin age* is simply the sum of the length of time the miner has owned each of their cryptocurrency units.)

For example, if Peter owned three units of Hybridcoin and they had all been in his wallet for five days, the coin age of that transaction would be 15 (5+5+5=15). If one of these three Hybridcoins had been in his wallet for four days, though, the coin age of the transaction would be 14 (5+5+4=14).

The higher the coin age of the transaction, the easier it is to find a hash that meets the target difficulty, meaning that miners with greater coin ages have a greater chance of winning than those with lower coin ages. Despite this, an element of chance still exists; a higher coin age significantly increases a validator's chances, but still doesn't guarantee their winning.

The first miner to solve the puzzle — to find a hash that matches the target — wins. That miner can now chain the latest block of transactions and will receive the block reward (the block subsidy and transaction fees) for doing this.

This system enables a miner to try their luck every second. Because they are sending the cryptocurrency to themselves in this process, it cannot be sent to anyone else and is effectively "staked" or locked to their account. Additionally, in most hybrid systems, when the miner finally does win this lottery, their cryptocurrency coin age is reset, reducing the likelihood that they will win the game again the next time.

HYBRID PROOF-OF-STAKE/ PROOF-OF-WORK REWARDS

So if a cryptocurrency uses proof of stake and proof of work, how do the rewards work? For most hybrid cryptocurrencies, the rewards are lumped together as a single sum and then split between the proof-of-stake validators and proof-of-work miners using a preset percentage. For example, say that the block subsidy is 10 Hybridcoin and the transaction fees in the new block equal 2 Hybridcoin, and there's a preset percentage split of 60 percent to the PoW miners and 40 percent to the PoS miners. In this scenario, the PoW miner who is creating and chaining the latest block earns 7.2 Hybridcoin, and the PoS miner who verifies the latest block earns the remaining 4.8 Hybridcoin. (If a node was both staking and mining, it would get the full amount, of course.) It is important to remember that the percentage split between types of miners can vary depending on the specific cryptocurrency, so always do your research!

Hybridized examples

DASH is the most successful hybrid of PoS/PoW. DASH's codebase is the basis for many other hybrid cryptocurrencies. Originally forked from Bitcoin around 2014 under a different name, and then later modified to allow hybrid PoS/PoW *master-nodes,* DASH offers returns of around 6 to 8 percent annually. DASH can handle quite a few transactions per second, but the masternode model is fairly centralized and will cost you a significant upfront investment to begin validating. This creates an underlying demand for that cryptocurrency, manipulating the purchase price in favor of existing coin holders.

PIVX is a fork of the DASH cryptocurrency. While it originally used proof of work, it now works on a proof-of-stake/proof-of-work hybrid model. Staking any amount of your PIVX will net you around 8 to 12 percent annually, paid in PIVX directly to your staked wallet.

At the time of this writing, Ethereum is still using a PoW system (Ethash), but plans to switch to a hybrid system at some future date. (The Ethereum community has been discussing the switch for quite some time.) The front runner for the beginning of the switchover (it will likely evolve over time) is currently known as Casper FFG, in which a PoS protocol runs alongside the Ethash PoW protocol, with a network of validators running a PoS checkpoint every 50 blocks.

Peercoin (PPC) was the first PoS cryptocurrency in operation (back in cryptocurrency ancient history, 2012). However, it is not a pure PoS currency; it is a PoS/PoW hybrid. Peercoin has been mimicked and built upon since then. You can still mine its hybrid proof-of-work and proof-of-stake implementation today for about a 1 percent return annually, assuming the coin price stays steady.

Upsides

Hybrid systems take the best of both proof of work and proof of stake. The PoW component provides security, while the higher efficiency of the PoS component allows a higher throughput of transactions and, therefore, lower transaction fees. The result is a secure and fast, albeit more centralized, cryptocurrency.

MASTERNODES

A *masternode* is a staking and validating node that holds a sufficient threshold of coins, often many hundreds or even thousands. This amount of coins allows the node to vote on code proposals as well as validate and propagate blocks to the network. DASH is the best-known blockchain using the masternode concept.

Downsides

Governance is difficult for hybrid cryptocurrencies. Because the reward split can theoretically be voted on and changed, there's a constant disagreement between the users who want more rewards for proof of stake and those who want a higher percentage for proof of work. While the hybrid approach has some of the benefits of each consensus system, it also carries many of the downsides of both proof of stake and proof of work.

Delegated Proof of Stake

Delegated proof of stake (dPoS) works similarly to proof of stake, but with a more centralized concentration of *block producers* or *witnesses* in the dPoS ecosystem. Block producers are elected and take sequential turns to add blocks to the blockchain. Generally, the cryptocurrency owners get to vote for the validators in proportion to the amount of the cryptocurrency they own. And there simply aren't many block producers, with the number being generally in the range of 20 to 100. (EOS has 21, for example.)

dPoS systems also have *validators* who validate that the blocks the block producers are adding are indeed valid; anyone can be a validator. (This shows what a confusing world cryptocurrency is, with different people using words in different ways. In some PoS systems, validators also add blocks to the blockchain.)

In dPoS, a voting mechanism allows witnesses (block validators) to vote for or against other witnesses if some become bad actors by corrupting the chain with invalid transactions or other damaging behavior.

The advantages and disadvantages of this system are very similar to typical proof-of-stake systems. However, a number of blockchains have actually been successfully deployed using this technology, the most noteworthy examples being EOS and Steem.

Delegated Byzantine Fault Tolerance

Delegated Byzantine Fault Tolerance (dBFT) is similar to dPoS. Its name refers to the Byzantine Generals Problem, which Bitcoin and other cryptocurrencies sought to solve. Its challenges include how to find consensus, with everyone working together for the good of the network, in a distributed computer network in which some parties may be unreliable, either because of technical faults or intentional malfeasance.

In dBFT, blocks are put forward by speaker nodes and voted on by delegate nodes. Consensus in dBFT is achieved when at least two-thirds of the delegate nodes agree on a proposed block. Any user can run a speaker node, but to be a delegate node requires being voted in by large token holders. The risk is that this may lead to centralization of power and vote manipulation in the future, but so far, dBFT implementations have maintained chain validity.

With dBFT, once a transaction is confirmed and the block recorded into the chain, it achieves total finality and is irreversible. This leads to almost no chance of forking between delegate nodes.

NEO is one of the few dBFT cryptocurrencies. In the *genesis* block (the first block of the NEO blockchain), 100 million NEO were created (premined), with 50 million sold to the public and 50 million locked up, then trickled out to the team working on NEO at a rate of 15 million per year. The stake you earn for running a speaker node is not paid in NEO. Rather, it is paid in GAS, which is a separate token used to fuel contracts on the NEO network. NEO has only seven voting delegate nodes. More may be added, in groups of three, to allow for the two-thirds agreement required. (The total number of delegates, minus one, can be divided by three, so a block is accepted when at least two-thirds of the delegates plus one vote for it.)

Proof of Burn

Proof of burn (PoB) is a consensus mechanism that proves that adequate resources are expended in the creation of a particular coin or token. This can be an expensive method to choose, but it can be effective for kickstarting a new cryptocurrency that utilizes the accumulated proof of work of a more secure chain. A PoB cryptocurrency typically sits on top of another, PoW, cryptocurrency blockchain.

Essentially, a coin that has been created in the proof-of-work blockchain is sent to a verifiably unspendable address (sometimes known as an *eater address*) — that is, to a blockchain address that the community has verified as being unusable. Such an address may have been created randomly, rather than through the usual process of creating a private/public key pair and then hashing the public key. If the address was created randomly, then the private key cannot be known, and thus the address is unspendable. Thus, any cryptocurrency sent to that address can never be used again. (There's no private key that can be used to send the cryptocurrency to another address.) The cryptocurrency has been, in effect, burned!

Thus, launching a PoB cryptocurrency begins with buying PoW coins and sending them to the eater address. In return, the buyer gets the right to mine. For example, that's how the Counterparty (XCP) cryptocurrency began, back in January 2014, when miners sent Bitcoin to an eater address and in return were issued Counterparty coins, which gave them the right to participate in Counterparty mining.

The benefits of this method include the ability to use the burnt coins' PoW as security for the PoB chain, but the downsides include the fact that the PoB network cannot exist independently of the PoW coin and requires the trust and utilization of the underlying cryptocurrency asset that was burnt.

And More . . .

There's more, of course. There's *proof of capacity* (PoC), where miners save a database of puzzle solutions to the node's storage, and when a block contest runs, the node accesses the puzzle solutions to find the correct one. There's *proof of elapsed time* (PoET), where nodes are randomly assigned a wait time and then blocks are added, based on the sequence of wait times (the lowest wait time goes first). There's also *proof of activity* (PoA), a particular form of hybrid PoW/PoS, *limited confidence proof of activity* (LCPoA), and so on.

And more models turn up all the time. There is no perfect consensus mechanism, so the evolution goes on, as new ideas arise and new models are tested.

2

The Evolution of Cryptocurrency Mining

Chapter **5**

The Evolution of Mining

For the first few years of Bitcoin's existence, the network was not widely known, and very few users were running nodes or mining. The hardware used to mine was also very basic: general-use computer equipment not designed specifically for mining. Due to this, the amount of computational resources that were being dedicated to mining blocks and securing the network was very small in comparison to today. It was also viewed by most participants in the ecosystem during this period as an experiment and was not something that many believed was worth devoting significant amounts of resources to. These factors combined to create a very low block difficulty environment for early Bitcoin miners.

In this chapter, we look at the history of Bitcoin mining, the evolution of computational hardware, the progression of mining software, differing techniques to mining, and how the various components function together. To get an idea of the best approaches that might work well for a miner going forward into the future, it is often good to know the past and present state of the industry and technology.

Proof of Work Mining Evolution

The Bitcoin mining saga all started on a computer operated by Satoshi Nakamoto, with what's known as the *genesis block* — the first Bitcoin brought into existence. At this time, the beginning of Bitcoin mining, the block difficulty was pretty low — that is, it didn't take much computing power to be able to win the contest and add a block now and then. That afforded virtually any user running a Bitcoin full node the opportunity to mine a block and collect the associated reward. The second confirmed node operator and Bitcoin miner was a fellow by the name of Hal Finney. In these early days, the network comprised as few as two nodes at times, but since then the node network has grown to more than 100,000 full nodes. At one point, there were more than 200,000!

Over the first ten years of Bitcoin mining, the competition for finding blocks steadily increased as network popularity and notoriety increased. Miner ingenuity combined with increasing economic incentives led to the development of more efficient mining. The decade between 2009 and 2019 saw a computational arms race incentivizing the construction, acquisition, and operation of the most effective and efficient mining hardware.

CPU mining

Personal computers consist of a few key components chief among which is the central processing unit, the CPU. Central processing units are very flexible computer chips, good at computing a wide variety of tasks from email to web browsing to word-processing. They are capable at performing all these tasks, but aren't exceptionally efficient or specialized in any of them.

An off-the-shelf CPU today could perform roughly 20 to 200 hashes per second (H/s) when pointed to a proof of work mining protocol. However, deploying a CPU to mine on the Bitcoin network today would be an exercise in futility, like going into battle against a modern army, equipped only with arrows and spears. A CPU simply can't compete against the specialized equipment in use today. However, there are still cryptocurrency blockchains with lower network hash rates and unique mining algorithms that can be effectively mined with a CPU.

Adoption of GPUs

Beginning around 2011, Graphics Processing Units (GPUs) became the mining hardware of choice on the Bitcoin network (though they were somewhat obsolete by 2013). GPUs are pieces of hardware designed to manage the kind of calculations required for computer graphics. Gamers and graphic designers often upgrade their desktop computers by buying graphics cards to improve their systems' performance. Graphics in computer games would display more quickly, and the huge graphics files produced by graphic designers could be managed more quickly and easily. GPU cards are also designed to run for long intervals while dissipating heat through large heat sinks and fan cooling systems.

From the cryptocurrency miner's perspective, these cards had the additional advantage of being able to hash more quickly, with a lower energy expenditure per hash than a CPU. This allowed miners to increase their overall hashing power while maintaining relatively low power usage.

REMEMBER

Miners are in competition with each other. The more quickly a miner can hash, the more likely the miner is to win the hashing competition. Hash power is everything!

The total Bitcoin network hashing power as well as block difficulty increased substantially during these years, essentially pushing CPU mining into the history books on the Bitcoin blockchain.

Rise of the FPGAs

Another mining device used to increase hash rate was the Field Programmable Gate Array, or FPGA. These devices can be rapidly reconfigured, or field programmed, to process different algorithms at a more efficient rate without the need to design and manufacture circuit board chip sets designed for a specific algorithm. These types of mining rigs are still popular and used to mine cryptocurrencies that change their Proof of Work algorithm frequently in an attempt to prevent hardware specific mining equipment from proliferating.

Dominance and efficiency of ASICs

As mining cryptocurrency became more widespread and profitable, suppliers began developing hardware specifically designed to mine cryptocurrency.

REMEMBER

CPUs are designed to do a wide range of tasks reasonably well, and consequently do none of them really well. This new hardware was designed to do just one thing really well — process the algorithms required for mining a specific cryptocurrency.

Thus, the FPGA developments quickly gave way to the development and manufacturing of Application Specific Integrated Circuits, or ASICs for short. These chips were deployed for a single purpose, which was to mine proof-of-work cryptocurrencies, such as Bitcoin. These ASICs would do a poor job of word-processing, email, or web browsing, but were orders of magnitude more effective and efficient at cryptocurrency mining. The increases in chip efficiency can be seen in Figure 5-1, which graphs popular and widely used chips during the 2014 to 2017 period. As you can see, the amount of power used to process a terahash (a billion hashes) dropped dramatically as ASICs were designed specifically to process these algorithms. Today's state of the art ASICs are even more capable.

The rise of ASICs led to an enormous increase in the network's hash rate. The network *hash rate* is the number of hashes that can be done every second by the combination of all the miners working on a network. The chart in Figure 5-1 shows that the Bitcoin network hash rate peaked at more than 120 million TH/s — that is, 120 million terahashes per second. A tera is a trillion, so a terahash is a trillion hashes; thus, 120 million TH/s means that the entire combination of all the miners on the network could, at the peak, run 120,000,000,000,000,000,000 hash operations in a single second, a truly vast amount of computational power!

FIGURE 5-1:
A chart depicting the energy (joules) needed to produce the same amount of hash power from some of the more popular ASIC chips as they evolved and become more efficient over time.

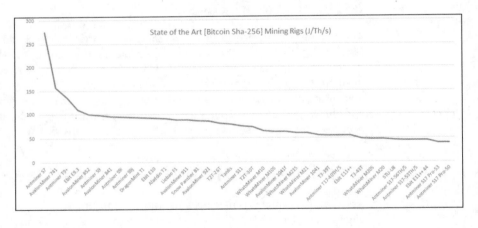

You can see how quickly processing power on the Bitcoin network grew, in the logarithmic chart in Figure 5-2. (You can see the latest data at www.blockchain.com/en/charts/hash-rate?timespan=all.)

WHY NOT EXAHASHES?

120,000,000,000,000,000,000 hash operations is 120 quintillion hashes. So why don't we say 120 QH/s? Well, first, the correct notation would be 120 EH/s; that is, 120 exahashes a second, because *exa* is used to denote quintillion in the same way that tera denotes trillion. But, more importantly, terahashes is just what is perhaps most frequently used when discussing these vast numbers of processes occurring every second. Terahashes is also the unit most manufacturers use to describe the specifications on the latest and greatest Bitcoin mining ASIC rigs. Whether it's terahashes, or thousands of terahashes, or millions of terahashes, we most commonly measure this processing power in terms of terahashes, or TH/s. But sometimes you will see exahashes here and there.

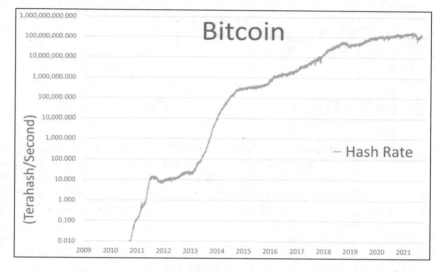

FIGURE 5-2: A chart showing the immense hashing power — and its dramatic growth — of the Bitcoin network over time.

The Days of Solo Mining

During the early days in Bitcoin's history, the network hash rate was very low. This gave virtually any miner running the Bitcoin core-client software with a laptop or desktop during 2009 to 2011 a very good chance of minting a new Bitcoin block now and then and collecting the associated block subsidy and fees. This was done by simply enabling mining in the core client software after it had synced with the Bitcoin blockchain.

Some large miners still elect to solo mine, choosing to bet on their slim odds of finding a block in the hopes of minting a block and retaining all its associated coin rewards. It is not as popular an option today, but with a significant portion of the network hash rate and enough time, a block can still indeed be found by individual miners. (They fatten up these slim odds by investing huge sums of money into their mining equipment.) Today, this method is not recommended for the novice miner. Most hobbyist miners choose to work with mining pools.

As mining hardware evolved into the ASIC realm, it became harder and harder for the layman to mine, for Mom and Pop operations to mine. Equipment got more expensive, and to compete, miners needed more and more equipment, they needed more space for the equipment, they needed cooling for the equipment, they had to put up with the noise and deal with complex hardware and software configurations, and so on. Mining became expensive and complicated. Pool mining and cloud mining were developed as a way for the little guy to get involved in mining, without all the hassles. (And for the pool- and cloud-mining companies to make money, of course.)

Pool Mining

Bitcoin mining is inherently competitive, in an adversarial environment — which is what makes pool mining so interesting, as it is a microcosm of cooperation inside this highly competitive space. Each individual miner participating in a pool works for the collective benefit and shares the reward, in proportion to their contribution, with all those who contributed hashing power toward finding minted blocks.

What is a mining pool?

The users who participate in mining pools pool their computational resources together and work as a team to find blocks. If a mining pool user were to find a block, but at the time is only contributing to ~5 percent of the total pool hash rate, that user would collect ~5 percent of the total block reward associated with that block. This distributes the costs and gains in a very fair manner across the pool based on each miner's contribution.

By the way, even though the thousands of participants in a pool think of themselves as miners — and for the purpose of this book, we're going to call them miners — from a system standpoint, they are not. A miner is really a mining *node*, and from the perspective of the cryptocurrency network, the pool itself provides a mining node, and the individual members of the pool are really invisible to the network, behind the node. That is, you're not setting up your own node; pool mining is far simpler than solo mining! You're not carrying out every task required of a real miner. The individual pool members provide their computers' processing power to the mining operation, but there's really, from a technical perspective, a single miner, the pool operator, who has to manage the entire process and run the node. The pool provides the tools for you to work with them. Figure 5-3, for example, shows Antpool's statistics page.

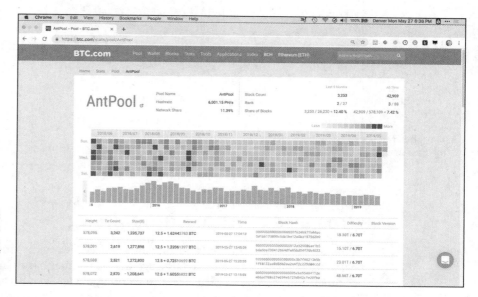

FIGURE 5-3:
Antpool's statistics page; Antpool is one of the largest Bitcoin mining pools.

Choosing a pool

Many different pools are in the Bitcoin and cryptocurrency mining industry today. Some of them are very altruistic in nature, and others could be considered bad actors.

TIP

It is important to select a mining pool that reflects your values. If not, the pool could be utilizing your hashing power in a manner that does not coincide with your goals. (You can find out more about picking a pool in Chapter 7.) You can employ lots of tools to help you make the right choice. Figure 5-4, for example, shows a chart on the Coin Dance website that displays blocks added to the Bitcoin blockchain over the previous 24 hours, broken down by the mining pool.

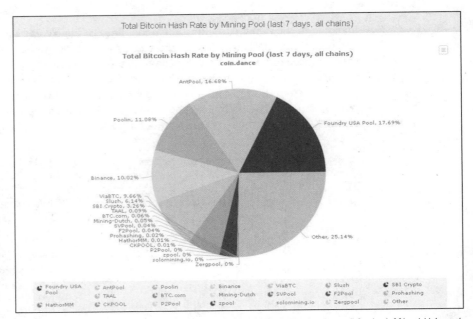

FIGURE 5-4:
A pie chart that displays the percentage of blocks found by mining pool over the past seven days.

Source: https://coin.dance/blocks/allhashthisweek

Pros and cons of pool mining

Pool mining allows a miner to consistently collect rewards for the work provided toward the network, even though the average pool miner has such a low hash rate that they aren't likely to earn a reward working alone. Even if you never actually find the hash to win the reward, as long as you are contributing processing power, you'll still share in the profits.

Of course, if you are the lucky miner finding the winning hash, you don't get to keep the entire block reward; you share it with all the other miners, each according to the proportion of contributed hash power.

The pool also takes a small fee for providing their service. That is, the block rewards — comprising the block subsidy and transaction fees — that are earned are not shared out equally among everyone; the guys running the pool take their cut, of course (hey, it's business!).

One criticism of pool mining is that it is leading to the concentration of power in a small number of hands (the various pool operators). For example, when nodes vote on a blockchain network's policies, it's just a few pool operators that get to vote for tens of thousands of individual pool members.

This has become obvious during code improvement debates where mining pools were voting for code proposals that individual users on those pools may not have agreed with. Misuse of hash rate was also apparent when some pools were mining blocks that did not include any significant amount of transactions in an attempt to clog the mempool, increase transaction fees, and congest the network. By not adding transactions to blocks, the mempool isn't cleared as fast, and precious blockspace is wasted. This situation backlogs transactions and causes finality of settlement to be delayed. It was a tactic used to push Bitcoin alternatives with larger blocksizes and is also used to push transaction fees up, increasing rewards for miners. Miners select transactions from the mempool that they want to include in a block. Most choose to load blocks to their maximum with the largest transaction fees for more profit to themselves, but sometimes miners and pool conglomerates have other political motives.

TIP

These downsides can easily be overcome by users, however, by simply pointing their mining hardware to a different pool that more closely aligns with their objectives and goals. As the mining pool is providing a service, if a user doesn't like the way the pool operates, that user can take their hash rate and go elsewhere. This free market pool ecosystem normally acts as a check and balance against pool operators and creates incentives for pool behavior that benefits the cryptocurrency instead of hurting it.

Cloud Mining

Cloud mining operations are *mining farms* — data centers dedicated to mining — that sell or lease hashing power. The essence of the service is that a third-party hosts mining equipment and provides access to the rewards associated with the equipment. This method has many advantages and disadvantages. For one, the user must trust the cloud provider in a space ripe with scams and frauds. The user is not in control of the equipment or how it is used.

The advantages, of course, are not having to fill your home with computer equipment, not having to deal with the noise, the heat, the power consumption, and the upkeep of the mining equipment, and so on. Essentially, you outsource the work.

Pool mining versus cloud mining

So what's the difference between pool mining and cloud mining? In both cases you're working with a third party:

>> With **pool mining**, you need your own mining rig, and through the use of the pool's software, you contribute your mining rig's processing power to the mining operation. You'll need to deal with buying and managing equipment, running the equipment, cooling the equipment, keeping a solid Internet connection up and running, and so on.

>> With **cloud mining**, you are essentially an investor in a mining operation; all you provide is money. Cloud mining companies sign up thousands of individuals to invest various sums into the operation and who take a cut of the proceeds in return. All you need to do is find a reputable cloud-mining operation (be careful!), send them money, and go about your daily business while they manage everything.

Pros and cons of cloud mining

Cloud mining has similar pros and cons to pool mining, of course. You don't get to keep blocks you mine (you have to share them); you have to pay the cloud-mining firm a fee to play (but think of all the hassle you avoid!), and like pool mining there is the danger of concentration of power into a small number of hands.

You may also find switching more difficult, as some cloud contracts require a longer term commitment; you may not be able to jump ship quickly. Also, on occasion, if mining the particular cryptocurrency becomes unprofitable (as sometimes happens), the operator may cancel the contract. Carefully do your homework and research on cloud mining firms prior to investing any significant amount of money into these services.

Chapter **6**

The Future of Cryptocurrency Mining

What does the future hold for the now budding Bitcoin and cryptocurrency mining industry? It has been thriving as of late, and the future appears to be as bright as the past 13 years.

Incentivization of Energy Exploration

The process of Bitcoin mining is inherently an energy-intensive process, by design, to prevent malicious actors from co-opting the system for their own personal gain. The most economically effective miners tend to be those that find the most cost-efficient sources of electricity.

One study found that on a per-unit economic basis, in 2018, mining a dollar's worth of Bitcoin was four times as expensive as mining a dollar's worth of gold. (Based on the price of Bitcoin at the time of writing, it would, today, be a little less than twice the price.) However, a recent study estimated that *gold mining* uses much more energy per year — perhaps twice as much — as Bitcoin mining.

(Skeptical? See www.nasdaq.com/articles/research%3A-bitcoin-consumes-less-than-half-the-energy-of-the-banking-or-gold-industries.) This, of course, has led to one of the biggest criticisms of proof-of-work cryptocurrencies, such as Bitcoin — that they use vast amounts of energy, in a world that sources most of its electricity from fossil fuels, contributing to the climate crisis.

However, there's another possible future for cryptocurrency. Today, some of the cheapest and most abundant electricity does not come from fossil fuels, but instead from renewable sources, such as hydro, wind, solar, and even nuclear. As the future progresses, more miner facilities will push the envelope on clean and cheap electricity to gain a larger competitive advantage.

The best examples today of wasted and stranded energy resources range from underutilized hydroelectric dams and thermoelectric facilities in El Salvador to flared methane from wells drilled in the shale-oil boom occurring across the United States and Canada. There are also examples of wasted solar and wind energy, as some electric utilities are forced to curtail and waste the electrons being produced from solar farms during low consumption periods of the day.

Some cryptocurrency miners have been seeking out these kinds of energy opportunities. The most economically effective miners tend to be those that develop, deploy, and utilize the most cost-efficient sources of electricity, and presently some of the cheapest power is being sourced from renewables or otherwise wasted energy resources. (This is a subject you can find out more about in Chapter 17.)

Underutilized hydroelectric dams

A huge proportion of cryptocurrency mining (perhaps 70 percent) over the last decade or so occurred in China, partly due to its monopolization of computer chip manufacturing facilities, but also due to the affordability and abundance of cheap hydroelectricity that would otherwise be wasted. However, China banned Bitcoin and cryptocurrency mining in 2021 so most miners were forced to migrate and find new sources of excess energy. Many relocated to Russia and the United States.

During large rainfall periods, many hydroelectric facilities are forced to release water through their spillways, not generating as much electricity as they otherwise would in some of these regions, most notably the Sichuan area, but this is also a common occurrence in the Northwest United States and some remote areas of Canada where hydroelectric capacity is often underutilized. Bitcoin miners in these areas have been able to capitalize on the excess energy and repurpose the wasted hydroelectricity to lower their energy costs.

Oil and gas flaring

Oil and gas exploration and extraction has increased across North America in remote parts of Texas, Colorado, North Dakota, and portions of Canada. One of the sources of waste for that industry lies in the fact that massive quantities of methane, also commonly referred to as natural gas, are uneconomical to transport for sale and utilization in the market. This forces many operators to flare off and burn otherwise completely usable energy.

A few enterprising Bitcoin mining operators have co-located with these facilities and sourced their energy for mining directly from the otherwise wasted and flared excess gas. (Really! Go check out one company that specializes in building mining rigs that can be placed right next to oil-field flaring at `https://blog.upstreamdata.ca`; see Figure 6-1.)

FIGURE 6-1: Some enterprising miners position their mining rigs near oil rigs, so they can capture the flared off methane and use it to run generators.

Source: `https://blog.upstreamdata.ca`

They get cheap power, *and* (in cases in which gas is merely vented rather than burned) actually help the environment by converting methane into water and carbon dioxide. (As methane is a global-warming gas 23 times more potent than carbon dioxide, this is a dramatic reduction in harm.)

Unique applications will continue to provide advantages to mining operators as well as benefit the energy companies that are traditionally wasting these excess resources. This trend will continue going forward and will help contribute to the mining ecosystem as it becomes cleaner and more efficient.

Continued Computational Efficiency Improvements

As cryptocurrency mining has progressed, chip processing capability has skyrocketed. Efficiency levels have been increasing at a rate that echoes Moore's Law. Moore's Law was proposed by a gentleman by the name of Gordon Moore, who observed the number of transistors in computer circuitry doubling roughly every two years. With each doubling, the capability of computer chips has increased, while consuming similar energy levels. This increases the efficiency for standard computer chips, and the phenomena has held true for the ASIC mining hardware deployed to mine cryptocurrency.

There is much speculation as to if this trend will continue further into the future. However, it has so far.

Doing more with less

The first Bitcoin ASICs began hitting the market around 2013. Each subsequent mining equipment iteration has brought more hashing power online and has resulted in less energy consumption per hash. This has given miners who choose to upgrade an advantage over those who have not.

For example, an off-the-shelf Bitcoin ASIC mining rig today could have a hash rate that is greater than the entire network hash rate from early 2013. As energy consumption is one of the largest costs of running a cryptocurrency mine, the miners who seek the most efficient and effective equipment have been able to stay up and running and have not been priced out by the block difficulty (see the section "Block difficulty," later in this chapter) or the amount of energy it takes to hash and mine a block.

Approaching the limits of physics

As computer chips and the mining equipment that utilizes them have advanced, chip manufactures have slowly approached the physical limitations of matter. This is one of the main reasons that many experts believe Moore's Law will not hold true much further into the future. The current state of the art for Bitcoin ASIC chip fabrication is placing different circuitry about 5 to 7 nanometers apart from each other. This is down from 11 to 17 nanometers just a few years ago.

To put this in perspective, a sheet of paper is roughly 100,000 nanometers thick. This is an incredibly small distance for electrical circuity proximity and is very quickly approaching the limitations of our physical universe. To put this number in perspective, early ASIC chips had distances of nearly 130 nanometers separation between layers on the printed circuit board. Today some manufacturers in the space use a common chipset with 7 nanometers of distance between layers; that is about 15 atoms of silicon separation between electrical components (silicon is utilized as the electrical insulator between the various conductive portions of these circuits).

Eventually, these incremental improvements on chip capabilities will not be physically possible as there will not be enough silicon matter between circuits to adequately insulate components from each other. Once the limitations of physics are met, chip efficiency gains will be slower and much harder to come by.

Corporate and Nation State Participation

As Bitcoin and cryptocurrencies have progressed over the years, there have been many examples of corporations and nation states participating in the space, in ways that lend legitimacy to the technologies.

Nation states

Some countries are taking a hands-off position on Bitcoin and cryptocurrencies, while others either restrict usage or outright ban their citizens from using these systems. Cryptocurrency is downright illegal in Algeria, Egypt, Morocco, Ecuador, Nepal, and many other locations. China has now banned Bitcoin (though it has had an on-again, off-again relationship with Bitcoin in the past), but that hasn't stopped many Chinese mining companies from operating (some have closed, but Bitcoin and cryptocurrency mining still continues).

Countries such as Vietnam and Brunei allow citizens to own Bitcoin, but prohibit the use as a payment tool. And then there are the more open states, such as those in most of Europe and North America, where much more flexibility regarding the use of cryptocurrency is allowed — though these states are trying to get to grips with questions such as how profiting from cryptocurrencies should be taxed.

Some states may also be classified as crypto-friendly, passing laws that encourage the use of development of cryptocurrencies. Switzerland, Germany, Singapore, Slovenia, and Belarus have very friendly Bitcoin and cryptocurrency tax laws.

(Want to see Bitcoin legal status across the world? See `https://en.wikipedia.org/wiki/Legality_of_bitcoin_by_country_or_territory`. This list applies specifically to Bitcoin, though in general it will also apply to cryptocurrency of all flavors.)

Then there are the states that are getting actively involved in cryptocurrency. One of the earliest examples of a nation state participating and supporting the validity in the Bitcoin and cryptocurrency space began in 2014, and involves the United States Justice Department, which has utilized the U.S. Marshals Service to publicly auction off nearly $1 billion dollars' worth of Bitcoin and digital currencies that were seized from alleged criminals over the years.

Another example that stands out is Venezuela, which tried to launch its own cryptocurrency, albeit somewhat hastily, called the *Petro,* in an attempt to fix its failing Bolivar and circumvent sanctions and the U.S. dollar (see Figure 6-2). It was unsuccessful. Some nation states, such as Iran and Estonia have announced deals on electricity in an attempt to court Bitcoin and cryptocurrency miners to their territory. However, these electricity deals come with steep contracts, caveats, and limitations. Other countries, such as North Korea and Iran, are rumored to be mining cryptocurrency themselves in a more official capacity; Iran has reportedly created its own cryptocurrency, PayMon, backed by gold. Peer-to-peer cryptocurrencies are difficult to control and allow the owner to route around traditional financial institutions. They may be a tool in the fight against sanctions and economic blockades to which these countries are subject, but like all national central bank digital currencies (CBDCs), they suffer from traits inherent to the incumbent national currencies they would seek to replace.

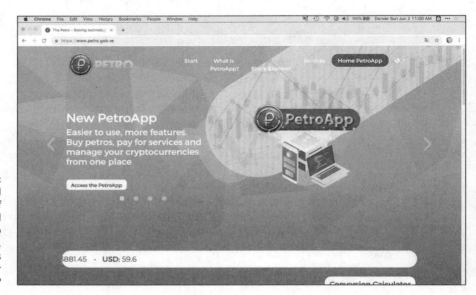

FIGURE 6-2: The official website of Venezuela's failed Petro cryptocurrency. Will other CBDCs suffer a similar fate?

You may have heard that cryptocurrency is treated by Japan and Australia as *legal tender*. This is a myth (driven by the low standards of so-called journalism in the cryptocurrency field!). However, this misunderstanding arose from both countries announcing that they would not stand in the way of cryptocurrency being used as a *legal payment method*. (*Legal tender* is a more specific classification, meaning that a particular form of money *must be* accepted by a creditor if a debtor wishes to pay using that form; nobody in Japan or Australia will be forced to accept cryptocurrency!) Bitcoin *is* regarded as legal tender in El Salvador, though it's not clear that this experiment will turn out well.

Corporations

Many mainstream corporations have benefited from the cryptocurrency boom. Some of the obvious early winners were providers and manufacturers of GPUs, such as Nvidia and AMD. Other computer hardware providers have also seen the increased demand for components that is the symptom of the hardware arms race that cryptocurrency miners contribute to. Some other noteworthy companies, such as Samsung, Taiwan Semiconductor Manufacturing, and GMO Internet, Inc., have actually begun producing chips and printed circuit boards specifically for Bitcoin ASIC mining hardware. Other large companies, such as Square, Fidelity, and the Chicago Board of Exchange (CBOE), have Bitcoin products. These companies and their actions have further expanded upon the credibility of cryptocurrency technology.

In fact, many major corporations have jumped into the blockchain field, with some delving into cryptocurrencies. IBM, for example, has made a major, multi-billion dollar bet on blockchain, including developing *World Wire*, a cryptocurrency token designed to make international money transfers fast and cheap. More recently, Intel has announced that it has gotten into the Bitcoin ASIC chip manufacturing industry with its BMZ1 and BMZ2 bonanza miners.

Future speculation

Going forward, more countries could begin to crack down on Bitcoin and cryptocurrencies as they may become viewed as a threat to fiat currencies issued by governments and their central banks. On the other hand, we might see other countries loosen up restrictions and draft cryptocurrency-friendly tax and legal tender laws similar to the initiatives by Japan or Germany mentioned in the previous section.

Because Bitcoin and cryptocurrencies are borderless and easy to transport, cryptocurrencies become attractive in countries with significant financial problems: countries with hyperinflation such as Venezuela, high-inflation nations such as

Turkey and Zimbabwe, and in countries such as Greece with moderately high inflation but worries about the stability of the banking system. Some people in these areas have sought financial stability in cryptocurrencies as they flee their collapsing currency, and some have been able to recapture portions of their wealth. If countries attempt to ban the utilization of these technologies within their borders, entrepreneurial people will simply leave and take their talents and capital elsewhere. The nature of cryptocurrency is such that it's very hard for a government to ban its use. How does a government in Latin America, for example, stop an Internet-savvy citizen from buying Bitcoin and transferring the Bitcoin to another country?

As far as companies are concerned, many have already released branded tokens on top other cryptocurrencies or launched entire systems of their own. That includes companies such as Kik messenger, Circle, Coinbase, Gemini, Wells Fargo, and JPMorgan Chase, among many others. Even Facebook (now Meta) planned to release a cryptocurrency, Diem (originally Libra), though the project was cancelled after much congressional and regulatory pushback. However, as we were finishing up this book, it began to look like Diem might be revived; in January 2022, the Diem assets were sold to Silvergate, a public company (SI) and Federal Reserve member bank, which plans to continue development and launch a stablecoin in 2022.

The advantages these systems have may include value stability and one-to-one redeemability compared to a national currency, such as the dollar. They also may include brand recognition based upon the trust of their parent companies.

The drawbacks, however, in some cases are vast. These systems may be more centralized than a typical cryptocurrency, making them easy to seize, censor, and restrict. They may also be saddled with security and privacy flaws that make their usage less than ideal. Another downside to these company issued assets is that they cannot be mined as a single entity controls their issuance.

The Mythical Miner Death Spiral

In recent years, especially when the value of Bitcoin and other cryptocurrencies goes down, there has been speculation on the possibility of a *miner death spiral*. The theory is that as the price drops, and as the Bitcoin and cryptocurrency that miners generate becomes worth less, miners are forced to trade their mining rewards for local currencies at prices that may not be able to cover operating expenses (data center fees, electricity costs, equipment maintenance, and so on; see Part 4).

As miners dump cryptocurrency, the market price of the cryptocurrency further drops, making mining even less profitable, forcing miners out of business. If enough miners shut down and liquidate their cryptocurrency holdings, it will cause a *miner death spiral* that will further reduce Bitcoin and cryptocurrency prices, causing more miners to shut down.

In fact, if enough miners shut down, the theory goes, blocks will cease to be mined and confirmed, and the cryptocurrency system will stop propagating and fail.

Block difficulty

In proof of work–based consensus algorithms, the amount of computational effort that is needed to find the correct nonce that creates a hash for the current block is commonly referred to as the block difficulty (see Chapter 2). When the Bitcoin genesis block was created, the very first block, the block difficulty target was 1. If the block difficulty was at 100, it would be 100 times harder to find the correct hash to create the block compared to a difficulty of 1.

The block difficulty is a unitless number, and at the time of writing, the Bitcoin block difficulty stands at 27,967,152,532,434 or roughly 27 trillion times harder to find a block when compared to the block difficulty of that genesis block.

Imagine, then, a situation in which many miners shut down their computer systems. The block difficulty would be so high that it would be virtually impossible to create a block. There simply wouldn't be enough processing power on the network to do so.

Block difficulty adjustment algorithm

Never fear! The Bitcoin network alleviates this block difficulty cliff by readjusting the block difficulty threshold every 2,016 blocks, or roughly every two weeks. This period is referred to as a *Bitcoin mining difficulty epoch*. The difficulty adjusts and retargets at the end of the 2,016 block period based upon how fast or slow blocks were created during the previous epoch, with a goal of generating blocks at about 10 minutes per block.

If the previous 2,016 blocks were generated at an average interval of about 10 minutes, the block difficulty will stay roughly the same. If the previous 2,016 blocks were created at a rate that is longer than 10 minutes on average (the 2,016 blocks were generated in a period longer than two weeks), the difficulty will go down. If the 2,016 blocks were created on average quicker than 10 minutes (the 2,016 blocks were generated in a period faster than two weeks), the block difficulty will adjust upward to compensate.

You may be able to find charts showing the latest difficulty and the fluctuation over time. See, for example, `https://bitinfocharts.com/comparison/difficulty-hashrate-btc.html` and `www.blockchain.com/en/charts/difficulty`. You can see a two-year chart of block difficulty in Figure 6-3.

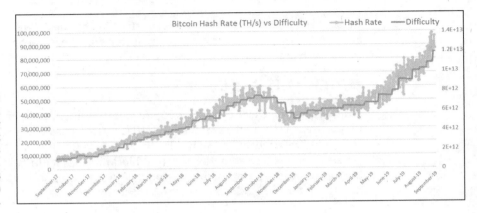

FIGURE 6-3:
Bitcoin Block Difficulty usually goes up, but sometimes comes down. Block difficulty is shown over a two-year period.

In general, if more hash power is being pointed to the network over the two-week period, the difficulty will go up, and vice versa. Mathematically, if the miner death spiral were to occur and half the miners on the network suddenly shut off at the beginning of a new difficulty epoch, the 2,016 blocks would take about twice as long to find (roughly four weeks instead of two), and at the end of the period the difficulty would adjust again to allow block creation at a rate of about one block per ten-minute period.

Imagine if 90 percent of the miners stopped mining for blocks and shut down; what would happen? It would take the remaining 10 percent of the network ten times as long to find the 2,016 blocks (roughly 20 weeks, or 4 months, to get to the next difficulty adjustment period). What would the network do? Transactions would backlog, fees would increase for the duration of the period, but it would eventually adjust difficulty!

As mining gets less profitable, miners leave, the block difficulty goes down, and the remaining miners find the mining is cheaper, making it more profitable. It's a self-regulating system.

Take a look at Figure 6-4; you can see how block difficulty has changed over time for Bitcoin. Notice the big dip in 2018. That's a perfect example of the self-regulation of the block difficulty on the Bitcoin network. You'll recall that there was a precipitous decline in Bitcoin pricing early in 2018. What happened?

1. **The price of Bitcoin dropped.**

2. **This made mining cryptocurrency less profitable.**

3. **Some miners stopped mining.**

4. **That meant less hash power applied to the proof of work.**

5. **So it took longer to add a block than the targeted ten minutes per block.**

6. **So block difficulty was automatically reduced, making it easier to mine and remain within the ten-minute target.**

7. **As the price of Bitcoin stabilized and later rose, more miners entered the business.**

8. **This meant more hash power . . . and blocks were being added more quickly than every ten minutes.**

9. **So the block difficulty went up again, making it harder to add blocks, again moving back to the ten-minutes-per-block target.**

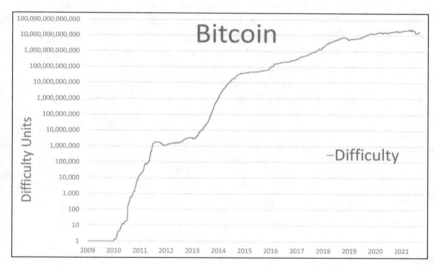

FIGURE 6-4: This figure is a graph of the Bitcoin network's block difficulty over time logarithmically, growing immensely over the decade the cryptocurrency has been in existence.

Miners of last resort

There's another reason the mythical miner death spiral is unlikely to happen. There are actors in the Bitcoin ecosystem, as well as other cryptocurrency systems, that mine on principle and ideology as opposed to mining purely for profit. They mine to support their networks and to further system decentralization. And yes, they also mine out of their own selfish interests seeking reward and profit. However, they may measure their profit in Bitcoin or other cryptocurrencies instead of the current exchange rate as measured in local fiat currencies. They also believe in cryptocurrency and its future value, so they regard their mining losses as an investment in future profits.

These users could be deemed *miners of last resort.* Their hashing power may not shut off when the exchange price in local currency falls. In fact, they may choose to increase their mining hash capability during these times as difficulty sinks, blocks become easier to find, and hardware prices fall due to lack of demand. Some of these miners of last resort were supporting and mining the network before there was any real demand for Bitcoin, and for others, even before there was a valid exchange rate. For these miners of last resort, the best time to start mining was a decade ago, and the second-best time to start mining is today.

CRYPTO ANARCHISTS!

There's a very definite crypto anarchist or crypto libertarian thread running through the history of cryptocurrencies. A *crypto anarchist* is a person who sees in cryptography a way to keep Big Brother off our backs! Crypto anarchists see in cryptography a way to communicate with others in a manner that the state cannot listen in, to keep private information private, and, in the case of cryptocurrency, to even stop the state knowing how much we own and what we do with our value and money. So many early cryptocurrency enthusiasts were in it for political ideals, not monetary gain (the profits they make are icing on the cake, I guess!). Still, just as the early Internet had an anti-establishment undercurrent and yet was co-opted by major corporations, the cryptocurrency space is likely to be co-opted by large companies and the banking system. (The crypto anarchists, however, might claim that a time-bomb is being planted in the world's finance system; large corporations can use cryptocurrency in their own ways, but that doesn't stop the progress and development of peer-to-peer, decentralized, and anonymous currencies.)

3

Becoming a Cryptocurrency Miner

Chapter **7**

Mining Made Simple: Finding a Pool and Preparing an Account

For most small-scale miners, who seek consistent and predictable cryptocurrency mining rewards in today's incredibly competitive cryptocurrency mining industry, the best route to secure steady rewards from mining is to utilize a mining pool service for their mining equipment's hashing power. Unless you're wielding an immense amount of hash power — a considerable portion of the estimated network hash rate (anything nearing a single percentage point in this case would be considerable) — solo mining is a very risky venture and should probably be avoided if you are an entry-level novice miner.

We regard mining pools as a great way to get started in cryptocurrency mining, and for many miners, it's the last stage, too. Even if you plan to move on to solo mining, pool mining is a good way to begin, to test the cryptocurrency mining waters and get your feet wet. Pool mining also helps you discover the hash rate of your equipment, which you need when you read Chapters 8 and 9. You find out more about how everything works, and, in combination with other information in this book, what you find out here can help you decide whether it makes sense to solo mine, and, if you think it does, what it will take and what it will cost to do so. You must learn to walk (pool mine) before you can run (solo mine).

We also look at a related concept in this chapter, cloud mining. In cloud mining, you essentially invest in a mining operation and earn a proportion of the operation's revenues. It's a hands-off situation where you provide money, and they buy and manage the computing equipment.

Understanding How Pool Mining Works

Pool mining involves a group of miners acting as a team to find blocks. The block rewards are proportionally split across all miners who contributed to the pool's hashed proof of work; that is, the more hashing power you provided to the operation during a particular time period (*the pool mining duration* or *mining round*), the higher the share you receive for block rewards won by the pool during that time period. (More specifically, shares are calculated a number of different ways, as you find out later in this chapter, but in general, you're rewarded according to the proportion of the hash power you provide to the pool.)

Typically, the mining duration or mining round is the period of time between blocks being mined by the pool. That is, a round begins immediately after the pool has won the right to add a block to the blockchain and stops when it adds a block to the blockchain the next time. The round can range anywhere from a few minutes to many hours, depending on the pool size and the pool's luck.

Here's essentially how this all works:

1. **You sign up with a mining pool.**
2. **You download and install the mining pool's software on your computer.**
3. **The software on your computer communicates with the mining pool's servers; in effect, your computer has just become an extension of the mining pool's cryptocurrency node.**

4. **Your computer helps with the mining operations, contributing spare processing power to the pool's proof-of-work (PoW) hashing.**

5. **When the pool wins the right to add a block to the blockchain, and earns a block reward — the sum of the block subsidy and transaction fees — you get to share in the earnings based upon your individual contribution.**

6. **Periodically, the pool transfers cryptocurrency to your wallet address. Either you're paid in the cryptocurrency you helped mine, or that cryptocurrency is converted to another form (typically, Bitcoin) and the converted sum is transferred to you.**

Regardless of the hardware you plan to mine with or the cryptocurrency you end up choosing, there's a mining pool for you. Whether you have cryptocurrency Application Specific Integrated Circuit (ASIC) hardware, a graphical processing unit (GPU) mining rig, or just a typical desktop computer with both a central processing unit (CPU) and GPU onboard, pool mining is the best method of consistently earning mining rewards for small operators.

REMEMBER

Mining pools provide a way for the small operator to get into the game when their processing power is so low that solo mining simply isn't practical. In Chapter 8, you find out about *mining calculators,* web pages into which you enter your hashing power, and from which you get a calculation of how profitable mining a particular cryptocurrency would be, as well as how long it would take to mine your first block. These calculators simply work on a statistical calculation based on various numbers: the *overall network hash rate* (that is, the combined hashing power of all the computers mining that cryptocurrency), your level of hashing power, how often a block is mined, the block reward, and so on. The calculators take all these numbers, and output the answers based on pure statistical probability. They tell you what you're likely to earn over a particular period, but your results can vary. You might mine your first block immediately, or you might mine your first block in twice the predicted time.

For many small operators, these calculators can be a shock. You may discover, for example, that mining Bitcoin using your paltry processor may result, statistically speaking, in your first block being mined 100 years from now. In other words, solo mining simply isn't practical for you. In such a case, if you really want to mine Bitcoin, you have to join a pool.

By design, mining pools are very simple for the miner to use, as they take a lot of the technical details and headache out of the mining process. Mining pools provide a service to individual miners, and miners provide hash rate to the pools.

Choosing a Pool

This chapter provides links to a variety of mining pools. Which one you choose to work with depends on a variety of criteria. Here are the Big Three criteria.

>> **Your equipment:** Some mining pools require that you have an ASIC mining rig. Slush Pool, for example, mines only Bitcoin and Zcash, so if you want to work with Slush Pool, you'll need the appropriate ASICs for those currencies. Other mining pools support alternative hashing algorithms and let you provide hash power from your CPU or GPU.

>> **The cryptocurrency you want to mine:** To begin with, you'll probably want to simply jump into a pool that looks easy to work with, just to get your feet wet. At some point, however, you may want to target specific cryptocurrencies.

>> **Payouts:** Different pools pay in different ways and charge in different ways. For example, with some you'll share in the block subsidy but not the transaction fees. With others, you'll share in both. Some pools charge a higher fee — keeping a proportion of the mined cryptocurrency — than others, some charge withdrawal fees, and so on.

Many pools have multiple cryptocurrencies available to mine, while others list only a small number of specific coins that are available for miners to work with. For example, NiceHash (www.nicehash.com) works with literally dozens of different mining algorithms, for around 80 different cryptocurrencies, while Slush Pool (SlushPool.com) offers only Bitcoin and Zcash mining pools.

Slush Pool was the first cryptocurrency mining pool, way back in 2010, so it has a proven track record. Many other pools have since been created, and pool mining is now the dominant form of cryptocurrency mining. Some are also designed for lower hash rate CPU or GPU mining applications, and others have software suites that are more useful for specialized ASIC hardware. At this point in the evolution of cryptocurrency mining, most proof-of-work blockchains require the use of ASIC hardware; these machines are so efficient that you simply can't compete using a CPU or GPU. However, you can find opportunities to mine with standard off-the-shelf desktop computers or custom-built GPU mining rigs. These other opportunities include special types of pools that mine a variety of obscure cryptocurrencies but pay out rewards to miners in more common cryptocurrencies such as Bitcoin.

Pools that are good starting points

If you are using nonspecialized computing hardware, then here are a couple of popular and easy-to-use pools that are really good starting points:

>> **BetterHash** (www.betterhash.net) provides mining software for Windows machines.

>> **Cudo Miner** (www.cudominer.com) allows users to easily mine with their CPU or GPU for Bitcoin.

>> **Kryptex** (www.kryptex.org) gives you the ability to mine using your desktop computer on whatever cryptocurrency is most profitable, but they pay out rewards in Bitcoin.

>> **MinerGate** (https://minergate.com) mines about a dozen cryptocurrencies.

>> **NiceHash** (www.nicehash.com) allows users to buy and sell hash rate for a wide variety of different cryptocurrencies.

These types of pools act as hash rate marketplaces, allowing you to maximize return on your nonspecialized computer as mining hardware. These hash rate marketplaces and mining services allow for easy and quick mining access for beginners, and they can make any desktop or even laptop computer a mining device.

WARNING

You can find many more services like the ones listed in the preceding list, but some are risky, not as reputable, and can result in loss of funds. Choose carefully!

TIP

If you already have your heart set on a specific cryptocurrency, your choice can help dictate which set of pools are most appropriate for you to use. Ideally, you want to choose a fairly popular pool that mines blocks frequently, but you may want to avoid the very largest pool to help mitigate centralization issues and prevent a theoretical 51 percent attack. (A *51 percent attack* occurs when a malicious party takes over 51 percent or more of a blockchain's hashing power, giving it the ability to, in effect, disrupt the blockchain.)

A few of the largest pools

The following sections show some of the largest pools that are mining for some of the most popular proof-of-work cryptocurrencies.

Other factors should also help dictate your choice in mining pools beyond popularity and percentage of network hash rate. These factors include miner incentives and reward types, pool ideology, pool fees, and pool reputation.

Bitcoin (BTC)

Following are some of the largest pools mining for Bitcoin, listed in alphabetical order.

>> **Antpool:** https://v3.antpool.com

>> **Binance Pool:** https://pool.binance.com

>> **BTC.com:** https://pool.btc.com

>> **F2Pool:** www.f2pool.com

>> **Foundry USA Pool:** https://foundryusapool.com

>> **Poolin:** www.poolin.me

>> **Slush Pool:** https://slushpool.com

>> **ViaBTC:** www.viabtc.com

Litecoin (LTC)

Following are some of the largest pools that are mining for Litecoin, listed in alphabetical order.

>> **Antpool:** https://v3.antpool.com

>> **F2Pool:** www.f2pool.com

>> **LitecoinPool.org:** www.litecoinpool.org

>> **Poolin:** www.poolin.me

>> **ViaBTC:** www.viabtc.com

Ethereum (ETH)

Following are some of the largest pools that are mining for Ethereum, listed in alphabetical order.

>> **Ethermine:** https://ethermine.org

>> **F2Pool:** www.f2pool.com

» **Minerall:** https://minerall.io

» **Mining Express:** https://miningexpress.com

» **Nanopool:** https://eth.nanopool.org

Zcash (ZEC)

Following are some of the largest pools that are mining for Zcash, listed in alphabetical order.

» **FlyPool:** https://zcash.flypool.org

» **Nanopool:** https://eth.nanopool.org

» **Slush Pool:** https://slushpool.com

Monero (XMR)

Following are some of the largest pools that are mining for Monero, listed in alphabetical order.

» **F2Pool:** www.f2pool.com

» **MineXMR.com:** https://minexmr.com

» **Nanopool:** https://xmr.nanopool.org

Incentives and rewards

Different pools use different methods for calculating payouts. Each mining pool's website provides information about which payout method it uses and how they specifically implement the method.

The following list shows a few of the most popular payout-calculation methods. The premise of these methods is that miners are paid a proportion of the gains made by the pool over a period of time. That period of time is known as the *mining duration* or *mining round*. For example, https://slushpool.com/en/stats/btc shows Slush Pool's mining results. In Figure 7-1, on the right side, you can see how long the current round has been operating, and the length of the average mining round (2 hours 56 minutes).

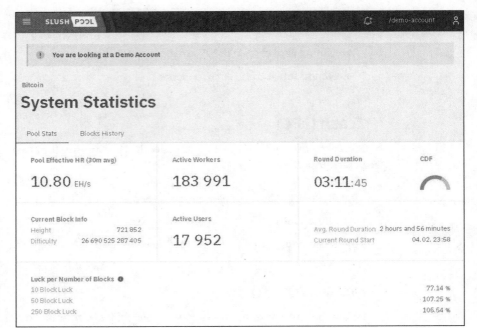

FIGURE 7-1:
The statistics
page at Slush
Pool, showing
information from
the current
mining round (or
mining duration).

On the left, it shows the average hash rate (10.80 EH/s) — that is, 10.8 exahashes per second, or 10.8 quintillion hashes per second (10,800,000,000,000,000,000 hashes per second). Now, 17,952 miner accounts are providing hash power to the pool (see on the left side; the number of "workers" are individual computers owned by those 17,952 miners), so for Slush Pool, on average, each miner is providing about 0.00557 percent of the pool's hashing power.

Say that you provide that proportion of the hashing power during the mining round; you'll earn 0.00557 percent of the payout from that mining round (after fees have been taken out by the pool operator). Your hashing power may not have been involved in the actual winning blocks (perhaps your computer was operating at times when the pool did not win the right to add a block, for example), but because you provided hash power during the mining round, you earn your proportional payout.

TIP

Payout calculations are often (as everything in cryptocurrency mining is!) more complicated than a simple proportional payout. The following list describes a few popular methods for calculating mining pool payouts. The term *share* refers to the proportion of the total hashing power during the mining duration that your mining rig contributes to the pool.

>> **Pay-Per-Share (PPS):** With PPS, miners earn a guaranteed income based on the *probability* that the pool mines a block, not the actual performance of the pool. Sometimes the pool will do better than the statistical probability, sometimes worse, but the miner gets paid based on their contribution to the average hash rate required to mine a block.

>> **Full Pay-Per-Share (FPPS):** FPPS is very similar to PPS. However, with FPPS, the pools also include transaction fees as well as the block subsidy in the payout scheme. This usually leads to larger cryptocurrency rewards for pool participants when compared to standard PPS.

>> **Pay-Per-Last N Shares (PPLNS):** The PPLNS structure pays out rewards proportionally looking at the last number (N) of shares contributed. It does not consider *all* the shares during the entire mining round, but rather considers only the most recent share contributions at the time of block discovery. (How many recent shares? Whatever number is set by N.)

>> **Shared Maximum Pay-Per-Share (SMPPS):** SMPPS is a similar reward method to PPS, but it rewards miners based on the actual rewards earned by the pool, and thus never pays out more than the pool earns.

>> **Recent Shared Maximum Pay-Per-Share (RSMPPS):** This reward scheme pays out miners in a similar way to SMPPS. Rewards are paid out proportionally to the total number of shares contributed during the mining pool, but with more weight on *recent* hash rate shares. That is, shares that were contributed early in the round would be worth a little less compared to shares that were contributed closer to the discovery of a block.

>> **Score Based System (SCORE):** This reward system pays you according to your proportion of hash rate provided, but gives more weight to more recent hash rate shares than earlier shares in the mining round. That is, if your hashing was made early in the period and a block was won later in the period, your hash power earns a lower proportion than if it were provided closer to the time of the winning block. So this is similar to RSMPPS, but the scoring hash rate is roughly a rolling average of your mining hash rate. If your mining share is steady and constant, your scoring hash rate is roughly constant as well. But if your mining rig is offline when a block is found by the pool, then you don't earn a reward equivalent to the total hashing you contributed over the block duration; instead, you earn an adjusted rate.

>> **Double Geometric Method (DGM):** This reward scheme is a cross between PPLNS and a geometrically calculated reward that equalizes payouts depending on mining round duration. This creates lower mining rewards during short duration rounds and larger reward payouts for longer rounds.

Each of these payout methods was conceived and deployed in an attempt to maintain fairness between pool operators and in pool mining reward distribution to the individual miners contributing to the pool. Some are more successful than others. However, they all have aspects of impartiality that balance the playing field for all the miners participating in the system.

TECHNICAL STUFF

For a more detailed discussion of pool-payment methods and various pools, see https://en.bitcoin.it/wiki/Comparison_of_mining_pools.

Pool ideology

An often-overlooked aspect of selecting a pool to contribute your hash rate and mining power to is pool ideology. Ideology can be a tricky concept to nail down, especially when businesses are involved, and that's what mining pool operators are: for-profit businesses. Some are benevolent actors, and some have ulterior motives beyond mining reward and revenue.

Some pools have even historically attempted to undermine the cryptocurrencies they support. This can be seen in pools mining empty blocks in an attempt to game transaction fee rewards, clog transaction throughput, and push alternative systems. Other mining pools have used their hash rate and influence to stall updates to the system or instigate and propagate forks on the blockchain they are mining.

TIP

There's no tried-and-true or easy way to measure mining pool ideology. However, community sentiment and historical actions are often a good barometer to measure if a mining pool is acting in a way that supports the wider ecosystem. The best way to sift through mining pool ideology is to stay up to date on cryptocurrency news, and to peruse online forums, such as Bitcoin Talk (https://bitcointalk.org), or social media sites like Twitter and Reddit.

Overall, ideology is a less important factor when you're considering pools compared to mining reward process and pool fees. After all, cryptocurrency is an incentive-based system, and selfishness drives the consensus mechanisms and security of the various blockchains.

Pool reputation

Another important factor in pool selection is pool reputation. Some mining pools propagate scams and steal hash rate or mining rewards from users. These types of pools don't last long, as news travels fast in the cryptocurrency space and switching costs for pool miners are very low, making it easy for users to leave pools that cheat miners. However, despite this, there have been many examples of mining pool and cloud mining service scams. Some of the more noteworthy instances have involved Bitconnect, Power Mining Pool, and Mining Max. The best way to detect a scam may be the old-fashioned mantra, "If it sounds too good to be true, it probably is!" (Strictly speaking, Bitconnect wasn't a mining pool, but it was a service that promised returns on a cryptocurrency investment. A Bitcoin investor could lend Bitcoin to Bitconnect and in return earn somewhere between 0.1 percent and 0.25 percent *per day....* Yep, up to doubling their money each month. Of course, many investors never got their money back from this Ponzi scheme.)

TIP

Other clear hints of mining pool or cloud mining scams include, but aren't limited to, the following.

>> **Guaranteed profits:** Pools or cloud services that offer guaranteed profits are selling more than they can provide. Again, you know the old saying: if it sounds too good to be true. . .

>> **Anonymous perpetrators:** Pools or mining services that are owned and operated by anonymous entities or individuals can sometimes be shady — buyer beware.

>> **Multilevel marketing schemes:** Some mining pools or cloud mining services offer larger rewards for those who recruit others into the scheme. This may not always mean the operation is a scam, but do your research carefully if MLM (also known as a pyramid scheme) is present. (Many online companies pay recruitment bonuses, but MLM takes it to another level.) Mining Max, for example, was a pyramid scheme: Miners would pay to get into the pool and then get paid recruitment bonuses. Reportedly, $250 million went missing.

>> **No publicly auditable infrastructure:** Pools or cloud mining services that aren't *transparent* — that don't publish videos of their mining facilities or publicize hash rate data, for example — may be scams.

>> **No hash rate proof:** Some pools publish provable hash rate data, proof that can't be counterfeited and can be independently verified by any prospective miner. On the other hand, some pools simply publish their hash rate data without any kind of evidence, hoping you'll just trust their claims. (For an example of how hash rate data can be independently verified, see Slush Pool's explanation at https://help.slushpool.com/en/support/solutions/articles/77000433900.)

>> **Unlimited hash power purchases:** If a cloud mining service offers very large, unrealistic amounts of hash power to purchase, then they may just be trying to secure your cryptocurrency for themselves instead of offering any long-term services. Be wary of services that offer sizable packages; it may be more than they can deliver.

In the cryptocurrency mining industry, a good reputation is hard to gain, but very easy to lose. For this reason, many of the pool operators functioning today that have acquired large hash rate percentages on the cryptocurrency networks they support aren't scams. If they were in fact scams or illegitimate actors in the space, then enterprising miners would have already switched to a better pool. This doesn't always apply to cloud mining operators (we discuss cloud mining services in more detail later in this chapter), as the switching costs for cloud mining contract purchasers are much higher, so this doesn't mean you can let your guard down. Vigilance and due diligence are a must and highly recommended in this space.

TIP

How do you check on a pool's reputation? Visit the mining forums and search on the pool's name to see what people are saying about it.

Pool fees

Pools charge fees in various ways, and these fees are paid by the miners to the pool operator. Most pool fees are in the range of 1 to 4 percent of total pool earnings. These fees are used to maintain the pool infrastructure, host servers for web interfaces, and run full mining nodes and other equipment needed to keep the pool operational — and, of course, to pay a profit to the pool operator.

WARNING

Don't be fooled by pools that claim they charge no fees. (No fees? How do they stay in business? They're not charities, are they!?) Obviously, the pools have to make money, so somehow you're going to pay.

Pools make money in two ways when they mine a block:

>> Through the block subsidy

>> Through transaction fees from the individual transactions entered into the block

So a pool may take a percentage of the total value — block subsidy and transaction fees — for itself and then share the rest with the miners. Or a pool may share the entire block subsidy among the miners, but keep the transaction fees for itself (these pools are most likely claiming to be "zero-fee" pools). Or perhaps they keep the transaction fees and a portion of the block subsidy. But one way or another, you're paying a fee!

Pool percentage of the total network

A pool holds a percentage of the overall network hash rate. How does that affect you? A large pool is going to take a larger proportion of the money being made from mining than a smaller pool. However, over time, this shouldn't affect how much you earn. Here's why. Remember, the network hash rate is the number of hashes contributed, by all miners and all pools, to mining a block. Depending on the cryptocurrency, it may take quintillions of hashes per second, for perhaps ten minutes on average, to mine a block (that pretty much describes Bitcoin mining, for example).

So, you have all these machines, possibly tens of thousands of them, hashing. Who gets to add a block to the blockchain? That's a factor of the amount of hashing power provided, in combination with luck and chance. That means that the miner or pool that gets to mine the *next* block is very hard to determine. It may be the pool that contributes more hashing power than any other pool or miner; but there's chance involved, too, so it could be the miner with the tiniest contribution in the entire network. It probably won't be, but it *could* be. That's the way chance (probability) works.

TIP

Think of it as a lottery. The more tickets you have, the more likely you are to win . . . but you may win if you only have one ticket. Chances are you won't . . . but it could happen.

Over the short term, then, it's impossible to predict who is going to win the hashing contest, or even, over a few mining rounds (or even a few hundred mining rounds), what proportion any pool is likely to win.

However, over the long term, the hashing percentage comes closer to the percentage of wins. So, if your pool contributes 25 percent of all the hashing power, then, over time, the pool is going to mine 25 percent of the blocks.

Here's another analogy: It's like tossing a coin. What proportion of coin tosses are heads, and what proportion are tails? Over the short term, it's hard to tell. Toss twice, and it's entirely possible that it's 100 percent one way or the other. Toss ten times, and it's still unlikely to be 50:50. But toss a thousand times, and you're going to get very close to that 50:50 number (assuming clean tosses of a balanced coin).

So, over time, a pool that represents 25 percent of the network hash rate should mine 25 percent of the network's blocks, and a pool that represents 10 percent of the network hash rate should mine around 10 percent of the blocks.

All right, back to the question: Should you go with a big pool or a small pool? A big pool, over time, will win more blocks than a small pool. But, of course, you're going to get a smaller proportion of the winnings than you would in a smaller pool.

Over time, this means there's no real difference. Whatever the size of the pool you join, *your* hashing power is the same percentage of the overall network, and thus, over time, you should earn the same percentage.

REMEMBER

There is one difference. The larger the pool, the more frequently you'll earn a cut. That means more frequent earnings than from a smaller pool. Those earnings will be smaller, though; you can't beat the math. You're not going to earn more than your percentage of the earnings represented by your percentage of the hash rate. (Over the long term, that is; over the short term, you may earn considerably more or considerably less, whichever choice you make.)

So you may prefer to go with a larger pool just so you see income more frequently, but don't expect that picking a larger pool will increase your earnings in the long term.

How do you find the relative size of the pools? Many sites provide this information, often in the form of pie charts. (We discuss how to find such information later in this chapter, in the section, "Researching Mining Pools.") For a historic graphical view of network hash rate percentages by pool on the Bitcoin network, see Figure 7-2.You can find this graph at `https://data.bitcoinity.org/bitcoin/hashrate/5y?c=m&g=15&t=a`.

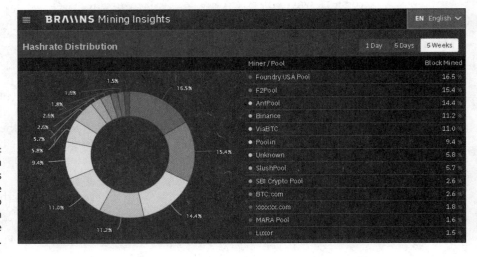

FIGURE 7-2:
A historical graph of each pool's hash rate contributions to the Bitcoin network over the past five weeks.

Setting Up a Pool Account

For the most part, after you decide which cryptocurrency is right for you (see Chapter 8) and after you select a pool to contribute to that resonates with you, creating and setting up a pool account is fairly simple. The process can be compared to creating an email account or other online web service, such as a social media account. The two requirements you need when setting up a pool account are an email account and a cryptocurrency wallet address. A few oddities and factors to consider during the pool account process include pool server choice, payout threshold, and reward payout addresses.

All mining pools, regardless of the cryptocurrency they happen to be mining, have easy, step-by-step directions to connect your suitable mining equipment (ASIC, GPU, or other) to the pool interface located on their website. You must set up an account, select a server, configure your mining hardware, and register a payout address. Most mining pools also have basic user manuals to help sift through the setup process, helpful FAQs for when you hit a snag, and, in many cases, detailed technical documentation for advanced users.

Server choice

For most mining pools, many different servers are up and running for you to connect your mining hardware to the pool infrastructure. The most important difference in servers is mainly geographical location. The most popular mining pools have servers based in locations across the globe, such as in Asia, Europe, and the Americas.

TIP

To reduce connection latency and avoid connectivity outages, connecting to servers that are in close proximity to your mining hardware is most beneficial for you.

Most ASIC cryptocurrency mining hardware allows you to set three separate servers or mining pools in the mining equipment user interface. Some miners point their equipment to multiple pools to avoid downtime in the event of a pool outage, while others simply point their hardware to different servers of the same pool.

Mining equipment pool settings

Specialized cryptocurrency mining hardware (covered in Chapter 9) is normally equipped with an easy-to-use graphical user interface (GUI). The mining equipment user interface can be accessed via any computer that's connected to the same Local Area Network (LAN) as the mining equipment. Simply open a web browser and type the mining equipment's Internet Protocol (IP) address into the browser to navigate to the user interface.

TIP

If you're unsure of the IP address for your mining rig, you can log into your home router to scan the connected devices on your network. Software such as Angry IP Scanner (AngryIP.org) can also assist you in doing an IP scan to nail down your device's local address if you're unsure how to access your home network modem or router. Your mining hardware user manual or guide should also have information to assist you in setting it up and logging into it.

Following is an example of the settings you'd need to input into your miner for a U.S.-based Bitcoin ASIC running on Slush Pool:

```
URL: stratum+tcp://us-east.stratum.slushpool.com:3333
userID: userName.workerName
password: anything
```

The specific mining pool you choose should provide details on connection settings via their website. For example, instead of requiring you to enter a user account, a mining pool may only need you to input your payout address for the cryptocurrency you're mining. Again, check your pool's documentation for details.

The URL you connect to depends on which location is closest to you. Your username is the same as your mining pool account, and you can get creative with what you decide to name your worker, or mining rig; however, don't duplicate worker names if you're connecting more than one piece of mining gear. (You can have multiple "workers" working within your single mining account, with each worker representing a particular mining rig.) See Chapter 10 for more information on setting up your mining rig.

Payout addresses

You can generate a cryptocurrency address to use for mining pool payouts from any cryptocurrency wallet. (See Chapters 1 and 9 for more on cryptocurrency wallets.) In the cryptocurrency space, it is highly recommended that addresses for transactions not be used more than once. This non-reuse of addresses is a best practice to help facilitate more privacy and transaction anonymity.

Actually, setting up a pool account can often be much easier than this, if you're using non-ASIC hardware. We show an example later in this chapter of setting up a pool account, which took around five minutes from reaching the website to beginning mining.

Payout thresholds

For cryptocurrency mining pools, one of the more finely tuned settings is the *payout threshold*. This is the amount you must earn while mining for the pool before the pool sends a reward to your cryptocurrency address on the blockchain. Most pools allow you to define how frequently you want to receive your earnings. Although some pools allow a manual trigger of mining reward payouts, most require you to set a payout threshold that indirectly determines your payout frequency, depending on your hardware capabilities and pool contribution.

If you select a payout threshold that's too low, you waste a large portion of your reward on transaction fees that may result in dust accumulating in your cryptocurrency wallet. (The term *dust* in the cryptocurrency realm usually refers to small or micro transaction amounts that may be unspendable in the future because the total amount held in the address is less than the transaction fees required to move it. Dust transactions are an occurrence you want to avoid.)

However, if you choose a payout threshold that's too large, you could leave your cryptocurrency rewards in the hands of the mining pool for longer than necessary, which makes them susceptible to theft through hacking or fraud.

TIP

A sweet spot exists — in other words, you can set your payout threshold value to an amount that helps to alleviate both problems. Normally, a good rule is to set your pool account payout threshold to the equivalent mining rewards projected to be earned from your mining equipment over a period of a few weeks to a month, similar to a traditional paycheck. This allows for enough cryptocurrency to be earned to make the transaction worth the effort and also doesn't leave your funds in the control of someone else for too long. Bottom line: You want steady rewards for your work that you contribute (in mining and labor), but hourly payouts for your day job or cryptocurrency mine don't make logical sense with the transaction fees and overhead involved.

Researching Mining Pools

A number of resource sites provide great information about mining pools, in particular for the Bitcoin network. When comparing alternative cryptocurrency pools, the information becomes less trustworthy and more difficult to come by. We recommend searching for the name of the cryptocurrency you're interested in and the term *mining pool* (for example, *DASH mining pool*, *Litecoin mining pool*, and so on), and visiting public forum sites, such as Reddit, Stack Exchange, and Bitcoin Talk, to find more information.

Here are a few Bitcoin resources:

>> https://coin.dance/blocks/thisweek

>> https://en.bitcoin.it/wiki/Comparison_of_mining_pools

>> https://99bitcoins.com/bitcoin-mining/pools

>> https://en.bitcoinwiki.org/wiki/Comparison_of_mining_pools

>> www.blockchain.com/pools

And here are a few for Ethereum and Litecoin:

>> www.poolwatch.io/coin/ethereum

>> www.litecoinpool.org/pools

>> https://litecoin.info/index.php/Mining_pool_comparison

Cloud Mining

Another option for aspiring cryptocurrency miners is to work with cloud mining services. Essentially, you fund a portion of a mining operation, and the cloud miners do the rest. You are, in effect, an investor in the operation.

These companies offer hash rate contracts. You buy a certain hash rate, for a certain period of time (see Figure 7-3), and you then benefit proportionally based on the percentage of the overall cloud mining operation that you've funded.

A huge advantage of these services is that it's totally hands off — no equipment to buy or manage, no space to find for the equipment, no equipment noise, no heat to deal with. Cloud mining services solve those issues for you.

However, cloud mining can also be somewhat risky. Many operations aren't profitable for the durations specified in the contract and can leave purchasers of these services losing money, in some cases, over the long run. Users may be better off simply purchasing the cryptocurrency that their mining contract mines. (That, of course, is often also true of pool and solo mining, but you can find out more about the economics of mining in Chapter 11.)

Other risks include outright scams. A common mantra in cryptocurrency circles is, "Not your keys, not your coin." In the case of cloud mining contracts, one might say, "Not your mining hardware, not your rewards."

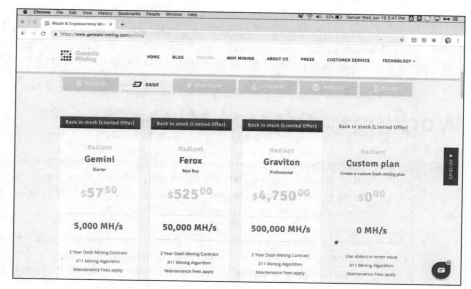

FIGURE 7-3:
Genesis Mining sells hash rate packages. DASH starts at 5,000 MH/s for two years, but you can also mine Bitcoin, Ethereum, Litecoin, Monero, or Zcash.

We believe the following services rank near the top of trustworthy cloud mining operators. However, *caveat emptor* (buyer beware). For *all* services we talk about in this book, you must do your due diligence, find out what the community is saying about them, and ensure that they are trustworthy and reliable.

» **Compass Mining:** https://compassmining.io

» **Genesis Mining:** www.genesis-mining.com

» **ECOS:** https://ecos.am/en/cloud-mining

» **Hashgains:** www.hashgains.com

» **HashNest:** www.hashnest.com

» **IQMining:** https://iqmining.com

» **Shamining:** https://shamining.com

This list is brief because we feel comfortable about only a few cryptocurrency cloud mining providers, as many of the rest aren't trustworthy and don't offer the services they advertise.

However, that doesn't mean the preceding services always provide *profitable* mining contracts. It just means that they do, in fact, deliver on the services that they offer — as far as we know, they provide the hash rates advertised for the period promised. But that doesn't mean profitability at all times.

The profitability of cloud mining contracts varies widely among services. To find out more on how to do a cost/benefit analysis on cloud mining services, pool mining deployments, or anticipated hardware rewards, refer to Chapter 11.

Working with Cudo Miner

Throughout this chapter, we provide a bunch of mining pools and resources to find out more. They all work differently, of course, so we can't possibly show you how to work with each one — it'll be a voyage of discovery for you. Spend some time getting to know the pool you picked.

In this section, we take a quick look at a popular and well-respected pool, Cudo Miner (www.cudominer.com), which has the advantage of being very quick and easy to set up and run. We're not recommending any particular pool, though (see earlier in this chapter for a few pool options) — we're just using this as an example.

As we explain at the beginning of this chapter, the pool mining software runs on your computer, contributing extra processing power to the Cudo Miner pool for hashing. You'll be involved in mining a variety of cryptocurrencies — in fact, Cudo Miner automatically switches between mining different cryptocurrencies based on what's the most profitable coin to mine at any moment. At the time of writing, the pool mines Bitcoin Gold, Ethereum, Ethereum Classic, Monero, and Ravencoin, and it pays miners in Algorand, Bitcoin, Ethereum, and Monero.

To get started with Cudo Miner, follow these steps:

1. **Go to** www.cudominer.com **and download and install the Honeyminer software.**

   There's currently a big red Sign Up and Download button in the middle of the Cudo Miner home page (and at various other places throughout the site).

2. **Sign up for an account (or sign in using a Google or Microsoft account).**

3. **After you've verified your email address, you'll be dropped into the console.**

   Look for the Set Up a Device button. You may have to scroll down the main Devices panel to see it, depending on what message boxes are displayed on the top of the screen.

4. Click the Set Up a Device button and click Continue.

You'll see Choose a Worker Type (see Figure 7-4), which is where you'll select your operating system. Notice that Cudo Miner has its own CudoOS operating system, optimized for mining; if you choose that option, you'll actually be downloading the operating system and the mining software. This is a more complicated process, of course, so we're not going into that right now. So, pick the operating system you're working with, then click the Continue button.

FIGURE 7-4:
Picking your
operating system
for the Cudo
Miner software.

5. Copy your organization username and click Continue.

Cudo Miner gives you a username (see Figure 7-5), so save it somewhere. (Click the little page icon on the right side of the text box to copy it to the Clipboard.) Then click the Continue button.

6. Click the Download Cudo Miner button.

Download the software (see Figure 7-6) and install it as you would any other program on your operating system.

TIP

If you see an "unidentified developer" message on the Mac, you can choose to proceed with the installation by going to System Preferences, opening Security & Privacy, selecting the General tab, and clicking Open Anyway.

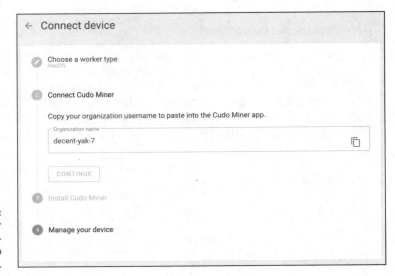

FIGURE 7-5:
Save your
username —
you're going to
need it later.

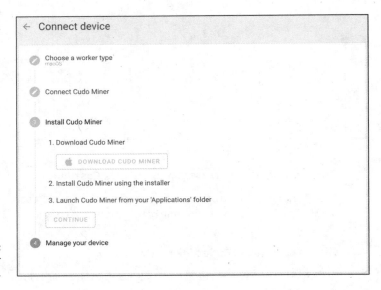

FIGURE 7-6:
Download your
software.

7. **Run the Cudo Miner app.**

Run the app (it may start automatically after installation). Then enter your organization username (see Figure 7-7) and click the Go button.

The app should start running. Now you have software running on your computer, mining the cryptocurrency, and in your Cudo Miner web console you can see the status. In the app, click your username in the upper right of the window and select Visit Console (see Figure 7-8) to go to the web console (shown in Figure 7-9).

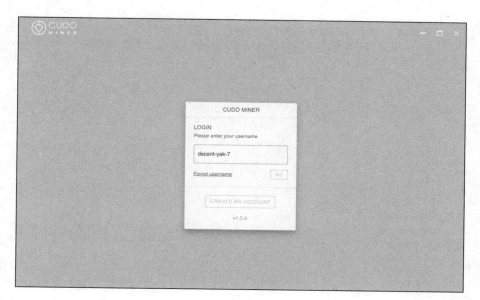

FIGURE 7-7:
Enter your
username to
log in.

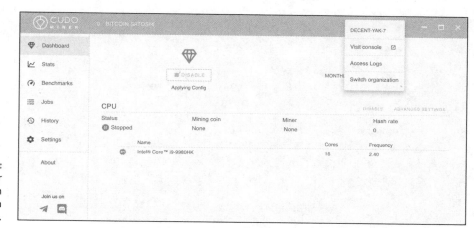

FIGURE 7-8:
The Cudo Miner
app works in
combination with
the web console.

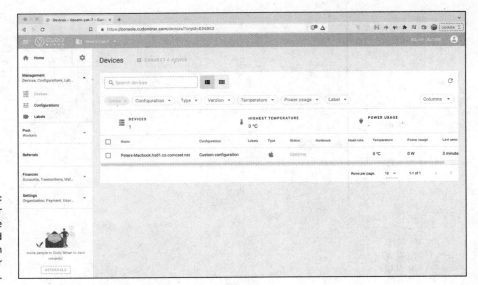

FIGURE 7-9:
The Cudo Miner
web console
provides detailed
information
about your
operations.

Chapter **8**

Picking a Cryptocurrency to Mine

C hapter 7 talks about an easy way to get into mining: using a pool. In this chapter, we discuss preparing to mine for yourself directly, by picking an appropriate cryptocurrency to mine. Of course, getting started is much more complicated than merely picking a target, and, in fact, we recommend that you don't actually begin mining until you finish this book, not just this chapter.

This chapter discusses the sort of factors that can help you find a good cryptocurrency to work with — one that is stable enough for you to be successful, for example. But we believe it's a good idea to understand more before you actually get started. This chapter helps you pick an initial target cryptocurrency, but your target may change as you discover more, such as the kind of equipment you'll need to use, for example (see Chapter 9) or more about the economics of mining (see Chapter 10). In fact, this decision-making process is a bit circular; the cryptocurrency you decide to mine determines the type of hardware you need, and the type of hardware you have (or can obtain) determines the cryptocurrency that makes sense for you to mine.

This chapter helps you to begin figuring out what cryptocurrency makes a good initial target.

Determining Your Goal

Whether you want to be a hobbyist miner or a serious commercial miner, or somewhere in between, you must ask yourself an important question before you go any further down the cryptocurrency mining path. Answering this question will enable you to properly determine which cryptocurrencies to mine, and will help you become the most successful crypto miner you can be:

What is your goal for mining cryptocurrency, and how will you reach it?

Let's break down this question and drill deeper into its component parts, by focusing on the following questions:

» **What do you want to get out of cryptocurrency mining?** Maybe you're looking to gain some insight into this whole cryptocurrency technology, or maybe you're motivated by the possibility of windfall profits. Are you wanting to support your cryptocurrency's ecosystem, or are you more concerned with it supporting you?

» **How much capital do you plan on using? Are you planning on betting the farm, or only wanting to dip your toes in to test the water?** It's always a good idea to start small and ease into the ecosystem, but depending on your financial situation, starting small may mean something completely different for you than for another investor.

» **How serious is cryptocurrency mining to you, and how much risk are you willing to take?** Markets go up, markets go down, and in cryptocurrency systems, they fluctuate more frequently than traditional financial assets. It's your savings on the line, so you should understand the risks. Consider the obligation and the stress to your life, and make sure you aren't overcommitting before you have enough experience and a feel for the complex systems. It's okay if you just want cryptocurrency mining to be a fun hobby experience, too!

» **What is the minimum return on investment (ROI) you must meet and in what timeframe?** In other words, what's it worth to you to get involved? Are you wanting to get rich quickly, or are you trying to secure some of your value and wealth long term? You should be prepared to try something different if this ROI isn't met, maybe even reduce the footprint of your operation. There's no shame in scaling down or calling it quits, either. Depending on market conditions, simply purchasing a particular cryptocurrency is sometimes cheaper than mining it!

» **Are you planning to measure your returns in your local fiat currency, or are you measuring your gains in the cryptocurrency asset you plan to mine?** The latter option only makes sense if you have confidence in the future value of the cryptocurrency, of course. For example, many miners, during Bitcoin's downturns, continue mining due to their strong belief that the price will increase again. As the value of the cryptocurrency drops, and some miners drop out of the business, the other miners' incomes — measured in cryptocurrency — go up, because the block rewards are being shared among fewer miners. At such a time, the remaining miners are increasing their stock of the cryptocurrency, and even though they may be losing money if measured in terms of fiat currency, they're okay with it because they view the cryptocurrency as an investment that will pay off in the future.

To help you answer these questions, we look at some hypothetical cryptocurrency mining stories.

First up is Kenny, an intelligent guy with a background in computers and IT. He knows his way around a datacenter, and to him, cryptocurrency mining is pretty similar to running a room full of servers. (Kenny is a tad overconfident, as running the mining equipment is only part of the battle when mining cryptocurrency.)

Kenny is looking to profit from cryptocurrency mining and views it as a challenge. With the savings from his tech job, he has set aside around $10,000 for his cryptomining venture, only a fraction of his overall savings. (We said he's smart!) He is very serious about cryptocurrency mining, and he views the undertaking as a challenge of his intellect and skill. The minimum ROI he has decided on is 20 percent annually on every penny he puts into mining, and he plans to adjust his mining strategy every day if he's not on track to meet this goal. Assuming moderate success on his ROI goals, he will do a full re-evaluation after one year to decide whether he continues mining.

Our second example is Cathy, a savvy investor who manages her retirement portfolio very successfully. For her, cryptocurrency mining is a way to experience and gain exposure to this new cryptocurrency technology; if it catches on, she doesn't want to miss the boat. She wants to profit but knows that she doesn't fully understand how cryptocurrency works, and she is excited to find out more. She is serious about doing the mining correctly and has initially set aside $500 to put toward cryptocurrency mining. She isn't going to freak out if it ends up not working out, though. She would like to see a 10 percent ROI annually, and after six months, she will decide whether she wants to continue mining. She plans to re-evaluate her strategy every two months.

The differences to highlight here are namely the amounts invested and the expectations that both Kenny and Cathy have set for themselves. Cathy is risk-averse in her approach, but has taken a lot of pressure off herself if things don't go as planned, by starting small with an amount she is willing to lose. She is also re-evaluating her strategy every two months, another way to reduce risk and exposure and to also make sure that she won't be too stressed if it doesn't work out.

Kenny has taken a riskier approach, but if he pulls it off, he will stand to profit much more than Cathy. It is important to note that Kenny has some prior experience with running networked computers, giving him a leg up and reducing some of his risk out of the gate. He is also taking a more hands-on approach with his two-week ROI evaluations, which is a good strategy because he's putting more on the line. However, Cathy has also hedged against failure by using less of an initial investment.

Both of these miners went on to reach their goals by the end of their predetermined timelines and ended up happy that they got into cryptocurrency mining. The moral of these stories is that none of your answers to the most important question are inherently wrong, but asking these questions is critical to your success. The questions and answers will play a major role when it comes time to choose the cryptocurrencies you'll mine and how you set up your mining rigs.

Mineable? PoW? PoS?

Many factors contribute to whether a cryptocurrency is a good choice for the aspiring miner. The first decision, of course, is whether it is possible to mine the cryptocurrency. Some cryptocurrencies cannot be mined. This is the case for some of the newest tokens and cryptocurrencies being created and promoted, especially centralized coin offerings and company-based tokens, as these are typically issued prior to release and work on systems more akin to a permissioned database than a decentralized cryptocurrency.

Furthermore, in general, we're going to ignore proof-of-stake (PoS) cryptocurrencies (see Chapter 4). While it is possible to mine PoS cryptocurrencies, PoS mining has some inherent problems that make it less attractive to most miners. First, you need a stake; in other words, you must invest not only in your mining rig, but also in the cryptocurrency you are planning to mine. (Note, however, that the equipment needed for mining PoS cryptocurrencies is generally cheaper than for proof-of-work (PoW) cryptocurrencies. It can generally be done on regular computers, even an old piece of computer hardware you have lying around.) Before you can start, you'll have to buy some of this cryptocurrency and store it in your wallet. Depending on the particular PoS cryptocurrency you've chosen, this could be a significant investment; the more you stake, the more often you will add a block to the blockchain and earn fees and perhaps block subsidies.

Secondly, the cards are already stacked against you. PoS systems have to have pre-mined currency; after all, if the system requires staking, it can't work unless currency is already available to stake. The founders of the currency will have awarded themselves large amounts of cryptocurrency right from the get-go, so they have a head start and will dominate the process. (Again, the more you have to stake, the more often you will win the right to add a block to the blockchain.)

Thus, PoS mining has this inherent problem for newcomers: You have to invest in equipment, but the ROI will be lower for you than for the cryptocurrency's founders, because they have a much larger stake and so will add more blocks. Hybridized proof-of-work / proof-of-state systems face many of these same issues, but with mining also involved, and so they tend to include many of the downsides of both PoW and PoS systems.

So, most mining is focused on PoW cryptocurrencies, and that's what we focus on here. As far as cryptocurrencies that do in fact have mining implemented and proof of work embedded into their deployed systems, we walk through a few factors that would make some cryptocurrencies better to mine compared to others.

Researching Cryptocurrencies

If you want to go deep and find out more about a cryptocurrency, you're going to need a few information sources. In this section, we look at a number of ways to uncover everything you need to know about a particular cryptocurrency.

Mining profitability comparison sites

So here's the first type of information source, which provides a shortcut around the whole "Is it mineable?" question. Refer to the mining-comparison sites. A number of these sites gather a plethora of data about mineable cryptocurrencies. Here are a few, and more will probably appear over time, so if any of these links break, do a search engine query:

>> **2CryptoCalc:** https://2cryptocalc.com/

>> **CoinWarz:** www.coinwarz.com

>> **Crypto-CoinZ:** www.crypto-coinz.net

>> **NiceHash:** www.nicehash.com/profitability-calculator

>> **WhatToMine:** www.whattomine.com

The first thing these sites do for you is to provide a list of mineable cryptocurrencies; if it's not on this list, it's probably not mineable, or not practical to mine. Some of these sites will have more cryptocurrencies listed than others, but in combination, they will give you a great idea of what's practical to mine right now. (What about the brand new coin that's coming out tomorrow? Sure, it won't be on those lists, but for a beginning miner, that probably doesn't matter, and in any case, consider the Lindy Effect, explained later in this chapter, in the section, "Longevity of a cryptocurrency.")

Take a look at Figure 8-1, a screenshot of WhatToMine.com. You can see that it's listing a variety of cryptocurrencies and comparing them to mining ether on the Ethereum blockchain. There's Metaverse, Callisto, Expanse, DubaiCoin, and so on. At the time of this writing, WhatToMine lists 62 cryptocurrencies that can be mined with graphics processing units (GPUs) and 59 that require application-specific integrated circuits (ASICs) to economically mine. (Look for the GPU and ASIC tabs near the top of the page.) In combination, these sites list around 150 different mineable cryptocurrencies.

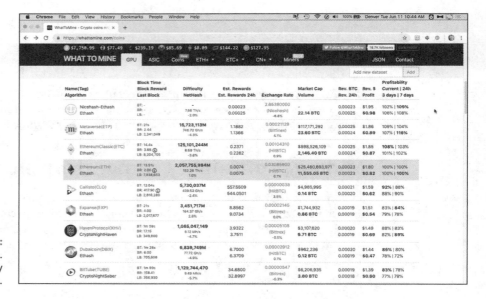

FIGURE 8-1:
The WhatToMine.com profitability comparison site.

In Figure 8-2, you can see CoinWarz.com, another very popular site; CoinWarz compares the various cryptocurrencies to mining Bitcoin, rather than Ethereum. CoinWarz has a much clearer table, allowing you to easily see a few important metrics:

>> Basic information related to the cryptocurrency, including the name, icon, ticker symbol (LTC, BTC, and so on), the overall network hash rate (the number of tera hashes per second; for more about hash rates, see Chapter 5), the block reward (though strictly speaking, what CoinWarz is showing is the block *subsidy*; the block reward is the subsidy plus the transaction fees), the number of blocks, and the time it takes on average to add a new block to the blockchain.

>> A chart showing the block difficulty and how it's changed over time.

>> An estimate of how many coins you could mine each day based on your mining rig's hash rate and the current block difficulty, and your hash rate and the average difficulty over the past 24 hours.

>> The exchange rate between each cryptocurrency and Bitcoin, and how it's changed over the last two weeks (the numbers are based on the best exchange for that cryptocurrency, which it names, so you can get the best rate when you sell your mined cryptocurrency).

>> The exchange volume over the last 24 hours — that is, how much of the coin has been traded.

>> The daily gross revenue, in U.S. dollars, that you would likely make (again, based on your hash rate), the cost for electricity, and the profit (or loss!) you would make each day.

>> Your daily estimated earnings, denominated in Bitcoin.

FIGURE 8-2: CoinWarz.com, another very popular profitability comparison site.

Okay, so about your hash rate. As noted, some of these calculations are based on your computer equipment's *hash rate* — that is, the number of PoW hashes it can carry out in a second (see Chapter 5). That's the basic information these sites need to know to calculate how often you're likely to win the game and add a block to the blockchain. Your hash rate is, essentially, the computational power of your computer.

These sites use default power settings, and the advantage of this approach is that you can at least get an idea of the relative profitability of the different cryptocurrencies, even if you don't know the power of your equipment.

Now, if you *do* know how powerful your equipment is, you can enter that information. In CoinWarz, this information is entered into the top of the page, as shown in Figure 8-3. What are all these boxes? For each mining algorithm (SHA-256, Scrypt, X11, and so on), you see three text boxes. You enter your processor's hash rate in the top box, in (depending on the algorithm) H/s (hashes per second), MH/s (mega hashes per second), or GH/s (giga hashes per second).

FIGURE 8-3:
The top of the CoinWarz.com page, where you enter your hash rate information.

The second box is *watts,* the amount of electrical power your processor is going to use; and the last box is the cost of that electricity, in $/kWh, dollars per kilowatt-hour. Well, that's a complicated subject, one that we get into in Chapter 10. Actually, some of these comparison sites provide data for common processors for you. For example, in Figure 8-4, you can see the calculator at Crypto-Coinz.net.

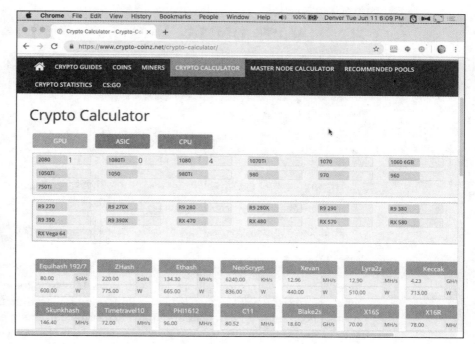

FIGURE 8-4:
Crypto-Coinz.net
actually provides
hashing power
information
for some
GPU, central
processing unit
(CPU), and ASIC
processors.

You can see that the GPU tab has been selected, so this area is showing commonly used GPUs in the cryptocurrency mining arena. These are powerful processors, set up to manage the heat that comes from constant processing. The top box lists a bunch of NVIDIA GPU model numbers; the bottom model numbers are AMD products. Find the models you have and enter the quantity you'll be using into the text boxes, and the site automatically enters the appropriate processing power into the boxes below.

TIP

All these sites work differently. We strongly recommend that you try a few, pick one or two that you really like, and then spend an hour or two digging around and figuring out how they function. They provide a huge amount of information, in many different formats, so play a while and really get a handle on them.

Algorithms and cryptocurrencies

When you first start working with these sites, they may seem to be speaking a foreign language. (That's why we suggest you spend a lot of time digging around in these sites, familiarizing yourself with the lingo, and fully understanding what's going on.) It takes time to get used to an arena in which every other word is new to you.

Refer to Figure 8-3, for example, and you see SHA-256, Scrypt, X11, and so on. What are these? They are the particular PoW mining algorithms. For each algorithm, one or more (generally more) individual cryptocurrencies exist that use the algorithm. The following sections provide a partial list of mineable cryptocurrencies and the algorithms they use.

The lists in the following section aren't everything; more algorithms, and more mineable cryptocurrencies, exist, but you can assume that if they're not on at least one of the comparison sites, they're not worth your attention. For example, at the time of this writing, a number of algorithms (X25, Keccak, SkunkHash, BLAKE2s, BLAKE256, X17, CNHeavy, and EnergiHash) are not being used by cryptocurrencies deemed worthy of these sites.

Notice another thing about the preceding list, something you may want to consider when picking a cryptocurrency that uses an algorithm that requires an ASIC. We have five ASIC algorithms listed, and below each algorithm, we have 7, 13, 8, 7, and 4 cryptocurrencies using each algorithm respectively. That is, the same ASIC — the same hardware — can be used to mine any of the cryptocurrencies using the algorithm for which the ASIC was designed.

So you could choose to mine, say, CannabisCoin, in which case you would need an X11 ASIC. If CannabisCoin went up in smoke (excuse the pun), you could switch to DASH, IDApay, or Startcoin. But if you bought an ASIC for the Scrypt algorithm, began mining one of the Scrypt cryptocurrencies, and then wanted to switch, you would have not 3 but 12 alternative choices.

Algorithms requiring a specialized ASIC

Following is a partial list of mineable cryptocurrencies and the algorithms they use. The first one, SHA-256, is the most popular algorithm — the one used by Bitcoin and all its derivatives.

» **SHA-256:**

- Bitcoin (BTC)
- Bitcoin Cash (BCH)
- eMark (DEM)
- Litecoin Cash (LCC)
- Namecoin (NMC)
- Peercoin (PPC)
- Unobtanium (UNO)

» **Scrypt:**

- Auroracoin (AUR)
- DigiByte (DGB)
- Dogecoin (DOGE)
- Einsteinium (EMC2)
- FlorinCoin (FLO)
- GAME Credits (GAME)
- Gulden (NLG)
- Held Coin (HDLC)
- Litecoin (LTC)
- Novacoin (NVC)
- Verge (XVG)
- Viacoin (VIA)

» **Equihash:**

- Aion (AION)
- Beam (BEAM)
- Bitcoin Private (BTCP)
- Commercium (CMM)

- Horizen (ZEN)
- Komodo (KMD)
- VoteCoin (VOT)
- Zcash (ZEC)

>> **Lyra2v2:**

- Absolute Coin (ABS)
- Galactrum (ORE)
- Hanacoin (HANA)
- Methuselah (SAP)
- MonaCoin (MONA)
- Straks (STAK)
- Vertcoin (VTC)

>> **X11:**

- CannabisCoin (CANN)
- DASH (DASH)
- IDApay (IDA)
- Petro (PTR)
- Startcoin (START)

Algorithms that may be mined without ASICs

The following algorithms may still effectively be mined without purpose-built, application-specific hardware, or ASICs.

>> **NeoScrypt:**

- Cerberus (CBS)
- Coin2Fly (CTF)
- Desire (DSR)
- Dinero (DIN)
- Feathercoin (FTC)
- GoByte (GBX)
- Guncoin (GUN)

- Innova (INN)
- IQ.cash (IQ)
- LuckyBit (LUCKY)
- Mogwai (MOG)
- Phoenixcoin (PXC)
- Qbic (QBIC)
- Rapture (RAP)
- SecureTag (TAG)
- SimpleBank (SPLB)
- SunCoin (SUN)
- Traid (TRAID)
- TrezarCoin (TZC)
- UFO Coin (UFO)
- Vivo (VIVO)
- Zixx (XZX)

» **Ethash:**

- Akroma (AKA)
- Atheios (ATH)
- Callisto (CLO)
- DubaiCoin (DBIX)
- Ellaism (ELLA)
- Ether-1 (ETHO)
- Ethereum (ETH)
- Ethereum Classic (ETC)
- Expanse (EXP)
- Metaverse (ETP)
- Musicoin (MUSIC)
- Nilu (NILU)
- Pirl (PIRL)
- Ubiq (UBQ)

- Victorium (VIC)
- WhaleCoin (WHL)

>> **X16R:**

- BitCash (BITC)
- CrowdCoin (CRC)
- GINcoin (GIN)
- GPUnion (GUT)
- Gravium (GRV)
- HelpTheHomeless (HTH)
- Hilux (HLX)
- Motion (XMN)
- Ravencoin (RVN)
- StoneCoin (STONE)
- Xchange (XCG)

>> **Lyra2z:**

- CriptoReal (CRS)
- Gentarium (GTM)
- Glyno (GLYNO)
- Infinex (IFX)
- Mano (MANO)
- Pyro (PYRO)
- Stim (STM)
- Taler (TLR)
- ZCore (ZCR)

>> **X16S:**

- Pigeoncoin (PGN)
- Rabbit (RABBIT)
- Reden (REDN)
- RESQ Chain (RESQ)

- » **Zhash:**
  - BitcoinZ (BTCZ)
  - Bitcoin Gold (BTG)
  - SnowGem (XSG)
  - ZelCash (ZEL)
- » **CryptoNightR:**
  - Monero (XMR)
  - Lethean (LTHN)
  - Sumokoin (SUMO)
- » **Xevan:**
  - BitSend (BST)
  - Elliotcoin (ELLI)
  - Urals Coin (URALS)
- » **PHI2:**
  - Argoneium (AGM)
  - Luxcoin (LUX)
  - Spider (SPDR)
- » **Equihash 192/7:**
  - SafeCoin (SAFE)
  - Zero (ZER)
- » **Tribus:**
  - BZL Coin (BZL)
  - Scriv (SCRIV)
- » **Timetravel10:** Bitcore (BTX)
- » **PHI1612:** Folm (FLM)
- » **C11:** Bithold (BHD)
- » **HEX:** XDNA (XDNA)
- » **ProgPoW:** Bitcoin Interest (BCI)
- » **LBK3:** VERTICAL COIN (VTL)

- **VerusHash:** Verus (VRSC)

- **Ubqhash:** Ubiq (UBQ)

- **MTP:** Zcoin (XZC)

- **Groestl:** Groestlcoin (GRS)

- **CrypoNightSaber:** BitTube (TUBE)

- **CryptoNightHaven:** HavenProtocol (XHV)

- **CNReverseWaltz:** Graft (GRFT)

- **CryptoNight Conceal:** Conceal (CCX)

- **CryptoNight FastV2:** Masari (MSR)

- **CryptoNight Fast:** Electronero (ETNX)

- **Cuckatoo31:** Grin-CT31 (GRIN)

- **Cuckatoo29:** Grin-CR29 (GRI)

- **Cuckatoo29s:** Swap (XWP)

- **Cuckoo Cycle:** Aeternity (AE)

- **BCD:** Bitcoin Diamond (BCD)

- **YescryptR16:** Yenten (YTN)

- **YesCrypt:** Koto (KOTO)

The cryptocurrency's details page

Another great place to find information about a particular cryptocurrency is on the currency's details page at the comparison sites. The comparison sites we looked at earlier in this chapter generally link to that page. In fact, refer to the image in Figure 8–1; if you click on a cryptocurrency name, you're taken to a details page that contains additional information about that cryptocurrency. For example, click Callisto (CLO), and you see the page shown in Figure 8–5.

This page contains stacks of information about the cryptocurrency, including statistics such as the block time (how often a block is added), the block reward, the difficulty level, and so on. It also lists mining pools that work with this particular currency (see Chapter 7).

CPU VERSUS GPU VERSUS APU VERSUS ASIC

Do you use a CPU, a GPU, an accelerated processing unit (APU), or an ASIC? First, some cryptocurrencies pretty much require an ASIC (see the prior list). You *could* mine using another processor, but there's not much point, because your processing power will be so low in comparison with the ASICs designed for the job that you may have to wait a thousand years to win the right to add a block to the blockchain. (No, we're not kidding, the disparity is on this scale.)

As the preceding list shows, other cryptocurrencies do not require ASICs; they can be mined using a CPU (your computer's main processor), a GPU (a specialized processor designed for managing computer graphics, which tends to be more powerful), or an APU (a processor that combines both the CPU and GPU on the same chip).

In general, CPUs don't make great mining processors, though it can be done. These comparison sites, and the mining calculators we look at later in this chapter, can tell you whether your particular CPU, GPU, or APU can be used. There's a huge range of processing power among processors; some will be useless, some will be viable. You can find out how to figure out the power of your processor in Chapter 9.

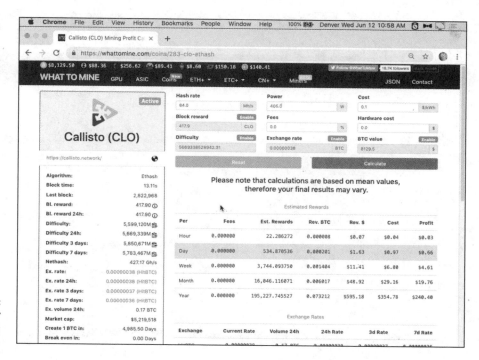

FIGURE 8-5:
A cryptocurrency detail page on WhatToMine.com.

Mining-profit calculators

If you want to know what the profit potential is for a particular cryptocurrency, you need to work with a mining-profit calculator. The mining comparison sites generally contain these calculators, though other sites also provide individual calculators without an overall comparison tool. (`www.cryptocompare.com/mining/calculator/`, for example, provides calculators for Bitcoin, Ethereum, Monero, Zcash, DASH, and Litecoin.)

For example, refer to Figure 8-5. At the top of the page, you can enter your hardware's hash rate, power consumption, and cost, along with the cost of your electricity, and the calculator will figure out how much you can make (or lose) over an hour, a day, a week, a month, or a year.

Figure 8-6 shows a simpler calculator, from `www.cryptocompare.com/mining/calculator/btc`, that displays potential revenue and profit from mining Bitcoin. This calculator even allows you to enter a pool fee, to include the costs of mining through a pool (see Chapter 7). This example, even though it shows you making a profit, is actually a losing proposition. (See the nearby sidebar, "Hash power envy? You'd better pool mine.")

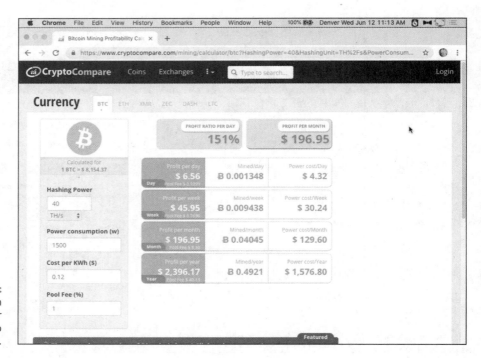

FIGURE 8-6: The Bitcoin calculator at Crypto Compare.com.

HASH POWER ENVY? YOU'D BETTER POOL MINE

In many cases, you're not going to like what you see in these calculators. If your hash power is simply not great enough, the calculators will implicitly — or, in some cases, explicitly — tell you not to even consider mining solo and direct you toward pool mining. For example, in Figure 8-6, you're being told that, using the hash power specified at the left of the page, you'll mine, on average, 0.4921 Bitcoin each year. Well, at present the block subsidy is 12.5 Bitcoin, and you can't get a partial block subsidy; you get all or nothing. Given that 12.5 Bitcoin divided by 0.4921 is 25.4, you're being told that if all things remain the same (which they won't), it would take your hardware 25.4 *years* to win the right to add a block to the blockchain. And that's just the average. Your luck may vary — it may take less time — but it could 30 years (or more) before you win a block subsidy! (What will change? The block subsidy will be reduced over time, more hashing power may enter the network, and so on.) In other words, you cannot practically mine Bitcoin with only 40 TH/s . . . so go join a pool if you want to mine Bitcoin (see Chapter 7) or up your game (your mining rig) dramatically (see Chapter 9).

Some calculators will actually be more explicit. The CoinWarz Bitcoin mining calculator (at `www.coinwarz.com/calculators/bitcoin-mining-calculator`) would present you with this information.

Bitcoin Mining Calculator Summary

Days to generate one block mining solo: 9,271.5 days (can vary greatly depending on your luck)

Days to generate one BTC: 741.72 days (can vary greatly depending on the current exchange rates)

Days to break even: N/A (can vary greatly depending on the current exchange rates)

The cryptocurrency's home page

Another great place to find information about a cryptocurrency in which you have some interest is, not surprisingly, the cryptocurrency's home page (though, of course, the information you'll find here will be biased toward optimism for the future of the currency). That's easy enough to find. The comparison site's cryptocurrency details pages (refer to Figure 8-5) generally have this information. You can also find this information at other sites, such as coinmarketcap.com.

REMEMBER

Many of these cryptocurrency systems are distributed with the aim of decentralization. This means that for most of these systems, no single party controls them, so many sites may claim to be the home page for that particular peer-to-peer cryptocurrency, with some having more validity to that claim than others. Always do plenty of research and tread lightly.

GitHub

Most cryptocurrencies you're likely to be mining have a GitHub page. GitHub is a software development platform and software repository, used by many open-source software projects. Although cryptocurrencies are not open source by definition, most of them are (in fact, any cryptocurrency you're likely to mine is generally open source). You can see an example — the Bitcoin GitHub page — in Figure 8-7.

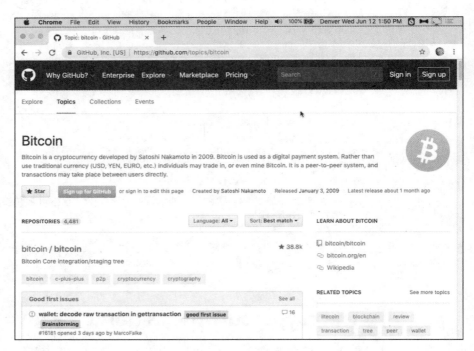

FIGURE 8-7:
Bitcoin's
GitHub page.

How do you find the GitHub page? Again, the details page at one of the cryptocurrency sites may hold a link to the currency's GitHub page, or it may not. You may be able to find a link to it in the currency's home page, or you can also search for it within GitHub.com.

At GitHub, you can review the actual source code of the cryptocurrency to see how it functions, if you have the skills to do so, but you can also get an idea of how active the community is, how many people are involved, how often changes are made to the code, and so on. For a deeper dive into the specific mechanisms and intricacies involved with GitHub, refer to *GitHub For Dummies* (John Wiley & Sons, Inc.) by Sarah Guthals and Phil Haack.

The cryptocurrency's Wikipedia page

Many, perhaps most, cryptocurrencies, have Wikipedia pages. These can be useful places to find general background information about a cryptocurrency, often more quickly than using other sources. These pages often provide a little history about the currency, information about the founders and the technology, controversies related to it, and so on. You won't find them for many of the smaller, more obscure cryptocurrencies, though, and the level of detail for the ones that are there ranges from sparse to exhaustive.

You can see an example in Figure 8-8, which shows Dogecoin's Wikipedia page. Notice the info-block on the right side, which provides a quick rundown of important information.

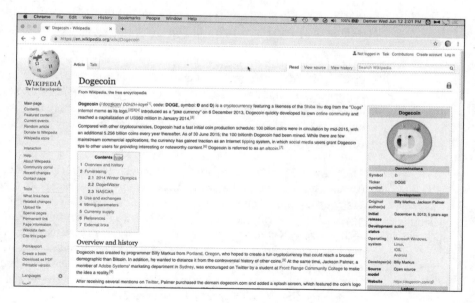

FIGURE 8-8:
The Dogecoin Wikipedia page.

Mining forums

Finally, don't forget the cryptocurrency mining forums, of which perhaps the most significant are the Bitcoin (BitcoinTalk.org) forums. You can find forums on numerous subjects here, related to many different Bitcoin and cryptocurrency issues. There's a Bitcoin Mining section, as well as an Alternative Cryptocurrencies section, and within that, a Mining subsection. The Altcoin mining section has more than 800,000 posts in more than 3,000 topic areas, and so a wealth of mining information is there to be digested.

Going Deep

After you know how to find the information on a variety of these cryptocurrency systems — if it's available, that is, because in many cases the information may be hard to find — you may want to consider several other factors.

Longevity of a cryptocurrency

To choose a cryptocurrency that is right for you, it is important to have confidence that it will be around and functioning during the period you choose to mine it, as well as the period in which you plan for the cryptocurrency to store your mining rewards.

Cryptocurrency systems that have withstood the test of time are more likely to continue to do so. There's a theory called the *Lindy Effect* that states that the life expectancy of certain things, such as technology, increases as they age. (The opposite is true for living things, of course; once they reach a certain age, life expectancy declines.)

The theory, by the way, is named after a deli in New York where comedians gather each night to discuss their work. Anyway, this theory suggests that the life expectancy of ideas or technologies (nonbiological systems) is related to their current age, and that each extra duration of existence makes it more likely that the idea or technology will continue to survive. Open-source systems such as Bitcoin or other similar cryptocurrencies are constantly being upgraded and improved ever so slightly by programmers and software enthusiasts. Each code *bug,* or error in the system, that is found and quickly *patched* (a software term for fixed) will leave the system tougher and less prone to error going forward. Software systems such as Bitcoin or similar open-source cryptocurrencies can be considered *antifragile,* with each flaw that is discovered and subsequently fixed leading to a stronger and less fragile technology.

It is important to choose a cryptocurrency to mine with enough perceived longevity, durability, and endurance to suit your specific risk profile.

Let us summarize with a question: Which cryptocurrency is likely to survive longer? Bitcoin, dating back to January 2009, or JustAnotherCoin, a (hypothetical) new cryptocurrency released to the world yesterday afternoon? *Bitcoin be a better bet*, if you'll excuse the alliteration. There are a couple of thousand cryptocurrencies; most are garbage, and can't possibly survive. A new one is likely just one more JunkCoin on the garbage heap.

On the other hand, sometimes apparently stable, long-lasting systems die. Who remembers DEC, WordPerfect, or VisiCalc, for example? (We bet that many readers have no idea what these words even mean!) And sometimes new systems appear in a flash and beat out well-established competitors. (Google, anyone? Facebook?)

But, to continue with the example of technology companies, most newcomers fail; most Internet startups in the 1990s Internet bubble went out of business, for example. Most obscure cryptocurrencies will fail, too. So, *in general*, a long-lasting cryptocurrency, such as Bitcoin, Litecoin, or ether, is a better bet than today's new entry into the cryptocurrency market.

How do you figure out how long the cryptocurrency has been around? It shouldn't be too hard to find. Check the currency's own website, its Wikipedia entry if there is one, and GitHub's history of software commits and releases.

Hash rate and cryptocurrency security

Another important factor involved with the choice of which cryptocurrency to mine is the security encompassing the blockchain being selected to mine. You wouldn't want to put your eggs (mining resources) in a basket (blockchain) with holes in it that cannot support the weight of your precious cargo (value).

This same idea applies to cryptocurrency systems, and security in this sense is relative. A cryptocurrency that has a low level of hash-powered proof of work is less secure than other cryptocurrencies that run on a similar consensus mechanism, as it's more easily hacked or manipulated. This puts the cryptocurrency's chance of surviving at risk and also puts your funds in that blockchain at risk.

Where do you find the level of hash power being used by the network? One great place to look for this kind of information is BitInfoCharts.com, which will let you select cryptocurrencies to compare against each other. This site provides a huge range of different cryptocurrency metrics, from pricing charts to market cap to lists of the richest blockchain addresses, for a large range of cryptocurrencies.

As shown in Figure 8-9, one thing you can do is select a bunch of cryptocurrencies and create a chart comparing their hash rates; see `https://bitinfocharts.com/comparison/bitcoin-hashrate.html`. You can also find individual hash rates from the comparison sites we look at earlier in this chapter (see the section, "Hash rate and cryptocurrency security").

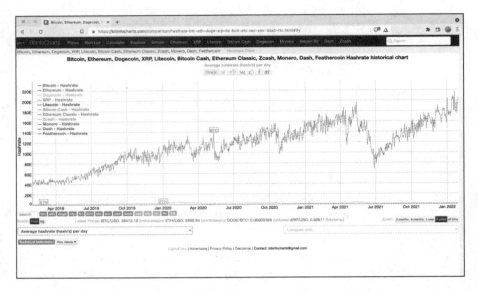

FIGURE 8-9:
BitInfoCharts.
com's hash-rate
comparison page.

In fact, hash rate is something you'll find on various sites. For example, you can find the hash rate for Bitcoin, Ethereum, and Bitcoin Cash at `www.blockchain.com/explorer`. The pool-mining services provide hash rate statistics for the cryptocurrencies they mine, and statistics sites such as Coin Dance provide some, too (see `https://coin.dance/blocks/hashrate`).

Community support

Another factor to consider and weigh when selecting which cryptocurrency is right for you is community support. Network effects of cryptocurrency systems are important, and wide adoption and utilization are key metrics to look at when choosing which blockchain to mine. Are many people involved in managing and developing the cryptocurrency? (A cryptocurrency with very few people involved is likely to be unstable.) And are many people using the cryptocurrency — that is, is there much trading going on, or are people using it to make purchases?

METCALFE'S LAW

Conceptually, Metcalfe's Law can be applied to any network, such as email networks or telephone systems, but also to cryptocurrency networks, such as Bitcoin. If only two users are on a telephone or email system, then there isn't much value in that network, but if there are four users, the value (along with possible network connections) is exponentially larger. If the system has 12 users, there are dramatically more possible connections, and thus more value (see the figure).

The same logic applies to cryptocurrency networks; each additional user adds a disproportional and exponential amount of potential connections. If the cryptocurrency system you select to mine doesn't have a large user base, there may not be enough possible connections to give that network adequate value for mining long term.

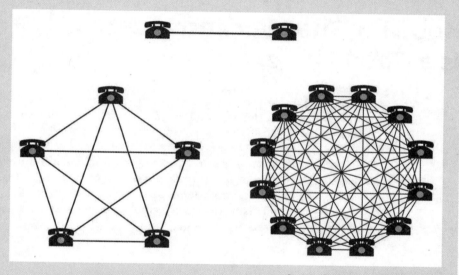

Courtesy of Woody 993 at English Wikipedia.

There's a concept known as *Metcalfe's Law* that explains network effects. The idea, proposed by Robert Metcalfe, one of the inventors of Ethernet, is that a communication system creates value proportional to the square of the number of users of that particular system. Essentially, the more users on a system, the more useful — and more valuable — the network becomes.

Community support is also important in other ways. It can be measured in the form of open-source developers actively contributing to the cryptocurrency's code repository. A healthy and robust cryptocurrency will have a diverse set of many individuals and entities reviewing and auditing the code that fortifies it.

Developer support is critical to the longevity and robustness of a cryptocurrency system. Note that many cryptocurrency systems created and issued by companies or consortiums are not open source, not mineable, and do not have a wide range of code auditors outside of the company reviewing and revising their walled-garden systems.

How do you measure community support? The cryptocurrency's GitHub page is a great start; you'll be able to see exactly how active the development process is, and how many people are involved. The currency's web page may give you an idea of activity, too, especially if the site has discussion groups. Another helpful tool to compare support across different networks can be found at www.coindesk.com/data, which shows a variety of rankings comparing top cryptocurrencies such as social, market, and developer benchmarks.

Knowing That Decentralization Is a Good Thing

In general, more decentralized cryptocurrencies are likely to be more stable and likelier to survive (long enough for you to profit from mining) than more centralized and less distributed cryptocurrencies.

In the cryptocurrency arena, the term *decentralization* is thrown around as an absolute: The system is either decentralized or it is not. This, however, isn't exactly the case. Decentralization, in fact, can be thought of as a spectrum (see Figure 8-10), and many aspects of a cryptocurrency system fall on different parts of the decentralization spectrum.

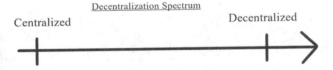

FIGURE 8-10: The spectrum of decentralization.

A major aspect of decentralized peer-to-peer blockchain-based systems is the fact that any user can spin up a node and be an equal participant in the network. Here are a few other factors that can also be used to rank cryptocurrencies on the decentralization spectrum.

>> **Initial coin distribution and coin issuance:** For a proof-of-work cryptocurrency with a predetermined issuance schedule, the distribution of coins can be considered fairer than a system in which a high percentage of the coin

issuance was pre-mined and distributed to a select few insiders. This would place pre-mined cryptocurrencies further toward the centralized spectrum than fairer and more decentralized coin-distribution models. To view a detailed breakdown of the Bitcoin network's coin issuance schedule, see Figure 8-11, which shows the interactive chart being dynamically created at `https://bashco.github.io/Bitcoin_Monetary_Inflation/`. (Go to the website and run your mouse pointer along the lines to see the exact numbers at any time.) The stepping line shows the block subsidy halving every 210,000 blocks, or roughly every four years. The upward curve line shows the amount of Bitcoin in circulation at any time. As for researching other cryptocurrencies, the comparison sites will show how often the currency's coins are issued.

>> **Node count:** The nodes are the gate keepers of valid transaction data and block information for blockchain systems. The more active nodes there are running on the system, the more decentralized the cryptocurrency. Unfortunately, this is a tricky one; it's probably pretty difficult to find this precise information for most cryptocurrencies.

>> **Network hash rate:** The level of the cryptocurrency's hash rate distribution among peers is also an important decentralization measurement for PoW cryptocurrencies. If only a few companies, individuals, or organizations (such as mining pools) are hashing a blockchain to create blocks, the cryptocurrency is relatively centralized. See the earlier section, "Hash rate and cryptocurrency security."

>> **Node client implementations:** Multiple versions of client, or node, software exist for many of the major cryptocurrencies. For example, Bitcoin has Bitcoin Core, BitCore, BCOIN, Bitcoin Knots, BTCD, Libbitcoin, and many other implementations. Ethereum has geth, parity, pyethapp, ewasm, exthereum, and many more. Cryptocurrencies with fewer client versions may be considered more centralized than those with more versions. You can probably find this information at the cryptocurrency's GitHub page and on its website. For an interesting view of the Bitcoin network client versions for nodes on the network, navigate to the following site: `https://luke.dashjr.org/programs/bitcoin/files/charts/branches.html`.

>> **Social consensus:** Social networks of users and the people participating in these cryptocurrencies are also very important in regard to the cryptocurrency decentralization spectrum. The larger the user base and the more diverse technical opinions on the system, the more robust the software and physical hardware are to changes being pushed by major players in the system. If the social consensus of a cryptocurrency is closely following a small set of super users or a foundation, then the cryptocurrency is, in effect, more centralized. More control is in the hands of fewer people, and the system is more likely to experience drastic changes in its rules. An analogy can be seen in sporting events; the rules (consensus mechanisms) are not changed by the

referees (users and nodes) halfway through the competition. The number of active addresses in the cryptocurrency's blockchain provides a good metric indicating social consensus and the network effect. This shows the number of different blockchain addresses with associated balances. This metric isn't perfect, as individual users can have multiple addresses, and sometimes many users have coins associated with a single address (when utilizing an exchange or custodial service that stores all its clients' currency in one address). However, the active addresses metric can still be a helpful gauge to compare cryptocurrencies — more addresses means, in general, more activity and more people involved. A helpful tool to find cryptocurrency active address numbers can be found at https://coinmetrics.io/charts/; choose Active Addresses in the drop-down list box on the left, and select the cryptocurrencies to compare using the option buttons at the bottom of the chart (see Figure 8-12). For smaller cryptocurrencies, this information may be hard to find, but the data would be accessible via a cryptocurrency's auditable blockchain.

>> **Physical node distribution:** With cryptocurrencies, node count is important, but it is also important that those nodes not be physically located in the same geographical area or on the same hosted servers. Some cryptocurrencies have the majority of their nodes hosted on third-party cloud services that provide blockchain infrastructure, such as Amazon Web Services, Infura (which itself uses Amazon Web Services), DigitalOcean, Microsoft Azure, or Alibaba Cloud. Systems with this type of node centralization may be at risk of being attacked by these trusted third parties. Such systems are more centralized than purer peer-to-peer networks with large node counts that are also widely geographically distributed. A view of the Bitcoin network node geographical distribution can be found at https://bitnodes.earn.com/. For the smaller cryptocurrencies, this information may be harder to find.

>> **Software code contributors:** A broad range of code contributors to the client software implementations — and code reviewers — is important for the decentralization of a cryptocurrency; the larger the number of coders, the more distributed and decentralized the cryptocurrency can be considered. With fewer contributors and reviewers, errors in the code can be more prevalent and intentional manipulation more possible. With larger numbers of reviewers and coders, mistakes and malfeasance are more easily caught. The developer count and activity on various cryptocurrency code repositories can be gleaned by exploring their GitHub pages. For Bitcoin's core repository, the link to find out more details is found at https://github.com/bitcoin/bitcoin/graphs/contributors. As an example, Ethereum averages just over 200 active repository developers per month, while the Bitcoin network averages just under 100. For most other cryptocurrency networks, that number is much lower. On average, at the time of this writing, about 8,000 developers are currently working on thousands of different cryptocurrency projects each month.

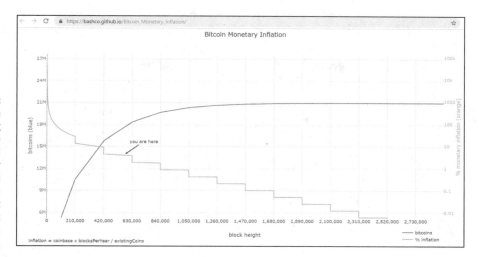

FIGURE 8-11:
Chart from
GitHub depicting
the coin issuance
schedule and
inflation rate for
Bitcoin. It has
served as a
model for most
proof-of-work
distribution
schedules.

FIGURE 8-12:
Coinmetrics.io
compares
active-address
quantities
between different
cryptocurrencies
(and provides
many more
statistics).

Finding Out It's an Iterative Process

Choosing a cryptocurrency to mine is an iterative process; it's a combination of all the factors we cover in this chapter, the hardware you're able to obtain (see Chapter 9), and the economics of the mining (Chapter 10). The economics will affect which mining hardware you can afford to buy, and what you can afford to buy will affect which cryptocurrency you choose. If you haven't already, we suggest that you read Chapters 8 and 9 to find out how all these factors fit together, and put off the final decision until you do.

» Finding a viable location to mine

» Choosing a wallet to store your mined cryptocurrency

» Finding other mining resources

Chapter **9**

Gathering Your Mining Gear

Mining cryptocurrency is easy; the mining hardware does most of the heavy lifting while you sit back and watch the coin accumulate. However, choosing the right miners, purchasing the gear, and setting up the necessary equipment is the hard part. Selecting the right cryptocurrency, selecting the correct hardware for that specific blockchain, and choosing a suitable location to deploy the mining equipment are early steps that are crucial for any gains and short- or long-term success.

We look at selecting a cryptocurrency in Chapter 8. In this chapter, we dive into the factors you need to consider when choosing mining hardware. (See also Chapter 10 for more information on mining hardware.)

Selecting the Correct Computational Mining Hardware

You can mine any cryptocurrency with any computing equipment (central processing units [CPUs], graphics processing units [GPUs], or application-specific integrated circuits [ASICs]), but if ASICs are available for a particular cryptocurrency's algorithm, in most cases using a CPU or GPU puts you at a huge disadvantage — perhaps such a big disadvantage that there's really no point in mining without an up-to-date ASIC.

Thus, the hardware you need varies for the different blockchains and their specific hashing algorithms. For example, the ASIC hardware needed to mine Bitcoin runs the SHA-256 algorithm, and there's no real point mining with a CPU or GPU; the disadvantage is simply too great. Ethereum uses the Ethash algorithm, and although Ethash ASICs are available, some miners still mine it using GPUs. Scrypt ASIC mining rigs are also available that can mine Litecoin or Dogecoin, and ASICs for the DASH and Petro cryptocurrencies use the X11 mining algorithm. (Of course, as we explain in Chapter 8, any American wanting to maintain their freedom should steer clear of the Petro; also see Chapter 8 for a list of numerous cryptocurrencies and their algorithms.)

For cryptocurrencies like Monero, however, an off-the-shelf computer with a functioning CPU and GPU (that is, pretty much any computer) can be used to mine it effectively.

REMEMBER

Don't forget the pool-mining services — such as NiceHash, Cudo Miner, and Kryptex — which let you use their software to point your off-the-shelf, common computer cycles toward a pool and cryptocurrency of their choosing, and then reward you for your contribution in a more stable cryptocurrency, such as Bitcoin. These services may be the easiest way to test out mining, by using your existing computational hardware that may very well sit idle most of the day on your desk. For those who want to test the waters before acquiring more expensive equipment, pool-mining services are highly recommended (see Chapter 7).

If you want to go further in your mining endeavors, possibly even buying specialized mining equipment — which, by the way, can be used for both pool mining and solo mining — you must consider a few rating factors.

Specified hash rate

The first and foremost factor when selecting mining hardware is the hash rate that the rig is stated to deliver. Normally, companies that provide mining hardware ASICs provide a guaranteed hash-rate value that the mining rig will output on average. Sometimes it may be slightly more, and other times it may be slightly less, but over longer periods of time, it should average out to the guaranteed rate.

For Bitcoin-based SHA-256 mining hardware — the most advanced and efficient equipment — this hash rate is typically specified in tera hashes per second, or TH/s. Figure 9-1 shows the specified hash-rate capabilities for some of the most capable Bitcoin SHA-256 ASIC mining hardware, released anywhere from 2017 to 2022. As you can see, the equipment varies greatly, from a low of around 1 TH/s to around 140 TH/s.

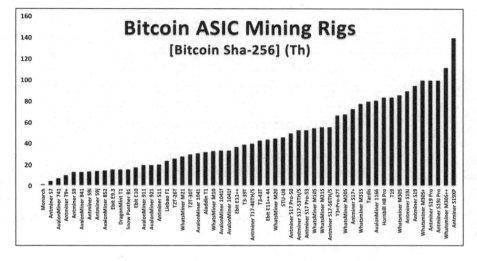

FIGURE 9-1:
A graph showing the highest hash-rate SHA-256 mining equipment being deployed on the Bitcoin network between 2017 and 2022.

Over the past few years, many different manufacturers have jumped into the Bitcoin-mining hardware-production game, increasing competition in the space and creating an ASIC-mining hardware arms race. This space has seen enormous growth, in terms of diversity of suppliers and hash-rate capability, within the last couple of years.

TIP

To stay competitive in the Bitcoin or other cryptocurrency mining realms, you need to use the latest and greatest hardware. Most proof-of-work blockchains have seen ASIC mining rigs developed for their network's algorithm. This is arguably a good thing for those blockchains (though many complaints still exist about it), as it provides greater security for the blockchain and decreases the likelihood of attack by increasing the resources needed to attack the blockchain. Remember, the whole point of proof of work is to make finding a block difficult so that it's not easy to attack the blockchain.

The danger in ASIC mining hardware when it is first released, however, is that the hardware will be quickly made obsolete . . . it will be superseded by new, more efficient products. You may think that, in order to stay ahead of the crowd, you should buy the very latest equipment, even pre-order equipment before it's ready.

However, that strategy comes with its own risks. Some shady manufacturers have sold mining hardware with long lead times and with implied or calculated earnings that will not match the earnings that the equipment will realistically gain once the mining hardware is delivered. As you wait for delivery, the blockchain's block difficulty and hash rate increase, perhaps dramatically during early-stage ASIC development. The longer you wait, the less competitive the ASIC will be once you get it into action.

Dishonest ASIC sales are not as bad a problem as they were in the past, at least for most mature proof-of-work blockchains, because of manufacturer diversification and the fact that, as ASICs mature, ASIC efficiency gains are harder to come by. However, for new algorithms that have not had ASIC-specific hardware developed, there may still be significant risks for early-edition hardware purchasers.

Specified power consumption

ASICs are far more powerful than your regular CPU or GPU, so they are able to hash much faster. That's the whole point, after all. However, nothing's free; ASICs can use a considerable amount of electricity. Each ASIC has a rated power consumption — that is, before purchasing it, you should be able to check the equipment specifications and find out how much power it's going to use when you start mining.

Power is measured with the International System of Units, using *watts*, and energy consumption is measured in watts per hour. Old-fashioned incandescent light bulbs typically consume about 20 to 100 watts — when you buy incandescent light bulbs, you're probably usually buying 60, 75, or 100-watt light bulbs — while today's LED light bulbs may output the same amount of light while using between 4 and 15 watts. Say that you have a 15-watt light bulb and run it for an hour; you've just used 15Wh — 15 watt-hours. What does that cost you? That depends on where you are. For example, in Denver, a watt-hour is about 0.01 cent, so running a 15W light bulb for an hour — consuming 15Wh — costs around 0.15 cent; run it for 100 hours, and it costs you about 15 cents.

A typical desktop computer with a CPU and GPU on board may consume anywhere from 400 to 1,200 watts, perhaps a little more. (The most recent Mac Pro uses around 900 watts.) Laptops generally use much less power; co-author Peter Kent's MacBook Pro has an 85W power supply, for example.

However, state-of-the-art ASICs now being deployed onto the Bitcoin network consume between 1,000 and 6,000 watts (1.0 to 6.0kW — that is, kilowatts; a kW is 1,000 watts). For a comparison of some of the Bitcoin SHA-256 ASICs being used on the network today, see Figure 9-2.

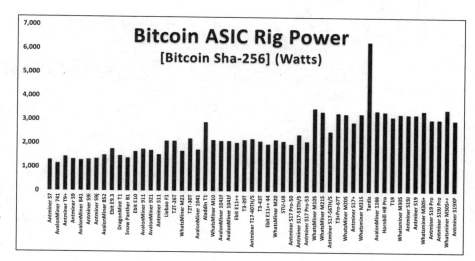

FIGURE 9-2:
Power
consumption for
a range of
SHA-256 ASICs for
Bitcoin hashing.

**TECHNICAL
STUFF**

How do you figure out your own power cost? Check your electricity bill, find your most recent paper bill, or log on to your power-company website account. You may have to look at the actual bill or you may find a summary. Figure 9-3 shows an example of the electricity consumption area on a bill.

Notice that the electricity is billed for kilowatt-hours, not watt-hours. Figure 9-3 shows that this utility company has billed a base rate of $0.05461 per kWh (with two different time periods — Non-Summer and Summer Tier 1, although in this case, the rate is the same for both periods). Then the utility has charged additional rates for various special fees: the *Trans Cost Adj*, the *Elec Commodity Adj*, and so on . . . whatever these things are (and we really don't care). We just add up the different rates — $0.05461, $0.00203, $0.03081, $0.00159, $0.00401, and $0.00301 — to come up with the kWh charge: $0.09606. That is, this utility charges 9.606 cents per kWh of power consumed.

Power consumption inputs and hash-rate outputs for mining hardware are important factors when considering which mining equipment is right for you. However, both of these metrics are more useful when combined. After all, what we care about is how many hashes we can get for a buck, as it were. What good is an ASIC that consumes almost no energy if it outputs almost no hashes? Or an ASIC that outputs a huge amount of hashes, but at twice the cost per hash of other equipment? What counts is how much we're going to have to pay for a particular hash output. We're concerned with *efficiency*. (Right now, we're talking about the cost in electricity, of course, not the cost of the actual equipment.)

Efficiency is typically defined as useful work performed divided by energy expended to do that work. However, when it comes to ASIC mining hardware, manufacturers often list this metric in reverse. ASIC mining equipment is often listed with the energy expended (in *joules*) divided by the work performed (tera hashes/second).

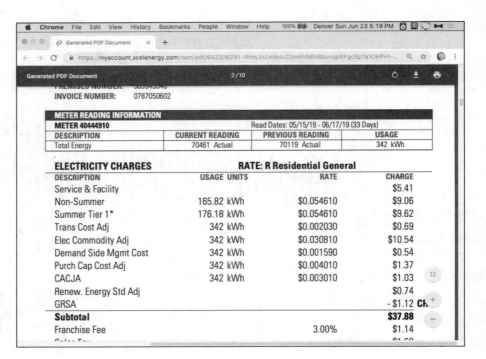

PREMISES NUMBER: 565545540

INVOICE NUMBER: 0787050602

METER READING INFORMATION

METER 40444910   Read Dates: 05/15/19 - 06/17/19 (33 Days)

DESCRIPTION	CURRENT READING	PREVIOUS READING	USAGE
Total Energy	70461 Actual	70119 Actual	342 kWh

ELECTRICITY CHARGES   **RATE: R Residential General**

DESCRIPTION	USAGE UNITS	RATE	CHARGE
Service & Facility			$5.41
Non-Summer	165.82 kWh	$0.054610	$9.06
Summer Tier 1*	176.18 kWh	$0.054610	$9.62
Trans Cost Adj	342 kWh	$0.002030	$0.69
Elec Commodity Adj	342 kWh	$0.030810	$10.54
Demand Side Mgmt Cost	342 kWh	$0.001590	$0.54
Purch Cap Cost Adj	342 kWh	$0.004010	$1.37
CACJA	342 kWh	$0.003010	$1.03
Renew. Energy Std Adj			$0.74
GRSA			- $1.12
Subtotal			**$37.88**
Franchise Fee		3.00%	$1.14

FIGURE 9-3:
You can find your electricity cost from your utility bill.

TECHNICAL STUFF

A *joule* is a unit of energy equivalent to a watt per second or 1/3,600th of a watt-hour. Wikipedia defines it as "The work required to produce one watt of power for one second, or one watt-second (W·s)." Thus, a watt-hour (Wh) is the equivalent of 3,600 joules (1 joule per second, multiplied by 60 seconds in a minute, multiplied by 60 minutes in an hour is 3,600; 1kWh would be 3.6 megajoules — 3,600,000 joules).

So ASIC manufacturers often show an "energy expended per output" value that allows users to easily compare mining hardware efficiency. ASIC specs are often provided in terms of *joules/hash*. For example, look at this excerpt from a review of mining equipment:

> "Thanks to the DragonMint 16T's new DM8575 generation of ASIC chips, the 16T has become the most electrically-efficient miner on the market. **Consuming merely 0.075J/GH, or 1,480W** from the wall, the 16T is 30% more electrically-efficient than the Antminer S9. . .. When compared to its closest competitor, the Antminer S9, the DragonMint 16T is the clear winner. It hashes at 16 TH/s, as opposed to the S9's 14 TH/s. Moreover, the 16T consumes **0.075J/GH, whereas the S9 consumes 0.098J/GH.**"

The review states that this particular miner (the DragonMint 16T) uses 1,480W, so over an hour, it would consume 1.48kWh of electricity. (In Chapter 11, you can see how that affects the cost of running the equipment.) But we're also told that it consumes 0.075J/GH. (That is, .075 joules per giga hash, or .075 joules of energy is consumed every time the device runs a million hashes.) As you can see, this data can be used to directly compare mining equipment; the S9 consumes 0.098J/GH. That is, the S9 consumes around 31 percent more energy for the same number of hashes.

For a ranking of the most recent SHA-256 hardware released to mine on the Bitcoin network, see Figure 9-4. On the left, you see the less efficient equipment. The Antminer S7 requires around 275 joules to output a tera hash per second, while at the other end of the charge, we see equipment that is outputting a tera hash per second while consuming around 20 joules.

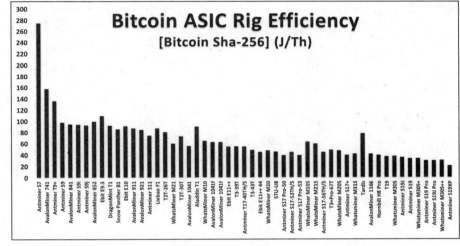

FIGURE 9-4: SHA-256 Bitcoin network ASIC mining hardware, ranked by efficiency in terms of joules per tera hash.

We've provided similar charts for a few other common mining algorithms. Figure 9-5 shows X11 ASIC miners designed to operate on the DASH network, Figure 9-6 displays Scrypt ASIC miners built to hash toward the Litecoin network, Figure 9-7 ranks Equihash ASIC miners that can mine on the Zcash network, and finally Figure 9-8 plots Ethash ASIC miners by efficiency. Miners on the left of these charts with a lower energy (joules) consumption per output (hash) would be more profitable to operate as electricity cost per work would be less. For more on the economics of mining, see Part 4 of this book.

REMEMBER

Mining equipment efficiency is a very important factor in deciding what hardware is right for you. The lower the energy usage per work output, the less power will be spent, the lower power bills will be, and the more cost effective the mining hardware will be.

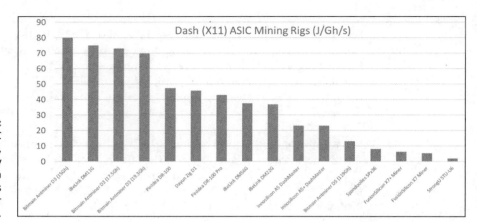

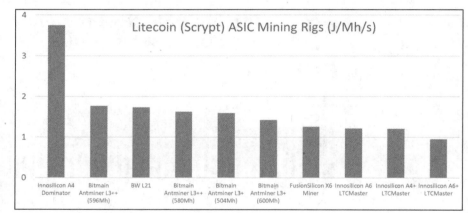

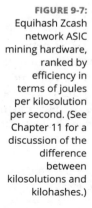

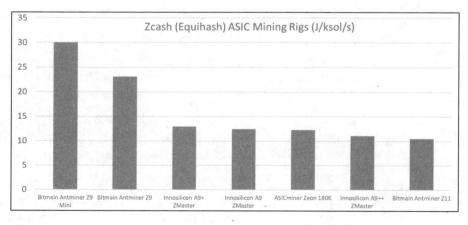

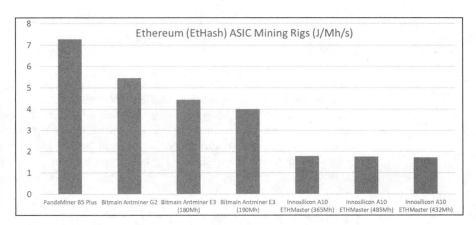

FIGURE 9-8:
Ethash Ethereum
network ASIC
mining hardware,
ranked by
efficiency in
terms of joules
per mega hash
per second.

Cost effectiveness is critical to long-term survival in the mining industry, whether you're deploying a commercial mining facility or becoming a home hobbyist miner. Over time, most of the costs will be from operational expenditures, of which the biggest part is the cost of electricity. For more on the economics of mining, refer to Chapter 11.

Equipment cost and other considerations

The cost and affordability of mining hardware fluctuates wildly, similar to the market capitalization of cryptocurrency assets. During some periods, the cost of mining equipment moves surprisingly in tandem with the market. If the price is going up, new and used mining equipment sells at a premium. If the price is down, the hardware sells at a steep discount as large mining firms and manufacturers liquidate equipment stockpiles.

In any market condition, however, the newest, most efficient equipment is always expensive. These high-efficiency mining rigs are in high demand, regardless of the price of the cryptocurrency they mine. At the time of this writing, the state-of-the-art SHA-256 ASIC equipment can range from a few hundred to a few thousand dollars.

TIP

For the best prices on new hardware, the most dependable route is to purchase straight from the manufacturer and avoid the middleman who sells hardware above the manufacturers' listed prices.

On the other hand, some manufacturers simply don't sell small retail quantities. Other manufacturers don't allow purchasers to use local fiat currencies to acquire their products, and sell their hardware only for Bitcoin or the cryptocurrency the hardware specializes in mining. Another thing to really carefully check is the lead time for delivery after purchase. If you're buying the latest and greatest piece of hardware at a premium, your advantage may be minimized if actual delivery is delayed for a long time.

You may also be able to buy used hardware. Check marketplaces, such as eBay, Amazon, Newegg, Alibaba, or Craigslist. However, beware of sellers on most second-hand markets, and remember that some markets are more reliable than others. (For example, on Amazon, you can return the equipment if it turns out to be faulty or oversold in some way.) Always do your research on the equipment specifications, such as hash rate, power consumption, and efficiency, before you buy.

Length of time your hardware will be viable

Another thing to consider is how long the ASIC equipment you're buying is going to be able to keep up and stay profitable. That is, as block difficulty and hash rate requirements increase, how long will it be until your hardware is hopelessly left behind?

A number of factors determine the viability of a cryptocurrency ASIC miner, including the network hash rate and thus block difficulty, market exchange rate for the cryptocurrency you're mining, mining equipment efficiency, and your time preference.

For the most part, network hash rate on any cryptocurrency lags the exchange price. Remember, network hash rate increases as more miners enter the network or existing miners buy more mining equipment, and network hash rate goes down as miners leave. So, if the cryptocurrency price soars for a month, the hash rate for the forthcoming months will most likely go up as more miners jump in, and vice versa; if the exchange rate falls, then in the following months, hash rate may also fall as miners shut down their unprofitable equipment.

During a period in which the cryptocurrency prices rise, you may earn less of the cryptocurrency — as miners bring more equipment online, your percentage of the network hash rate drops, leading to less frequently mined rewards — but you may still be earning more money in terms of dollars (or whatever fiat currency you work with). You mine fewer coins, but those coins are worth more.

The inverse is also true. During times of falling value of the cryptocurrency you're mining, and subsequent falling hash rate, your mining equipment will produce more reward when measured in the mined asset, but those larger quantities of cryptocurrency may be worth less overall when measured in your local fiat currency.

This is where your time preference factor comes in, in combination with your assessment of the future value of the cryptocurrency you are mining. *Time preference* is the value you place on receiving something now, as opposed to the value you would place on receiving it in the future. An individual with high time preference is more concerned with their present well-being and satisfaction when compared to a low time preference individual who would rather put that reward off until a later date when their satisfaction may be increased.

REMEMBER

If you believe in the cryptocurrency you're mining, and you believe that the price will go up in the long term, you may want to continue mining. Even during market downturns, as network hash rate comes down, competition is reduced. Your percentage of the network hash rate goes up, and so it costs you less to mine the same amount of cryptocurrency.

Here's an example. In December 2018, Bitcoin dropped below $3,300 (USD) per coin. For many miners, perhaps most, mining became unprofitable, but mining didn't stop. Why? Because the people who continued mining believed that the price would come back. They were right. A few months later, a coin was worth almost four times that value. So if you're willing to defer present gain for future gain, and if you're sure that there *will be* a future gain, then you'll want to continue mining through the bad times (which, if you're right, will eventually look like the good times!).

Cryptocurrency miners with a low time preference, and faith in the cryptocurrency, may continue to use slightly "unviable" mining equipment during what appear to be unprofitable mining conditions, because they anticipate profits in the future.

As network hash rate increases, and as competing mining equipment gets more efficient — as the newer equipment is able to output more hashes for each kWh of power consumption — your equipment will become less profitable. It will mine fewer coins than before, and each coin will cost more. At some point, it will make economic sense to replace the mining equipment with more efficient equipment.

A typical state-of-the-art Bitcoin or cryptocurrency mining rig today may have a viable life of four or more years. However, going forward, the viable life of an ASIC may increase as hardware efficiency gains of ASICs become slower and more difficult to come by. Refer to Figure 9-4 to see how efficiency gains have trended for mining equipment released over the past four years.

For example, the Bitmain Antminer S7 was released in late 2015, as the most efficient and capable miner on the market at the time. In some situations, if miners have a low time preference and access to abundant or cheap electricity, the S7 is still a profitable miner and is still being operated today roughly four and a half years later. The S7, however, is close to its end of life and is the least efficient Bitcoin ASIC miner listed in Figure 9-4. Compare the S7 (at 275 J/Th/s), with the Antminer S17 Pro-15, which uses around 40 J/Th/s. That is, the former uses around seven times the electricity to do the same work.

REMEMBER

Useful life spans of computer hardware are never guaranteed, especially in the fast-moving cryptocurrency mining industry, but with proper research, due diligence, and knowledge, these risks can be mitigated. Always perform product research prior to purchase and reference profitability projection tools to ensure life cycle profitability. See Chapter 11 for more information on calculating mining profitability.

Mining Equipment Manufacturers

Today, many manufacturers produce computer equipment (both ASIC and GPU) that is tailored to hash toward and mine various cryptocurrencies.

ASIC rig producers

Here's a list of some top ASIC producers who make the most capable equipment and the most efficient hardware, designed specifically to hash and mine towards Bitcoin and other cryptocurrencies that utilize the SHA-256 hash algorithm. For a list of other cryptocurrencies that use this algorithm, see the list in Chapter 8.

>> **Bitfury** (https://bitfury.com/crypto-infrastructure) is the manufacturer of the Tardis Bitcoin SHA-256 mining hardware.

>> **Bitmain** (https://shop.bitmain.com) produces the Antminer series of mining hardware and sells ASIC equipment that specializes in SHA-256, Equihash, and other popular mining algorithms.

>> **Canaan** (https://canaan.io) created and manufactures the Avalon series of SHA-256 Bitcoin miners.

>> **Ebang** (http://miner.ebang.com.cn) produces the EBIT line of ASIC miners that specialize in the Bitcoin SHA-245 hashing algorithm.

>> **Innosilicon** (https://innosilicon.com/html/miner) produces mining equipment that specializes in the Equihash, SHA-256, Scrypt, X11, and other popular mining algorithms.

>> **Whatsminer** (https://whatsminer.net/shop) makes the M series line of Bitcoin SHA-256 mining hardware.

Beware of new manufacturers selling ASICs with sensational specifications and industry-leading hash rate and efficiency numbers! A number of cases have occurred in the past (and we'll likely see more in the future) where newly created hardware manufacturing companies released a presale on new ASIC hardware with amazing specs. Often, these scams only accepted Bitcoin or other cryptocurrencies as payment for the presale. Of course, the hardware was never created or delivered, and the "manufacturer" was never seen or heard from again. (This is sometimes known as an *exit scam.*)

Mining container producers

Check out the following prebuilt mining hardware containers that provide "mobile mining units" for Bitcoin or cryptocurrency mining:

- » **Bitcoin Mining:** https://blog.upstreamdata.ca
- » **Bitcoin Mining Container:** www.bitcoinminingcontainer.com/bitcoin-mining-container
- » **Digital Shovel:** https://digitalshovel.com

GPU rig producers

Check out the following list of prebuilt GPU mining hardware providers.

- » The **Coinmine** (https://coinmine.com) is a GPU mining rig with an easy-to-use interface that has the ability to mine a variety of cryptocurrencies, such as Ethereum, Grin, Monero, and Zcash.
- » The **MineShop** (https://mineshop.eu) has many products for sale, including ASIC miners, large-scale cryptocurrency mining operations built into 20-foot shipping containers, and Ethereum GPU rigs.
- » **MiningSky** (https://miningsky.com/gpu) provides the V series of GPU miners with potentially eight onboard GPUs to amplify mining capability.
- » **Mining Store** (https://miningstore.com.au) provides prebuilt GPU mining rigs that can mine a variety of cryptocurrencies with 6, 8, or 12 onboard GPUs to maximize mining returns.
- » **MiningStore** (https://miningstore.com) provides a variety of different services, including mining hosting, mining containers, as well as prebuilt GPU and ASIC mining rigs.
- » The **PandaMiner B Pro series** (www.pandaminer.com/product) are prebuilt GPU mining rigs that can mine Ethereum, Grin, Monero, and Zcash.

Finding a Wallet to Store and Protect Your Private Keys

Besides the mining equipment itself, you're also going to need an address in the blockchain to which your mining profits will be sent, and a wallet to store your keys. Wallet security is everything. Lose your private keys, or have them stolen, and your cryptocurrency is gone for good, so the following is nothing more than a reminder and perhaps a way to spark ideas, but make sure you understand wallet security in depth! Consider, for example, viewing co-author Peter Kent's video course on cryptocurrency, *Crypto Clear: Blockchain and Cryptocurrency Made Simple*, which you can find at CryptoOfCourse.com.

Where to Mine? Selecting a Viable Location

Once adequate hardware is attained (both mining and key storage equipment), finding and securing a place to run your mining equipment becomes a priority. A few requirements for any cryptocurrency mining location include space, communication connectivity, proper ventilation or air-conditioning, and adequate power supply.

Vet your home for cryptocurrency mining

The easiest and most affordable place to start slowly testing the waters in cryptocurrency mining is at home. You already have the resources that would be required to start a cryptocurrency mine: Internet access, electrical power, and space.

Some homes are more suitable for mining than others. An apartment, for example, may not be the best location due to limited space and the noise of the mining equipment. A single-family house would be a better location when compared to a multifamily dwelling like an apartment; you wouldn't want to keep yourself or your friendly neighbors up at night while your mining equipment hums along.

Mining equipment, ASICs specifically, is typically cooled by an intake and an exhaust fan that run anywhere from 3,600 to 6,200 rotations per minute. (6,200 RPM fans produce 60 to 100 decibels or more!) These high-RPM cooling fans create quite a bit of noise and exhaust, and an even greater amount of heat. Some places in a home are better than others. For example, you wouldn't want a 6,200 RPM fan buzzing on your bedside table or in your kitchen.

TIP

The best places to run mining equipment in a residence, if that is the place you select, would be in a garage, an easily vented garden shed, or a cool basement with plenty of airflow for ventilation.

Regardless of whether your residence, an industrial facility, or some other suitable location is the place you select to deploy cryptocurrency mining hardware, there are a few things to consider in the space you choose. Ease of ventilation, cooling in hot months, Internet connectivity, and adequate power supply are all essential. Ventilation becomes easier and more affordable if the climate you're mining in is cool, cold, or mild for large portions of the year.

Communication requirements

Cryptocurrency miners have to connect to a global network of blockchain nodes, so communication connectivity is key. Most importantly, you need a reliable connection to the Internet. This connection can come in many forms, but for mining, you need to be able to send as well as receive information, so both upload and download links are important. A high-bandwidth connection is not absolutely required, but low latency in connectivity is often best as every millisecond (thousandth of a second) in the mining sphere counts.

Bandwidth is the amount of throughput: how much data can be transferred, often measured in megabits per second (Mbps). *Latency* is the time delay that the data takes to make it from A to B, often measured in milliseconds (ms) or thousandths of a second.

Traditional Internet access

The simplest method of connection for cryptocurrency mining is just traditional Internet access. Most broadband speeds today are more than adequate to satisfy the requirements for a cryptocurrency miner. In fact, a fully synced and decently connected Bitcoin node rarely goes above 10 to 50 kbps (kilobits per second) and could, in theory, be run on a 56 kbps dial-up modem from years past. (No, we're not advising this!)

Ideally your mining equipment would connect to your Internet service provider's modem with an Ethernet cable; you may need an additional router or network switch to connect multiple miners. You could, however, use a Wi-Fi connection if the mining hardware is not easily hardwired to your ISP's modem.

Satellite access

Remote areas that are otherwise suitable for mining equipment may not have hardwired Internet infrastructure, but alternatives are available. A few companies provide satellite-based Internet connections to areas otherwise unserved with Internet access. Search for *satellite internet* to find these services.

Power source thoughts

The place where you set up your mining equipment must have an adequate power supply for that equipment. If the mining you're planning to do is on a normal desktop computer, a typical 120-volt outlet can feed enough power to your computer's power supply. In the case of dedicated cryptocurrency mining hardware, the equipment consumes thousands of watts of electrical power to produce many trillions of hashes per second.

In addition to the 120-volt circuit that you plug most of your devices into — your TV, hair dryer, lamps, and so on — your home also has 240-volt circuits; that's what your air conditioning and clothes dryer connect to. A 240-volt circuit can feed the higher-voltage ASIC mining equipment you may use.

Still, you need a few pieces of electrical gear to ensure safe and reliable power delivery to any piece of cryptocurrency mining hardware. You need power delivery units (PDUs), properly rated power supply units (PSUs), and upline electrical wiring and breaker panel infrastructure.

Power delivery units

Power delivery units route power from electrical outlets to power supply units. These are typically 240-volt devices in the United States. They deliver power and protect against circuit overload. These PDUs may also be able to connect and feed multiple power supply units, depending on their rating. They typically have an internal 240-volt line-to-line electrical bus that feeds a few breakers providing electrical surge protection to the outlets they are feeding. You can see an example in Figure 9-9 shows a PDU from CyberPower.

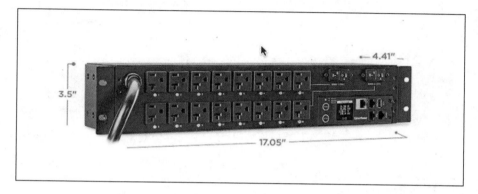

FIGURE 9-9: A PDU manufactured by CyberPower.

For example, an adequately rated electrical supply line, per the specifications in the National Electrical Code (NEC), feeding a PDU rated at 240 volts and 30 amps, may then feed three separate 240-volt 10-amp breakers in the PDU.

The equation to calculate electrical power (P, measured in watts) from voltage and amperage is fairly simple. We use P=V*I, where P is power (the rate of energy flow, in watts), V is voltage, and I represents current, measured in amps.

Using this equation, a 240-volt 10-amp PDU outlet would be able to provide about 2,400 watts (2,400W = 240V * 10 amps), and thus each PDU could power most of the ASICs specified in Figure 9-2 (shown earlier in this chapter), but not all of them. As shown in that figure, a few on the left side are going to require more power than that!

This configuration provides individual electrical overload protection to the three outlets on the PDU and helps isolate any equipment or electrical faults downstream of any of the outlets while maintaining power to the other two outlets.

PDUs are not always necessary, depending on the size and configuration of the mining equipment, but their use can provide additional electrical fault protection and safety to multiple pieces of mining equipment. PDUs are reasonably priced for the electrical connectivity, convenience, and peace of mind they provide, and can be purchased from many web-based suppliers.

Power supplies

Power supplies for the cryptocurrency mining space have come in all shapes and sizes, from a typical power supply unit (PSU) that would be found in a desktop computer all the way to dedicated pieces of hardware specially designed for cryptocurrency mining applications. See an example in Figure 9-10 for an example from Bitmain.

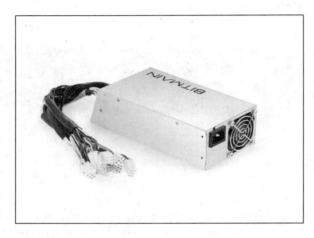

PSUs are often bundled with ASIC mining hardware in a package purchased directly from the manufacturer with the specific cryptocurrency mining hardware they can support. PSUs can also be found on many online marketplaces. Power supply units can come in 120-volt or 240-volt varieties, and some are able to be dual voltage (connecting to either voltage), depending on the outlet type you have available. If buying a PSU separately, you need to ensure that the PSU's rated wattage is greater than the maximum power consumption of the mining hardware it's going to power.

WARNING

The rated wattage of the power supply should exceed the rated maximum power consumption of the cryptocurrency mining hardware being used. Otherwise, the power supply won't be able to service the electrical load. This underrating could lead to electrical faults, frequent power supply failures, or mining rig failures. All of these outcomes are dangerous and costly, so you really need to use a power supply that's adequately rated for the hardware (the ASIC or GPU mining rigs) you're trying to power. Refer to the manufacturer's mining equipment manual for more specific information.

WARNING

Be really careful with your mining installations! An improperly configured and installed mining operation represents a serious fire risk. Don't think this can't happen to you; it's happened to others. If you're at all unsure of what you're doing, get a professional electrician to help you set up your gear!

Existing electrical infrastructure versus new installations

If you plan to use existing electrical infrastructure to serve your mine, it is important that the outlet, the wire from the panel, and the breaker panel from which you plan to feed your cryptocurrency mining equipment be properly rated for the electrical load. It is also important that the service wire from your utility and the transformer feeding it also be rated for the increase in load from your cryptocurrency mining gear. Consult your local electric utility as well as a local electrician to find out whether your proposed loading requires additional electrical upgrades.

WARNING

The conductor or electrical line and the breaker protecting the circuit in question also need to be adequately rated for the load you plan on feeding. The breaker in the panel feeding the wires may give you an idea of the maximum current, or amperage, that the circuit can carry. However, if you have any question as to the wire, breaker, or outlet rating, consult a local qualified and licensed electrician to ensure electrical safety and reliability, and to avoid electrical faults for your proposed mining hardware.

For larger deployments of dedicated cryptocurrency mining gear, especially with the power consumption involved with state-of-the-art gear, you're almost certainly going to need new circuitry and electrical installations. The typical home electrical service panel is rated around 100 to 200 amps, so the amount of mining hardware that can be installed in a typical residence is limited. Unless you're a qualified electrician, consult the experts and get in touch with a local licensed electrical expert to perform your electrical upgrades or new installations for you. For midsize or larger deployments, you may need to use a commercial data center, a mining hosting facility, or your own entirely new mining facility in a commercial space.

WARNING

Although this won't be a problem for most people, check with your power utility to see whether you're even *allowed* to run mining gear! In some localities, mining is banned in private homes, particularly in rural areas that have relatively little power demand and thus run the risk of being overwhelmed if a few miners set up shop. For example, a few years ago, Chelan County in Washington State, which is mostly national forest and has a population of little more than 70,000 people, required mining permits and at one point implemented a moratorium on cryptocurrency mining, as they were concerned that the mining operations in the county were a fire risk and also represented a burden on the electricity supply. On the other hand, Hydro-Québec welcomes cryptocurrency miners, but still requires that mining operations be registered with the utility.

Data centers and other dedicated commercial locations

Aspiring cryptocurrency miners who want to scale up to a significant mining deployment will find that commercial locations, such as warehouses or dedicated data centers, may be the best route. Large mining operations simply won't fit into your apartment or home.

You have essentially three options:

» **Build your own data center.** Find some warehouse space or a shipping container, for example, and build from scratch.

» **Work with a colocation center.** Colocation centers are all over the world, and are designed primarily to manage web servers. They come with reliable power, flood, and fire protection, redundant Internet connections, and so on. They charge for the space you take up in their racks and the bandwidth you use.

» **Work with a mining-service hosting company.** These services charge reasonable fees to host equipment that you own, including space and electrical costs in their tailor-made and ready-to-deploy commercial spaces. They are, in essence, colocation services, but designed specifically for cryptocurrency mining. Here are a few popular cryptocurrency mining equipment hosting services.

- **Blockstream:** https://blockstream.com/mining
- **Citadel 256:** www.citadel256.com
- **Compass Mining:** https://compassmining.io
- **Compute North:** www.computenorth.com
- **Core Scientific:** https://corescientific.com
- **Frontier Mining:** https://www.bitcoinmined.net
- **LightSpeed Hosting:** www.lightspeedhosting.com
- **Mining Colocation:** https://miningcolocation.com
- **MiningSky:** https://miningsky.com/miner-hosting

- **MiningStore:** https://miningstore.com/mining-services
- **TeslaWatt:** https://teslawatt.com
- **Upstream Data:** https://blog.upstreamdata.ca

Upsides

Whichever way you choose — build it yourself, use a colocation service, or work with a mining-service company — these types of bulk commercial deployments allow you to install vast amounts of cryptocurrency mining equipment. The latter two have the advantage of making it easy to get set up quickly. They may already be equipped with bulk access to the power grid and adequate internal electrical infrastructure to service your mining hardware needs. Colocation centers and mining-service companies also have powerful air-conditioning equipment to cool your valuable cryptocurrency mining equipment. (Some warehouse situations may, too.) They have lightning-fast Internet connectivity as well, allowing for lower-latency mining and giving you a slight edge. In other words, some of these locations can provide the entire package, everything required to hit the ground mining in a timely fashion; and in the cryptocurrency space, *time is coin*. Another thing to consider: The colocation and mining-service businesses are sharing the costs among all customers. If you try to build from scratch, the entire cost burden falls on you, and it's going to be expensive.

Downsides

The downsides for these types of installations can, in some situations, be significant. They may include cost, length of lease, and lack of direct control or access to your equipment. A warehouse may be cheaper . . . or not.

TIP

Often, building a very large mining operation in a dedicated location is cheaper. For small operations, however, working with a colocation center or service will likely be cheaper.

In hosted facilities, you may not have direct physical control of your equipment. In some cases, it may be at the whim of the service provider. If it is a commercial space or data center of your own deployment, extra costs (above what it would cost to run a cryptocurrency mining rig at your residence) may include Internet connectivity, space rental costs, and insurance fees. These may not seem like much, but if not adequately prepared for, they can add up to significant impediments to profitability in times when hash rate competition increases or when the market exchange rate falls.

» **Assembling your mining hardware**

» **Understanding mining software options**

» **Building a GPU mining rig**

» **Configuring your mining hardware**

Chapter **10**

Setting Up Your Mining Hardware

After selecting a cryptocurrency you intend to mine, acquiring all the needed supplies and hardware, and choosing a suitable location to run your mining equipment, the next step is to bring it all together and set up your mining rig. Whether you plan to use application specific integrated circuit (ASIC) mining hardware, or a custom-built graphical processing unit (GPU) mining rig, we look at how to assemble the mining equipment, hook up all the needed cables, and install and run the correct software.

ASIC Mining Rigs

ASIC mining equipment is manufactured in a prebuilt package that takes care of much of the technical software and physical setup requirements that make GPU cryptocurrency mining somewhat more difficult. ASICs are designed to be virtually plug and play. After all, ASIC mining equipment is specially intended and built for cryptocurrency mining, so it is designed to be easy to use in that very application. Your ASIC should come with an installation manual, of course, with detailed instructions. This chapter is more of an overview to give you a feel for what will be required.

CHAPTER 10 **Setting Up Your Mining Hardware** 175

Racks

Computer colocation facilities are full of racks that are a little over 19 inches wide and 40 to 50 inches high. A rack contains different customers' installed mining rigs, with one setup above the other. Each rack is subdivided into vertical units; 1U means a vertical space 1.75 inches high. Thus, computer equipment designed to fit into racks may be 1U or 2U or 3U, and so on. A piece of equipment that is 2U will fit into a 3.5-inch-tall space in the rack, for example.

Well, *some* ASICs are designed to be *rack mountable.* This typically means that the ASIC slots right into a standard 19-inch computer rack and may take up several vertical units. However, this is actually relatively rare. In general, ASICs are not designed to be rack mountable. You can see an example of the typical form factor of an ASIC in Figure 10-1.

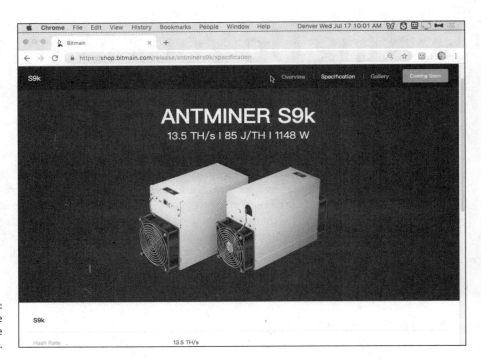

FIGURE 10-1:
A typical ASIC size and shape; the Antminer S9k.

So how do you rack-mount an ASIC that isn't rack-mountable? You use a case. A few companies sell rack-mount shelves designed to hold particular ASICs and mount them in server racks. For example, in Figure 10-2, you can see an example of a Gray Matter Industries rack designed specifically for the Antminer Bitmain S9 and L3 ASICs (www.miningrigs.net). This rack holds three Bitmain ASICs, and the PSU (power supply unit), too. The case is 7U tall.

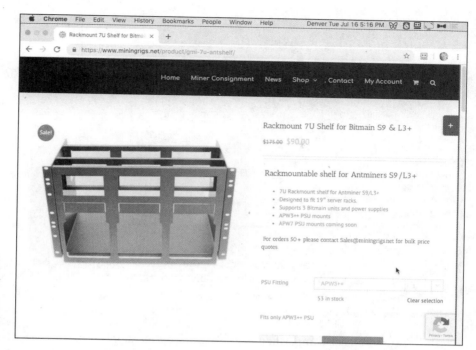

FIGURE 10-2:
A Gray Matter
Industries shelf
designed to hold,
and rack mount,
three Bitmain
ASICs and a PSU.

These rack-mount shelves are not terribly expensive (usually less than $200), and if you are running a large mining operation, with dozens of ASICs, you'll probably want to use some kind of mounting equipment. However, there's no need to go overboard if you have a small mining operation! There's nothing wrong with sitting a couple of ASICs on a table, or perhaps on utility shelving from your local hardware store or big box outlet. Computer server racks in data centers are typically electrically grounded, and if you are using a metal rack or shelving, it should also be grounded so you and your equipment are safe.

Power supply

Most ASIC mining rigs use external power supply units (PSUs); you can see an example in Figure 10-3. In general, when you buy an ASIC, you'll probably get an appropriate PSU bundled with it — not always, though, so if not, you'll need to carefully select the right PSU and buy it separately.

Power supplies convert the alternating current (AC) supplied from the electrical utility to direct current (DC) electricity, used by computer equipment. So, you'll connect your ASICs directly to the appropriate PSUs.

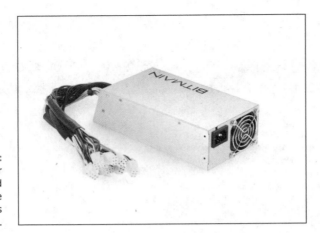

FIGURE 10-3:
A Bitmain power
supply, designed
for use with the
company's
Antminer ASICs.

WARNING

It is critical that you ensure that none of your devices are plugged into a wall socket before you begin connecting components. Connect the power supply to the ASIC first and then the power supply to the PDU prior to connecting the PDU to the wall outlet.

It is also important to only use one power supply per mining rig. Trying to connect a single ASIC miner to multiple power supplies can be dangerous and lead to equipment failure or electrical faults. Also, be aware that while some power supplies are equipped with a power switch, others are not and will power on as soon as you connect them to the outlet. (See Chapter 9 for more information on the electrical requirements and equipment.)

TECHNICAL
STUFF

Power supplies are equipped with PCIe (Peripheral Component Interconnect Express) power cables that allow for easy and quick connection. If you've worked on personal computer hardware, you'll be familiar with these. There are many variations of PCIe cables, but for mining power supplies, the 6-pin version is typically used.

Your ASIC will have multiple PCIe connectors. Each hash board has several PCIe plugs — likely at least 2, maybe 3 or 4 — and each mining rig has about three hash boards (though some may have more) for a rough total of 6 to 12 PCIe ports for hash boards per ASIC. Each ASIC mining rig also has a control board that must be powered, so you'll also see a PCIe connection for that board. In Figure 10-4, you can see a page from the installation manual for the Antminer Z9 ASIC, in which power connections are discussed.

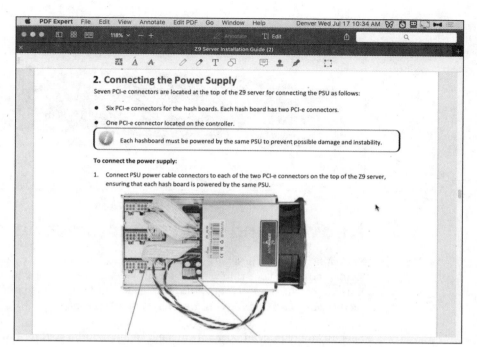

2. Connecting the Power Supply

Seven PCI-e connectors are located at the top of the Z9 server for connecting the PSU as follows:

- Six PCI-e connectors for the hash boards. Each hash board has two PCI-e connectors.

- One PCI-e connector located on the controller.

> Each hashboard must be powered by the same PSU to prevent possible damage and instability.

To connect the power supply:

1. Connect PSU power cable connectors to each of the two PCI-e connectors on the top of the Z9 server, ensuring that each hash board is powered by the same PSU.

FIGURE 10-4: The Antminer Z9 ASIC documentation showing the power connections.

PDUs

Power delivery units, or PDUs, are not necessary for running cryptocurrency mining equipment, especially in small installations. However, they are recommended, as PDUs make the connection of multiple mining PSUs easier and safer.

To install your PDUs, they must be connected to the mining PSUs, via cables that are typically provided with the purchase of the PSU. Once that is complete, you can connect the PDUs to the electrical outlets. We discuss electrical infrastructure requirements in more detail in Chapter 9. For a view of a typical PDU, see Figure 10-5.

WARNING

Fire risk is real (see Chapter 9). You must make sure you're using the right equipment, configured correctly. If you're not sure, you *must* get the assistance of a professional electrician. Keep a fire extinguisher accessible, but not too close, to your mining rig.

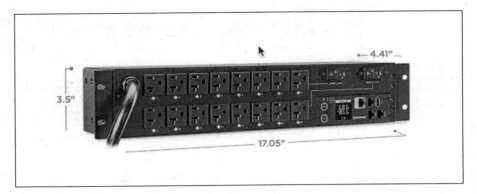

FIGURE 10-5:
A typical PDU.

Network and Ethernet connection

Your ASIC mining hardware needs Internet access, of course. You'll need some kind of box that your Internet service provider gives you (or you buy so you don't have to pay the monthly rent) that connects your home (or whatever other kind of facility you are using for your mining) to the Internet.

Specifically, you need both an Internet modem and a router, and these days you typically get a single box that has both functions built into it. Anyway, that's up to you and your ISP.

Your modem/router, whether you own it yourself or it is provided by your Internet service provider, has multiple Ethernet ports. Ethernet is a connection standard used in most local area network (LAN) applications. An Ethernet port looks a little like a phoneline port, but is slightly larger and can be found on most desktop and many laptop computers.

ASIC control boards are equipped with Ethernet ports as well and must be connected to your Internet modem to access the Internet. Connections to your miner and the Internet modem can be made either via direct Ethernet connection or through a network switch.

Once your power supply and Ethernet connections are hooked up to your miner, the next step is to power the equipment on. Make sure everything is properly connected — ASIC PCIe cables are connected to the PSU, and the PSU is connected to the PDU. Then, and only then, should you plug the PDU into the wall socket and turn everything on.

A computer to control your rig

To access the control board and the installed GUI of specialized cryptocurrency mining ASICs, you will need to access it via any computer that is connected to the same local area network as the mining equipment. Any laptop or desktop will work. Even a cell phone can connect as long it is on the same LAN. The computer managing your ASIC doesn't need to be powerful. It's just used to set it up and get it running; the ASIC itself is doing all the work.

Open up a web browser and type the ASIC's IP address into the browser to navigate to the user interface.

Where do you find the IP address? You can use software, such as the free Angry IP Scanner (https://angryip.org), or log on to your network's router and scan. Your ASIC manufacturer may provide a tool to find the IP number. For example, some of the Bitmain Antminer ASICs work with a Windows program called IP Reporter (downloaded from the Bitmain website). You run the software and then press the IP Report button on the ASIC, and the ASIC reports its IP number to the software (see Figure 10-6). You can then take that IP number, enter it into a web browser, and connect to the ASIC. Refer to your ASIC's documentation; each ASIC is going to function a little differently.

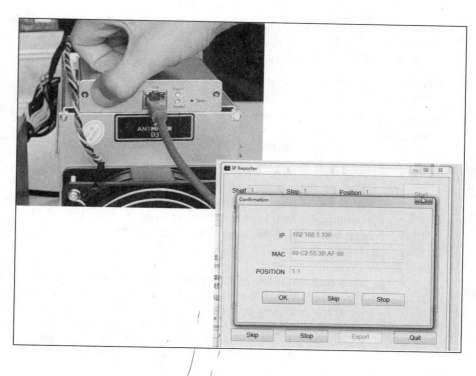

FIGURE 10-6:
Bitmain Antminer's IP Report button on the ASIC which reports the ASIC's IP number to the IP Reporter software.

You'll then use the ASIC software, accessed through your web browser, to point to the pool you're working with. Here's an example of the settings required to input into your miner for a United States–based Bitcoin ASIC running on Slush Pool:

```
URL: stratum+tcp://us-east.stratum.slushpool.com:3333
userID: userName.workerName
password: [yourpoolpassword]
```

In Figure 10-7, you can see the Bitmain Antminer ASIC user interface in the pool configuration screen.

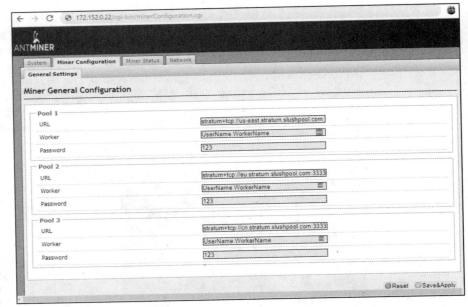

FIGURE 10-7:
The Bitmain ASIC configuration settings screen where you can set the pool, username, and server URL for pool mining with your ASIC rigs.

The specific mining pool you choose will also provide details on connection settings. Sometimes, for example, instead of requiring you to enter a user account, a mining pool will need you to input only your blockchain payout address for the cryptocurrency you are mining. Again, check your pool's documentation for details.

The server you connect to depends on which location is closest to you; your pool will provide you with several options. In general, you'll pick the one closest to you geographically, but you may want to test a few to see which is really the fastest connection; you'll use the *ping* command. For example, say you're in Australia and you're not sure if you should use NiceHash's U.S. server or Japanese server. If you have a Windows computer, you could open the Windows command line and run these two commands, one after the other:

```
ping -n 50 -l 128 speedtest.usa.nicehash.com
ping -n 50 -l 128 speedtest.jp.nicehash.com
```

On the macOS, you can use the Network Utility app's Ping screen. For each one, you'll get a response something like this:

```
50 packets transmitted, 50 packets received, 0.0% packet loss
round-trip min/avg/max/stddev = 62.156/67.665/83.567/7.214 ms
```

For Linux machines (Ubuntu, Debian, and so on), you'll just need to open the terminal and run these two commands (after 10 to 15 seconds, you'll need to press CTRL+C to obtain a report of the ping test):

```
ping speedtest.usa.nicehash.com
ping speedtest.jp.nicehash.com
```

You can then compare the average ping time to find the fastest connection (the smaller the number, measured in ms, or milliseconds, the faster the connection, of course). That's the server you'll want to use because with cryptocurrency mining, every fraction of a second is important.

If you need to enter a username rather than your blockchain address, it will be the same as your mining pool account. You can get creative with what you decide to name your worker, or mining rig, but do not duplicate worker names if you are connecting more than one piece of mining gear. (You may have multiple workers — individual GPU rigs or ASICs — working within your single mining account. See the particular pool's instructions to find out how to provide this information.)

GPU Mining Rigs

If you bought a prebuilt GPU mining rig, setting it up is as simple as setting up an ASIC. Building it yourself requires a lot more work and planning.

Getting your GPU rig online

Some mining-equipment providers sell preconfigured GPU mining rigs (see the list of prebuilt GPU mining rig manufacturers in Chapter 9 for some popular equipment providers), but these preassembled mining rigs come at a premium cost when compared to the sum of the cost of the computer parts. These preassembled rigs are easier to set up and get mining, of course, and are similar to ASIC miners — they're essentially plug and play. Figure 10-8 shows you a prebuilt 8-GPU mining rig with slots for eight individual GPUs. You will essentially treat a preassembled GPU like an ASIC, with the exception that a GPU rig is itself a computer and does not need an external computer to manage it. Thus, you will do the following:

1. Place it on a table, in a rack, or on a shelf.

2. Connect it to a PSU.

3. Connect the PSU to a PDU.

4. Connect it to an Ethernet network.

5. Install an operating system (unless it came with one, as some prebuilt rigs do).

6. Connect a mouse, keyboard, and screen (unless it came with a screen).

7. Install mining software on the computer (unless the prebuilt rig came with the software already installed).

FIGURE 10-8: A preconfigured 8-GPU mining rig.

Building your own GPU miner

Prebuilt GPU mining hardware rigs can be expensive, so some aspiring miners acquire the parts needed off websites, such as Newegg and Amazon, or retailers, such as Micro Center or Best Buy, and assemble their rigs themselves. Building your own GPU mining rig comes at quite a discount compared to the prebuilt options. However, this route is also more complex, with some assembly required as well as sometimes fairly complicated software implementations.

A typical desktop computer will have space onboard for only a single GPU or two. Some custom-built computers have space for up to three in standard tower cases, but in general, for GPU mining applications, special mining rig frames and custom-assembled hardware are needed to be able to run 6 to 12 GPUs.

You can buy all these parts separately, or perhaps buy a bundle and put it all together. For example, gpuShack (gpuShack.com) sells bundles that come with a motherboard configured for 5 to 13 GPUs (depending on the bundle), RAM, and a small amount of flash data storage with the ethOS operating system already installed. These range from $189 to $399, but you'll still require riser cards, various cables, a rack, and so on.

WARNING

There are many different possible configurations, so our explanation here is really quite basic and just outlines the essential principles. Before you jump into building your own GPU mining rig, we strongly recommend that you spend some time viewing videos from people who have already done it so that you can get a really good idea of what it entails. You can easily find many examples and detailed guides by typing **build GPU mining rig** into your favorite search engine.

Mining rig frame

Gamers often custom-build their own high-power desktop computers, buying a tower case and all the individual components — motherboard, CPU, graphics cards, power supplies, and so on — that they place into the case. The principle is the same when building a GPU mining rig, except that you can't use a typical tower case because of the size limitations for multiple GPUs. Rather, you need a special mining-rig case or frame.

Simple mining-rig frames are around the same price as regular computer cases, or sometimes cheaper (depending on the type you choose), hold more GPUs, of course, and allow for greater ventilation to remove the heat from the GPUs. The frame allows you to connect a motherboard, a power supply unit, and multiple GPUs in a compact form factor.

However, there's a wide range of what you can get when buying GPU frames, from the very basic (just a metal frame with holes to help you mount components); to more expensive versions that come with a CPU, hard drive, RAM, fans, all the necessary connectors, and even an operating system (essentially everything but the GPU cards); to the full-blown GPU racks with everything ready to go. The MiningSky Mining Rig shown in Figure 10-9, for example, is $899, but comes ready to plug GPU cards into it, making it very simple to work with.

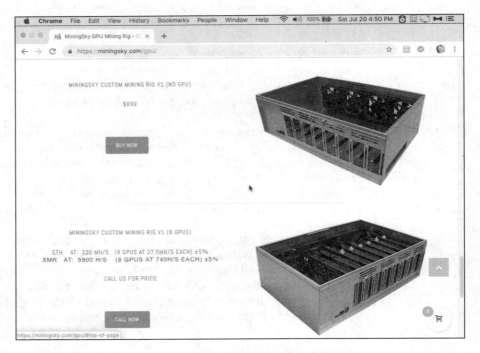

FIGURE 10-9:
The MiningSky V1 GPU Mining Rig — everything you need but the GPU cards.

Some frames are also designed to allow for stacking other frames on top, in case you want to deploy multiple mining rigs in a small space. Other frames can be mounted in a computer-server rack, allowing for scalability and easier deployment. Many online retailers sell mining rig cases or frames (Amazon, eBay, Newegg, Walmart, the mining-gear companies we mention in Chapter 9, and so on). The companies that sell preassembled GPU mining rigs generally also sell individual parts, including mining rig frames. (Some miners build their own frames to save on costs, though the extra hassle may not be worth it in many cases.)

Figure 10-10 shows a Rosewill GPU Mining Case, or Frame (see www.rosewill.com), which takes up to eight GPU cards and is also rack-mountable (6U tall). The diagram shows where the motherboard, GPUs, PSUs, and fans are installed. This case retails for around $100.

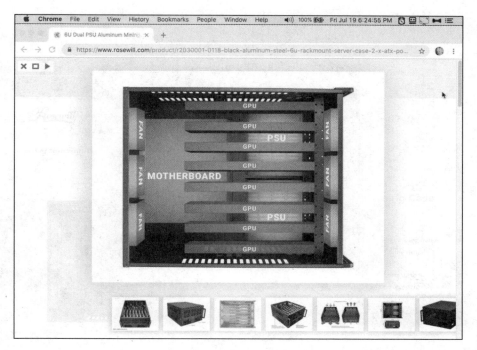

FIGURE 10-10:
The Rosewill 6U
Dual PSU
Aluminum Mining
Case.

In Figure 10-11, you can see an open-air design, which is popular with many miners. All you get is the bare frame, with space to mount everything you need, such as the motherboard, fans, GPUs, and so on.

Motherboard

The *motherboard* is the piece of computer hardware that ties everything else together. It provides connections on the board for installation of the CPU, the GPUs, and the power supply, as well as the RAM and hard drive.

It would be handy if your motherboard has plenty of slots for GPU cards. However, few motherboards have more than a couple of slots available. If you're using one of the more sophisticated, prebuilt mining-rig frames, that's okay — all the connectors are built in. You'll install your motherboard into the frame and connect it to the frame following the manufacturer's instructions. If you're using a simpler frame, then you'll need to use a riser card to connect your GPUs.

In fact, you may want to purchase a motherboard that is designed for cryptocurrency mining, which will likely have all the connectors you'll need. ASUS, the well-known computer company, manufactures a mining motherboard, the B250 Mining Expert, which you can see in Figure 10-12. This board allows you to connect up to 19 GPUs.

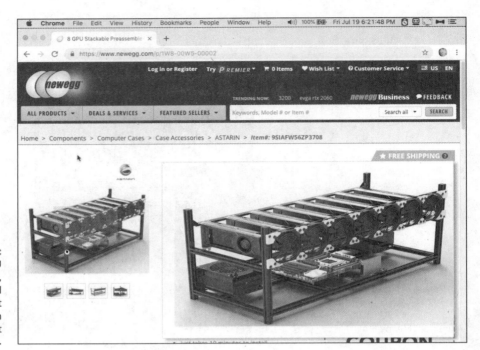

FIGURE 10-11:
An open-air GPU mining frame, shown after all the equipment has been mounted (it comes empty).

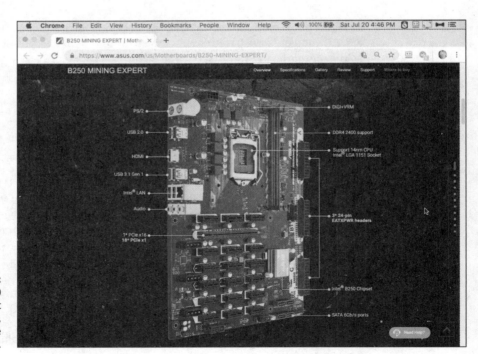

FIGURE 10-12:
The ASUS B250 Mining Expert motherboard, which can handle up to 19 GPUs.

REMEMBER

Make sure to securely mount your motherboard to your case or mining rig frame with the provided screws that come with the motherboard. Ensure the motherboard that you select is compatible with the CPU model you purchase.

Central processing unit

The *central processing unit* (CPU) is the main computer chip, the brain of your desktop or laptop computer. It serves this same function for GPU mining rigs. The individual GPU cards are the specialized processors, and they still need a CPU to manage them all.

In general, any off-the-shelf CPU is sufficient; it doesn't take much power to manage the GPU cards. However, in some circumstances, you may also use the CPU to mine, depending on the software you're using. Both the GPU cards and the CPU will be hashing. In such a case, you'll want a faster CPU. Faster CPUs will have many different cores (both physical and virtual) that will allow for more mining capability and hash rate from the CPU.

Make sure that the CPU you purchase is compatible with your motherboard. Some motherboards are usable with Intel CPUs, while others work with AMD CPUs. (The difference is in the number of pins for the CPU socket connection. The AMD chips use 938-pin sockets and the Intel chips use 1,366-pin sockets.) The manufacturer of the motherboard will list which CPU it is designed to work with. Figure 10-13 shows a fairly standard AMD CPU from Micro Center that would be able to run a GPU mining rig.

FIGURE 10-13:
An AMD CPU that would be suitable to run a GPU mining rig. This CPU comes with a fan.

Mount the CPU to the motherboard, following the manufacturer's instructions. It is best to also use a CPU fan and heat sink to cool the CPU chip. CPU fans are powered by a four-pin connection to the motherboard, and the fan pin will be labeled "CPU" on the motherboard. The heat sink and fan should be connected to the CPU via a heat sink bonding compound or paste, known as *thermal grease,* which allows for a proper connection and heat dissipation from the CPU to the heat sink and fan apparatus. Figure 10-14 shows a heat sink that is designed to attach to a motherboard and cool the CPU with an equipped fan.

FIGURE 10-14: A CPU heat sink with built-in fan (from Cooler Master). The pad shown directly under the fan sits directly on top of the CPU chip to pull the heat way from the chip.

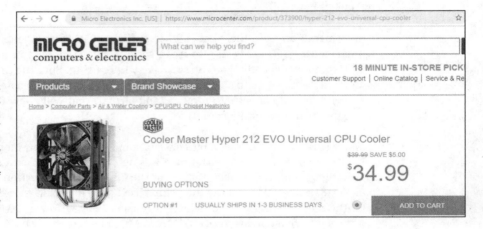

Graphical processing units

The *graphical processing units,* or GPUs, are the essential and keystone piece of equipment required for GPU mining rigs.

TIP

While other components needed for a GPU mining rig may not need to be top-of-the-line and you could get away with the purchase of cheaper components to save on mining rig costs, the GPU is the piece of computer equipment you may want to spend more on. It's the GPU that does the hashing, after all.

You can see an example of a GPU card that is often used for mining in Figure 10-15. This card was not cheap when it was new, but it's powerful. It has built-in fans and heat-sink cooling. In general, GPU frames are built to allow for the thickness of most common GPUs, though if you think your GPUs are particularly thick, you'll want to check the frame's specifications carefully.

Top-of-the-line GPUs are more efficient, so they require less power and output more hashes when mining. Figure 10-16 ranks popular GPUs used in cryptocurrency mining by price. These costs are an average from late 2019, but be warned: Prices fluctuate wildly over time, with supply, and between retailers.

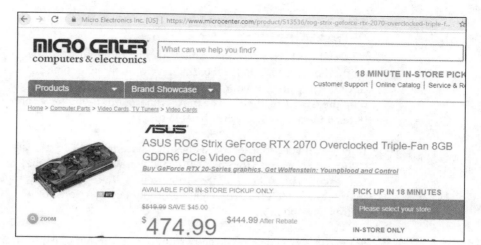

FIGURE 10-15:
GPU cards are popular among some miners.

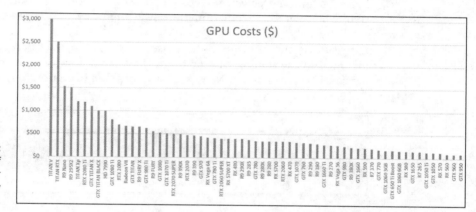

FIGURE 10-16:
Average price of popular GPUs for cryptocurrency mining in 2019.

WARNING

We recommend not mixing and matching GPU types on a single mining rig, as they may use different GPU drivers, which will cause problems. Sticking with the same brand and type will ensure that this will not be an issue.

See Chapter 11 for figures and more details on GPU mining hardware hash output, power consumption, and overall efficiency. Some GPU mining rigs are able to run up to 12 GPUs (see, for example, the prebuilt mining rigs from `https://mining store.com.au`). These mining rigs require larger frames, multiple power supplies, and, in some cases, two motherboards to run that many GPUs. Six GPUs is a common deployment and is near the limit that can be safely and easily powered by a single power supply.

Riser card and cables

A special GPU riser card and cables may be required to connect your GPUs to the motherboard. Most motherboards have only a few onboard PCIe connections for GPUs. Depending on your hardware setup and motherboard, you may be able to plug the GPU directly into the motherboard, but if you have more GPU cards than PCIe connections, you won't be able to.

However, if your motherboard doesn't have enough PCIe connections, you can use GPU riser cards, one for each GPU card you want to use. (They are around $15 to $20 each.) The riser cards are mounted on the frame; they then plug into the motherboard via USB (Universal Serial Bus) connections, of which most mother-boards have plenty.

Some GPUs are powered directly from the motherboard connection. However, the most modern and powerful GPUs (the ones best suited for mining) require the GPU to be powered directly from the power supply by a separate PCIe 6-pin cable.

Each GPU is then plugged into a riser card via the PCIe port, and physically mounted to the mining case or frame. You can see an example of a riser card, being sold on the popular Newegg electronics site, in Figure 10-17.

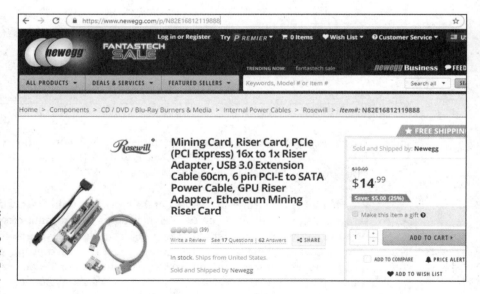

FIGURE 10-17: A riser card designed to connect a single GPU card to a motherboard.

Memory

Random access memory, or RAM, is needed for any computer as well as for a GPU-based mining rig. RAM is cheap, but mining doesn't actually need very large amounts of memory (unlike the graphics-intensive operations the GPU cards were originally designed for), so you won't need to go overboard. Still, your rig will run better with a decent amount of RAM, and anywhere from 4 to 16GB of RAM is most likely adequate.

RAM sticks or cards can be plugged directly into the motherboard, but be sure to follow your motherboard manufacturer's instructions carefully. For example, you may need to plug two chips into slots 1 and 2 with some motherboards, or slots 1 and 3 with others. Typical modern motherboards are equipped with four slots for expandable RAM, but because GPU-mining rigs do not require much RAM, you generally don't need to use all four slots.

Power supply

You'll need a power supply — maybe several. GPU-rig power supplies, similar to their ASIC counterparts, also come equipped with PCIe 6-pin cables, allowing for easy and quick connection to the various pieces of gear that require power.

REMEMBER

Make sure to properly calculate your mining rig's power supply needs before purchasing your power supplies. GPU manufacturers will list the maximum rated power consumption of their graphics cards. Multiply this number by the number of GPUs you have and install enough power to supply them all. Also account for the CPU, fans, and motherboard power consumption. The power requirements for these additional items should be provided in the manufacturer's documentation, but do not normally exceed 200 to 400 watts. Typically, computer power supplies range between 600 and 1,600 watts and can easily power between 3 and 8 GPUs, depending on the GPUs' electricity consumption. Refer to Chapter 11 for a ranking of popular GPUs' power consumption in watts when mining a cryptocurrency such as Ethereum.

Hard drive

The storage mechanism for digital data, the hard disk drive (HDD) is needed for any computer, and a GPU mining rig is essentially a specialized computer. Some solo miners, with their own full cryptocurrency node, use state-of-the-art solid-state drives (SSDs), but in pool mining this type of technology isn't needed. With pool mining, the pool is managing the blockchain itself. All your gear is doing is the hashing, so you don't need a particularly fast or large hard drive. A smallish HDD is fine.

For solo mining, though, it's a different matter. You'll have a full copy of the blockchain on the hard drive. What that means, as far as a choice between HDD and SDD is concerned, depends on the cryptocurrency you're mining. In the case of many smaller cryptocurrencies, the choice probably isn't terribly important. In some cases, though, in particular if you're mining the Ethereum blockchain using an *archival* blockchain (a copy of the blockchain that includes all historical data), the choice is more important. You'd need a multi-terabyte SSD, because the archival blockchain is huge, and an HDD really wouldn't be fast enough to keep up or sync. (On the other hand, it's possible to solo mine in the Ethereum blockchain using what is known as a *pruned* blockchain, one in which non-essential historical data has been removed, which is much smaller.)

SSD drives are more expensive than HDDs, but much faster, and can help solo-mining equipment quickly read and write block data into storage. This isn't needed for pool mining, but in solo cryptocurrency mining, every (split) second counts. If you're trying to download, sync, and verify an archival Ethereum block-chain, for example, you cannot even catch up to the real-time blocks being added to the chain without using an SSD, as an HDD is just too slow. (On the other hand, this isn't a problem with most cryptocurrencies.)

Drives are connected to the motherboard, generally using a Serial ATA (SATA) cable, as well as connected to the power supply via a six-pin PCIe power cable.

Fans

Air flow is essential for any mining application, as the computational processes generate quite a bit of heat. The GPUs best suited for cryptocurrency mining have built-in, on-board fans to cool off large heat sinks. You'll also need a CPU fan. The mining-rig frame itself may also be equipped with a place to mount a few external fans to the unit. These can be connected to the motherboard via four-pin fan power connections and will help dissipate heat off the mining rig and keep your equipment running optimally.

Ensure all these connections are firmly secured and plug in your GPU mining rig. Once online, the next step is to install the software to get your mining rig pointed to your cryptocurrency blockchain or pool of choice.

An operating system, mouse, keyboard, and screen

Unlike working with an ASIC, which requires an external computer to manage the ASIC, your GPU rig is going to be managed by an operating system stored on the HDD or SSD that you installed into the frame. The GPU mining rig itself is a computer. Just like your desktop or laptop PC, it has a motherboard, CPU, RAM, and a disk drive.

If you bought a prebuilt GPU rig, it likely already has an operating system included. The Shark Mining rig we looked at earlier in the section, "GPU Mining Rigs," has something called SharkOS installed, which is a Linux-based operating system with mining software included, and the MiningSky V1 GPU Mining Rig comes with Windows pre-installed on the disk (though not registered). Otherwise, you'll have to install an operating system, probably downloaded to the rig's hard drive through your Internet connection.

Note that some of the software we look at in this chapter is also, like the SharkOS, a combination of operating system and mining software. You install the operating system, and it comes with the mining functions ready to run.

You'll also need to control that GPU rig computer, so you'll need a mouse, keyboard, and display. (A few, like the Shark Mining rig, may have a built-in touch screen.)

CPU Mining

CPU mining was very popular and, in fact, was the only method of mining in the early days of Bitcoin and other cryptocurrencies, pre-ASIC. Since then, specialized mining hardware has evolved to be much more effective and efficient. However, it is still viable to CPU mine on a variety of smaller cryptocurrencies or cryptocurrencies that intentionally discourage the development of ASICs, such as Monero. These days, almost nobody builds CPU "rigs." Instead, you either use a spare computer that's sitting around or decide that if you have a GPU rig running, you may as well use the CPU in the rig, too. It's there, controlling the GPU cards, so why not use the additional computational power that is sitting idle to mine as well?

Still, the easiest way to mine using a CPU in a spare machine is by using pool software, such as NiceHash, Cudo Miner, and Kryptex. You can also use other programs, such as Easyminer and Hive OS.

If you want to solo mine, you'll generally install the cryptocurrency's core software on the computer holding the CPU you're planning to use, though a few other solo-mining programs are also available to use. We talk more about mining software in the next section.

REMEMBER

With any form of mining, you need to understand the numbers and whether you can mine profitably (see Chapter 11). This is even more important with CPU mining, which is far less likely to be profitable.

Mining Software

After you have your hardware running, you'll need to install the appropriate software. The software you'll use depends on whether you're pool mining or solo mining, your hardware setup (ASIC, GPU, or CPU), and the particular cryptocurrency you plan to mine.

In some cases, the mining software replaces the entire operating system (ethOS and Braiins OS, or Braiins OS+, for example), but in other cases, the software is application software that runs within another operating system, typically Windows, Linux, or macOS (such as MultiMiner, NiceHash, and Cudo Miner).

Pool mining

Pool mining is a cooperative mining system in which thousands of individual miners work together to mine blocks. They share in the rewards proportional to their individual contributions of hash power.

We recommend pool mining for steady and consistent mining rewards, and later in this section, we discuss some software options for getting your mining rig (CPUs, ASICs, and GPUs) set up and working with a mining pool. Some work with all three, while some only work with one of these systems.

REMEMBER

If you bought an ASIC or a prebuilt GPU rig, your rig most likely already has mining software installed on it. ASIC mining rigs generally come equipped with a manufacturer-provided operating system (running on the ASIC's control board), with a simple graphical user interface. You will work with this operating system from another computer, connected to your local network; you'll use a web browser to navigate to the unit's IP address on the LAN.

See the manufacturer's documentation to properly set up the mining software. For a view of a typical mining manufacturer's GUI, refer to the snapshot in Figure 10-6 showing the pool-configuration screen in the software that ships with Bitmain's ASICs, and the discussion earlier in this chapter in the section, "A computer to control your rig." If you purchased a prebuilt GPU frame, it most likely comes with an operating system and mining software, too.

However, many of these manufacturer-provided systems are not open-source. Some implementations have been prone to issues, such as backdoors, remote monitoring, and lack of full overclocking or other efficiency limitations, so miners often replace the manufacturer's software. (If you're interested in finding out more about possible efficiency limitations or backdoors, search for *Bitmain ASIC-Boost scandal* and *Antbleed scandal*.)

A lot of downloadable programs are specifically designed for mining cryptocurrencies. However, many of them are from unreliable sources, and some may include malware or other computer viruses. We have compiled this list of reliable mining software programs designed to mine towards pools.

>> **ethOS:** This Linux-based mining operating system for GPU cryptocurrency mining rigs is highly recommended for pool mining GPU applications and is easy to install, set up, and operate (for people who have worked with Linux software!). ethOS currently supports mining Ethereum, Zcash, Monero, and others. ethOS is free software licensed under the General Public License (GNU), but it is highly recommended that you purchase a copy to support the ongoing development of the software. (While free, it is not open source; it is, according to the website, provided under the "'Small Goat with Red Eyes' license. You should buy one ethOS from gpuShack.com per each rig on which you intend to run ethOS. If you don't, a small goat with red eyes will visit you while you sleep.") The software can be directly downloaded, or you can purchase a preloaded flash drive or SSD. Follow the documentation to get your mining rig fully set up and hashing (http://ethosdistro.com).

>> **NiceHash:** This is a pool-mining service and mining configuration software (which also allows people to buy and sell hash rate; see Chapter 7) that is used for a wide variety of different cryptocurrencies. It is specifically designed to mine via GPUs, ASICs, and CPUs and runs only on the Windows operating system. So, you could GPU mine by installing it into the Windows operating system that is installed in your mining rig, and CPU mine by running it on a Windows PC to use that computer's CPU. To ASIC mine, you use its instructions to point your ASIC rig to its server (see Figure 10-18). Follow the documentation to get your mining rig fully set up and hashing (www.nicehash.com).

>> **Easyminer:** This free, open-source mining tool allows for the mining of various coins, such as Bitcoin, Dogecoin, Litecoin, and others. It can be configured to mine with CPUs, GPUs, and ASICs and can mine pointed to a pool as well as solo mine. It runs only in Windows (www.easyminer.net).

>> **Hive OS:** Hive OS is a free operating system for up to three mining rigs, but requires a monthly fee for larger deployments. It can be configured to mine with CPUs, GPUs, and ASICs, and can mine a variety of different hashing algorithms (www.hiveon.com/os).

>> **Braiins OS:** Braiins OS is a great alternative to manufacturer-provided web-based GUIs when mining Bitcoin on ASIC rigs. It is an open-source, completely auditable, operating system designed for the Antminer S9 and the DragonMint T1 ASICs (and maybe more by the time you read this). In some hardware configurations, it allows for an increase in hash power with the same electricity expenditures, increasing your efficiency and returns. Follow the documentation and installation guide to flash the operating system

software to your mining rig's control board to get set up and hashing toward your chosen pool (https://braiins.com).

>> **Mother of Dragons:** Mother of Dragons is software that runs on your Linux computer (implementations such as Debian, Ubuntu, and CentOS) or other LAN-connected Linux-based device, such as a Raspberry Pi (a tiny, cheap, single-board computer; see www.raspberrypi.org). You enter your settings — pool server, user, password, clock speed, fan speed — and then the software automatically detects ASIC miners (DragonMint/Innosilicon) that are connected to your network and changes their settings. It has a built-in monitoring system and will also update firmware for your ASICs as well as reboot any miners that fall offline. It saves quite a bit of work, but is built for the expert user. Follow the documentation on the following GitHub page for setup instructions https://github.com/brndnmtthws/mother-of-dragons.

>> **MultiMiner:** MultiMiner is an open-source mining tool designed for Windows, Linux, and macOS. It is designed to work with GPUs, ASICs, and FPGAs (Field Programmable Gate Arrays). MultiMiner actually uses the BFGMiner mining engine (discussed in the later section, "Solo mining") in combination with an easy-to-use interface for simple configuration and monitoring. It can be configured to mine toward pools and, similar to Mother of Dragons, it has monitoring systems and automatic updates (https://github.com/nwoolls/MultiMiner).

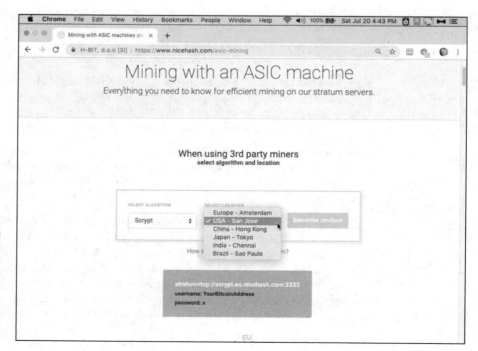

FIGURE 10-18:
To ASIC mine with NiceHash, pick an algorithm and server location, and NiceHash tells you how to configure your ASIC.

FPGA?

FPGA (Field Programmable Gate Array) chips are for really advanced, truly expert miners, not for beginners to dabble in, as they can be quite difficult to work with. FPGAs are configurable computer chips — blank slates, in effect. Unlike most computer chips that come from the manufacturer already configured and ready to use, FPGAs are designed to be configured by the user.

FPGA chips are sometimes used to mine cryptocurrencies, such as Monero, which discourages the user of ASICs. The Monero community changes the algorithm periodically to make it hard for manufacturers to design, build, and distribute ASICs for Monero. (By the time an ASIC can be brought to market, the algorithm changes again.) Expert miners use FPGAs as a more efficient way to mine Monero than CPU or GPU mining. These miners will reprogram the chips when the algorithm is changed. They are, in effect, homemade ASICs, though generally not as efficient as a true ASIC would be. They may also be used for smaller, unpopular coins that do not have a large enough market to encourage manufacturers to design ASICs for them.

TECHNICAL STUFF

Although setting up pool-mining software designed for Windows and macOS to run on your laptop or desktop PC is generally pretty simple (as you can see in Chapter 7, for example), working with some of these other systems can be far more complicated.

Setting up, say, ethOS or Braiins OS can be fairly straightforward for an experienced Linux user. However, if you've never left the Windows or macOS operating systems or your idea of dealing with a complicated software installation process is letting your employer's tech guy have the computer for the afternoon, then some of this stuff will be out of your zone of experience! You'll either need to find a friendly geek to help, or understand that you will have to read instructions very carefully and quite likely will expend serious amounts of time finding out how to get the job done.

WARNING

Most mining software is designed for ASIC and GPU mining because they are the most efficient systems and the sorts of systems used by most experienced miners. The non-ASIC cryptocurrencies, such as Monero, are an exception, as they are intended to be mined with CPUs and GPUs. (If you can GPU mine, you can CPU mine, too, but GPUs are far more powerful.) Some mining programs do work with CPUs. However, in many cases, miners who are CPU mining Monero or smaller cryptocurrencies simply use the *core software* — the software provided by the cryptocurrency itself — either on the cryptocurrency website or from the cryptocurrency's GitHub account. However, it is difficult to CPU mine profitably. Most Monero miners are GPU mining, though they often also use the CPU in the GPU rig.

It's generally not worth it to CPU mine. If you do intend to mine with your CPU, probably the only software it makes sense to use is NiceHash.

Solo mining

Solo mining is not recommended unless you have very carefully run the numbers (see Chapter 11) and are sure it makes sense. You need to fully understand and accept your odds (which may be low), or you need a significant enough network hash rate to ensure profitability. With that said, quite a few software implementations allow for configurable solo mining.

TECHNICAL STUFF

Most solo mining tools require that you download and sync a full node of the cryptocurrency you intend to mine on a separate computer system on your network, and then point the software running on your ASIC or GPU mining rig to the full node on that computer. Heavily research the documentation for the software you plan on using before firing up your mining equipment.

Check out the following list of solo-mining software.

>> **Core Cryptocurrency Software:** Some cryptocurrencies, such as Monero, have mining functionality built into the GUI of their core full-node software (Bitcoin also did at one point, though it's been removed). Simply download their core node, sync up to the blockchain (this may take a while), and enable mining under the Mining tab. Refer to the cryptocurrency's main site for the software download and documentation. (For example, for Monero, go to https://web.getmonero.org/get-started/mining).

>> **CGMiner:** CGMiner is open-source software created for Bitcoin mining with ASICs or FPGAs, and runs on Linux, Windows, and macOS. Its codebase is also open source (https://en.bitcoin.it/wiki/CGMiner).

>> **BTCminer:** BTCminer is a Bitcoin-mining software designed for FPGA mining that is open source. It runs on Windows and Linux (https://en.bitcoin.it/wiki/BTCMiner).

>> **BFGMiner:** This free and open-source software for Windows, macOS, and Linux can be configured for mining with CPUs, GPUs, FPGAs, and ASICs (https://en.bitcoin.it/wiki/BFGMiner).

4

The Economics of Mining

IN THIS PART . . .

Figure out whether mining is worth your effort.

Being efficient with your mining.

Manage your profits and keep the tax man happy.

Chapter **11**

Running the Numbers: Is It Worth It?

The best way to avoid making bad investments in the cryptocurrency mining industry is to do your homework and research before putting any considerable amount of funding into cloud-mining services, personal mining hardware, or hash-rate marketplaces. You really need to understand the numbers, so you can see whether you're likely to be able to make money.

In this chapter, we walk through the various aspects of cryptocurrency mining equipment and deployment benchmarks that can help you figure out whether your planned arrangements will lead to mining profitability.

Factors That Determine Mining Profitability

When you're calculating the rate of return on your investment (ROI), consider these factors:

» Cost of your equipment

» Hash rate of your equipment

» Efficiency of your equipment

» Maintenance costs

» Facility costs (renting space, cost of cooling the space, and so on)

» Electricity costs to run your equipment

» Total network hash rate of the cryptocurrency you're planning to mine

» If you're mining through a pool (see Chapter 7), the proportion of the total network hash rate provided by the pool and fees charged by the pool

» Block earnings (block subsidy and transaction fees)

» Conversion rate of the cryptocurrency into your local fiat currency

In the following sections, we look at these factors one by one and then bring them all together to help you calculate your potential ROI.

Cost of equipment

A significant factor determining mining profitability is the initial cost of your equipment. Equipment costs are often the largest portion of capital expenditures (CapEx) for cryptocurrency mining endeavors. *CapEx* is defined as costs incurred by businesses or organizations to secure equipment, assets, or locations.

New cryptocurrency mining equipment, both capable GPUs and application specific integrated circuit (ASIC) miners, fluctuate wildly in purchase price depending on demand and market sentiment. At the time of writing, the market prices for some top-of-the-line Bitcoin SHA-256 ASIC mining rigs varied from $20 to $100 USD per TH/s. (See Figure 11-1 for a visualization of this data for each mining rig, and see Figure 11-2 for a normalized cost per TH/s.) This variation in price mostly depends on the age of the equipment and unit efficiency (the amount of electricity consumed per TH/s; see Chapter 9) as well as its popularity and the age of the mining rig. Cost per TH/s is higher for newer, more efficient hardware. Older and less-capable mining equipment is generally sold at lower prices, and the newest and most electrically efficient gear is sold at a premium. In fact, it's sometimes hard to buy new ASIC releases at the manufacturer's intended retail price, as fresh inventory is often low and speculators snap them up and resell them at higher prices, in some cases two or three times the original manufacturer's suggested retail price (MSRP).

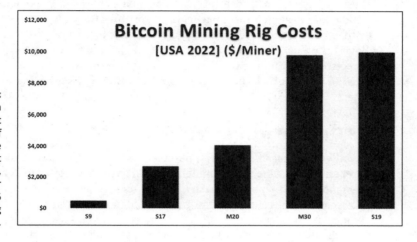

FIGURE 11-1: Purchase cost in U.S. dollars, at time of writing, of some of the latest, most widely available, and most popular SHA-256 Bitcoin-mining ASICs.

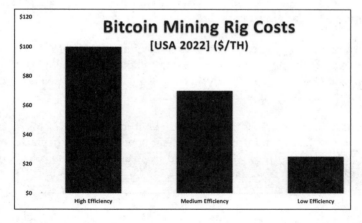

FIGURE 11-2: Purchase cost of SHA-256 mining ASICs, in U.S. dollars per hash rate (TH/s), of some of the latest and most capable Bitcoin-mining equipment at time of writing.

So there's a balance to be considered here. If ASIC A is cheaper than ASIC B in terms of TH/s, it may be because it is less efficient; that is, it may be costing you more in electricity for each tera hash per second (each trillion hashing operations per second). See Chapter 9 for a breakdown of mining gear efficiency for various hash algorithms.

Hash rate of your equipment

You need to know the hash rate of the equipment you own or the equipment you plan to buy. You can figure out the hash rate of equipment in a few ways.

REMEMBER

We want to reiterate that your equipment doesn't have an inherent hash rate. Rather, it has a hash rate specified for a particular mining algorithm. ASICs, of course, are designed for a particular algorithm. But CPUs and GPUs can be used with various cryptocurrencies and their algorithms. Thus, a GPU, for example, can have different hash rates depending on the different cryptocurrencies you're interested in mining. So before you can figure out a CPU or GPU hash rate, you need to know for *which* algorithm you're trying to discover the hardware's hash rate.

ASIC manufacturer ratings

If you've purchased, or plan to purchase, an ASIC, the job is easy; the manufacturer should provide the equipment's rated hash rate. (Refer to Chapter 9 for a list of manufacturer-specified hash rates, in terahashes per second, for some of the most capable Bitcoin SHA-256 mining ASICs on the market today.) As always, though, make sure to do your homework and due diligence. Research manufacturer documentation prior to purchase and study forums, such as BitcoinTalk.org, or social media sites, like Twitter or Reddit, to find discussions related to your prospective mining equipment.

In Figure 11-3, you can see shows a selection of ASICs for sale at Amazon. Notice the text in the product description stating the hash rate: AntMiner L3+ ~504MH/s, AntMiner V9 ~4TH/s, AntMiner S9 ~14.0TH/s, AntMiner V9 ~4TH/s (~ is the mathematical symbol for *approximation*).

TECHNICAL STUFF

What about the Innosilicon device that outputs 50Ksol/s? This means 50,000 *solutions* per second, a term you may hear sometimes, particularly in relation to the Equihash algorithm, which is used by Zcash and some other cryptocurrencies, such as Bitcoin Gold and Komodo. (See Chapter 8 for a breakdown of cryptocurrencies by algorithm.)

A retailer's website may not always list the hash rate of a device you're considering mining with. In that case, go to the manufacturer's website for the details. You can find a list of some of the most popular ASIC and prebuilt GPU mining equipment manufacturers in Chapter 9.

FIGURE 11-3:
A snapshot of an Amazon page showing ratings of various ASIC mining rigs.

Processor benchmarking sites

Another way to find your equipment's hash rate is to check out the third-party mining-equipment benchmark sites. These are particularly useful if you're planning to mine using CPUs or GPUs, for which the hash rate is not published by the manufacturers (because they're not designed for cryptocurrency mining!).

REMEMBER

The hash rate depends not only on the power of the equipment, but also on the cryptocurrency algorithm being used. A GPU will have a hash rate of x on cryptocurrency A, but of y on cryptocurrency B.

These sites can be very handy. However, they don't have every processor listed, so you may not be lucky enough to find the data you're looking for. (On the other hand, perhaps you can estimate — find equipment that *is* rated and that is similar to your hardware, based on more general CPU and GPU metrics.)

HASHES VERSUS SOLUTIONS

Unfortunately, there is a lot of confusion in the Equihash community about *solutions* and *hashes* and their relationship. This confusion exists because cryptocurrency algorithms are complicated, and it's possible to mine without understanding them. Miners need to understand how to set up and operate the relevant hardware and software, but not the function of the underlying, and highly complex, algorithm. Few miners intimately understand the algorithms they're using.

However, this lack of understanding has caused a little problem: While some equipment may be rated in *solutions per second,* some online mining calculators for Equihash cryptocurrencies require that you enter the *hashes per second* for your equipment. While MinerGate (`https://minergate.com/calculator/equihash`) uses solutions/second, for example, WhatToMine (`https://whattomine.com/coins/166-zec-equihash`), CryptoCompare (`www.cryptocompare.com/mining/calculator/zec`), and Minerstat (`https://minerstat.com/coin/ARRR`) all use hashes/second.

Solutions — or *sols*, as they're known in the Equihash community — are solutions to the Equihash proof-of-work challenge. Equihash's puzzle is a variation of what is known as the Birthday Problem (With *x* number of people in the room, what is the likelihood of two people having the same birthday?). Just like with Bitcoin's SHA-256 algorithm, in which every hash is tested against a target, with Equihash, each "solution" is tested against a target. In fact, Equihash doesn't use hashing in the same way SHA-256 does, and hashes per second is really an inappropriate metric; solutions per second is more correct.

Still, you'll sometimes see the hashes/second metric used in relation to Equihash and can usually assume it's being used to mean solutions/second. If you plan to mine an Equihash cryptocurrency, though, you should probably make sure of that when it really counts, such as when making calculations related to profitability based on expressed hashes/second.

Check out the following list of benchmarking sites for various devices, including CPUs, GPUs, and ASICs:

>> **CPU Benchmarks**

- Monero Benchmarks (`https://monerobenchmarks.info`)

>> **GPU Benchmarks**

- Bitcoin Wiki Benchmarks (`https://en.bitcoin.it/wiki/Non-specialized_hardware_comparison`)

- WhatToMine GPU specifications (https://whattomine.com)

- Miningchamp GPU lists (https://miningchamp.com)

>> **ASIC SHA-256 gear**

- Hash Rate Index (https://hashrateindex.com/machines)

- Bitcoin Wiki Benchmarks (https://en.bitcoin.it/wiki/Mining_hardware_comparison)

- Braiins Mining Inights (https://insights.braiins.com/en/#profitability_of_popular_asics)

You can also find tools that combine information related to the performance of the equipment with an actual profitability calculator. See, for example, https://whattomine.com/miners.

Mining pools

Another way to figure out the hashing power of your gear is to use it for mining. Find a reputable mining pool for the cryptocurrency you're interested in, create an account, set up your gear, and let it run for a while. The mining pool software will tell you what your hash rate is for that cryptocurrency. See Chapter 7 for more information on mining pools.

Downloadable processor testers

What if the equipment you're attempting to utilize for cryptocurrency mining doesn't have hash-rate specifications listed from the manufacturer and isn't listed on any of the preceding benchmarking sites? If you don't want to bother setting up a pool account, here's another way to discover your hash rate.

Search for *what is my hash rate,* or a similar phrase, and you'll likely find sites that provide programs that run on your system and check your hash rate. They generally do this by actually mining, so the site providing the download is using your processing power to actually mine and earn them cryptocurrency.

WARNING

However, be careful with such sites. They may also come with adware, malware, or worse! We don't advise using these services unless you're absolutely sure they're safe. (We don't feel confident enough in any of them to actually list them here, so definitely research them prior to using them and download them at your own risk.)

Mining rig efficiency

Behind operational expenditures (which we discuss further in the section, "Cost of electricity") and capital expenditures, the next most important factor in a cost/benefit analysis for your mining operation is your mining equipment efficiency. This number is determined by your mining equipment hash rate (hashes per second) as well as the unit's power consumption, normally measured in watts.

Remember from Chapter 9 that these two pieces of data can be combined to form an efficiency metric for each piece of equipment. This mining rig efficiency is typically specified in joules per tera hash per second (or, depending on the equipment, joules per giga hash, or joules per mega hash). You'll recall from Chapter 9 that a joule is a unit of energy, which can be considered equivalent to a watt of power consumption per second. A tera hash is a trillion hashes, a giga hash is a billion hashes, and a mega hash is a million hashes. See Chapter 9 for figures showing mining rig efficiency of popular ASICs running on some of the more common hash algorithms.

Hash-rate capability

Mining rig effectiveness, and thus its profitability, hinges on the hash rate that the equipment can output toward the blockchain proof-of-work algorithm for the cryptocurrency you choose to mine — that is, how many hashes the equipment can process each second. The more hashes your equipment processes every second, the higher your proportion of the network hash rate, which translates to you earning more of the mined cryptocurrency. (Remember, as we explain in Chapters 8 and 9, that in general and over a long enough period of time, you earn a proportion of the network's mining rewards equal to the proportion of the network hash rate that you provide.)

See Chapter 9 for a graph of the hash-rate rankings of a range of popular Bitcoin SHA-256 mining ASICs as well as other common hash algorithms. For a quick summary of estimated GPU mining hash-rate capabilities toward the Ethereum Ethash algorithm, see Figure 11-4. These ratings range anywhere from 20 to 120 megahashes per second; note that they do not include GPU overclocking and act only as an estimation.

TECHNICAL STUFF

Overclocking is a term used to describe increasing the output of a computer processor above the standard manufacture rating by increasing its clock rate, or frequency, which can sometimes be done through the BIOS or through manufacturer's software. For example, to overclock a piece of hardware, you could increase the frequency of the equipment in the settings from 600 MHz to 750 MHz. (*MHz or megahertz* is a unit of frequency cycle time measuring a million times per second.) Overclocking produces more heat, consumes more electricity, and ultimately produces more hash-rate capabilities in a cryptocurrency-mining application. The practice of overclocking is hard on processing units and can reduce the life of equipment, though miners sometimes do overclock. Miners may overclock a piece of equipment they know is coming to the end of its life, for example, because its hash rate is quickly dropping as a percentage of the network hash rate.

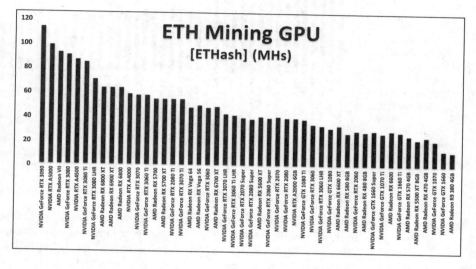

FIGURE 11-4: Hash rates for a range of common GPU cards at time of writing, mining ether using the Ethereum proof-of-work algorithm Ethash.

Efficiency

The combination of the mining equipment's hash rate with the mining equipment's power consumption provides you with an important metric to determine your hardware's efficiency. The more efficient your mining equipment is, the more profitable it will be.

As discussed in Chapter 9, efficiency is typically defined as useful work performed divided by energy expended to do that work. However, when it comes to typical mining hardware, manufacturers often list this metric in reverse. Mining equipment efficiency is often listed as the energy expended (joules) divided by the work performed (hashes/second).

For an efficiency comparison of a range of popular Bitcoin network SHA-256 and other common algorithms' ASIC mining hardware, see Chapter 9. In Figure 11-5, you can see an efficiency comparison for a variety of top GPU cards when used to mine Ethereum's Ethash hashing algorithm. The typical unit used to rank these graphics cards by efficiency is joules per mega hash per second or J/MH/s.

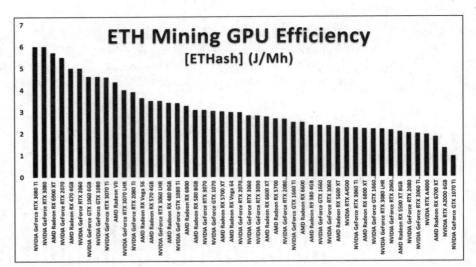

FIGURE 11-5:
A comparison of efficiency (in J/ MH/s) of various GPUs mining the Ethereum blockchain's Ethash proof-of-work algorithm at time of writing.

Cost of maintenance

While most of the mining equipment on the market today is highly reliable, failures still occur, and so a maintenance cost is associated with those breakdowns. The most likely components to fail on cryptocurrency mining hardware, for both ASIC and GPU deployments, are the fans that distribute air to cool the heat sinks. These fans spin at thousands of rotations per minute and, with 24/7 operation, they are likely to fail every once in a while. Luckily, these fans are standardized, very affordable (ranging anywhere from $15 to $25), and can often be found at the manufacturer's website, any electronics store, or your favorite online marketplace.

ASIC mining hardware has a control board that senses fan failure, safely shuts down mining, places the hardware into a failure alert state, and (normally) displays a red LED light. This is to alert the equipment operator of the failure and protect the equipment. For GPUs, the boards will lower their output to what the thermal management system can handle while the fan has failed. Unfortunately, GPU fans are not as standardized or easy to fix and will most likely warrant an entire GPU replacement upon failure.

Another component that sometimes fails is commonly referred to as a *hashing board*. ASIC mining rigs normally have three or so of these hashing boards, and a single board can contain many ASIC chips. The hashing boards connect directly to the ASIC controller. (In general, the controllers do not seem to fail very often, as they're not running the processes that heat up the ASIC mining chips and lead to failure.) However, when the control boards do fail, their replacement price can range anywhere from $150 to $750 (these are commonly sold by the original equipment manufacturer [OEM]).

The hashing boards can be replaced fairly easily, and many manufacturers or online marketplaces have them for sale independently of the mining rigs. The fans, control boards, and hash boards have quick connection plugs to allow for easy and fast replacement and cable termination. On average, the total maintenance costs should not exceed more than roughly 5 to 10 percent of the mining hardware purchase price over a one-year period.

Mining hardware that is operating in a clean environment requires only limited care and maintenance beyond fixing broken components. If the hardware is running in dusty or otherwise contaminated areas, it will sometimes also need to be cleaned.

TIP

The best way to clean dusty and dirty mining hardware is with an air compressor, canned air, or other high-velocity blowing device. This allows most of the contaminants to be cleared away and allows your mining hardware to continue hashing along.

Cost of facilities

If you choose to deploy your mining hardware at home, the majority of your facility costs should already be taken care of in your normal expenses. Some hosting or mining service providers, however, charge anywhere from $100 to $160 USD per month to run your equipment at their facilities, electricity not included. See Chapter 9 for popular cryptocurrency mining hosting providers.

A commercial data center may, however, charge a much steeper fee. In any deployment case, how you cool your equipment — whether by exhausting wasted heat, cooling it with an air conditioner, or using the heat to warm the space — also determines your facility's cost. Cooling your equipment and space with an air conditioner would be the most effective but also the most expensive method. If you can find some way to re-use your exhausted heat, you may be able to enjoy significant savings.

Predicting exactly how much cooling you'll need is difficult, but consider this. You can assume that all the electricity that goes into your mining equipment comes out as heat. Thus, if you are running a 1,500W ASIC, it's the equivalent of running a 1,500W room heater (a pretty common spec for a room heater, and in fact, if you visit your local hardware store, you'll probably find that most of the heaters they sell are 1,500W or less). So you can at least get an idea of how much heat you're going to be creating, and perhaps that can help you determine how much cooling you'll need.

Cost of electricity

One of the most important costs that goes into your mining profitability calculations is the cost of electricity. In fact, the cost of electricity for cryptocurrency mining equipment and operations *is* the largest part of your mining operational expenditures.

These operational expenditures, commonly referred to as *OpEx*, are the recurring expenses or costs of running a business, venture, or, in this case, a cryptocurrency mining operation. In fact, electricity costs are so significant in mining that cryptocurrency miners often go out of their way — literally — to seek cheap electricity. Cheap access to energy allows a cryptocurrency mine to remain profitable with even less-than-optimal hardware. This is why you may have heard of people, such as students mining in college dorms, stealing electricity to mine with. You can't get cheaper — and thus more economically efficient — than sourcing electricity for free! (No, we are not recommending this.)

To further reduce energy bills, you could develop your own auxiliary energy sources with no fuel costs, such as renewables, hydroelectricity, wind, or solar. Other mining deployments use resources, such as flared, unmarketable, and otherwise wasted natural gas (methane), and repurpose that energy toward mining cryptocurrencies. A cryptocurrency mining company that has made its mark specializing in this type of deployment is Upstream Data Inc. (www.upstreamdata.ca).

Wherever you're getting your electricity, your operation's cost of electricity depends on two things: how much electricity you're going to use, and how much you're going to be charged for each unit of electricity.

Measuring your power consumption

Similar to manufacturer-specified hash rate, most ASIC mining equipment has a rated power consumption value in watts from the manufacturer. (Refer to Chapter 9 to see a list of some of the more popular SHA-256 Bitcoin network mining hardware and its manufacture-rated power consumption ranked in watts.) This data is helpful in planning electrical infrastructure as well as calculating cryptocurrency revenue and ROI.

Finding this data is more of a problem when mining using CPUs or GPUs. In fact, they use different amounts of electricity when mining different cryptocurrencies, as the algorithms require different levels of processing power.

You can estimate power consumption for GPU and CPU hardware by using the manufacturer's maximum power rating associated with these processor devices. However, in many cases, this may overestimate power utilization and won't be a precise number, and so it will affect your ROI calculations. In Figure 11-6, you can see estimated power consumption for some of the more popular GPU cards when they're mining the Ethereum Ethash mining algorithm.

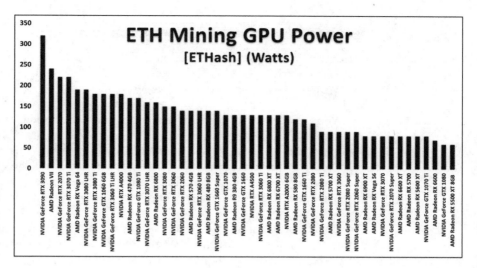

FIGURE 11-6: Estimated power consumption of a variety of popular GPUs on the market at time of writing, mining with the Ethereum Ethash mining algorithm.

The best way to figure out your gear's power consumption is to measure it directly. Ideally, of course, you would measure the power consumption while it's actually hashing the particular algorithm used by the cryptocurrency you want to mine . . . but if you haven't started mining yet, um, you can't do that.

If you're already mining, you can buy a power delivery unit (PDU; see Chapter 9) with a built-in watt meter.

TIP

We recommend a simpler device, though: a basic electricity usage meter (which you can often find for around $30 at your local hardware store or online), such as the Kill A Watt meter. Plug the device into a 120V wall socket and then plug your computer equipment into the socket on the front of the device, and it will show you real-time power consumption.

Finding the cost of electricity

After you determine how much electricity you'll use, you need to figure out the unit cost of the power. Electric utility providers generally bill in total consumed kilowatt-hour (kWh) energy increments over a monthly billing period. To find what your energy charge is per kWh, study your electric bill at the location where you intend to mine, check the utility's website, or call your electric utility provider. (See Chapter 9 for more information on finding your electricity cost.)

On average in the United States, electricity ranges from $0.08 to $0.15 per kWh, not including any connection or service charges. For our example calculations here, we will assume $0.10 per kWh.

Estimating monthly energy usage and cost

After you have an estimate or measurement of your mining equipment's instantaneous electrical power consumption, measured in watts, extrapolating that to kWh is a matter of simple arithmetic.

A kWh is 1,000 watts of consumption over a one-hour period. There are 24 hours in a day, as you probably know, and on average, about 30 days in any given month (30 days and 10 hours, if you want to be more precise). This makes for about 720 hours in the average month (okay, 730). This value allows you to multiply your measured or estimated mining hardware power value in watts by 730 hours for a quick estimate of monthly energy consumption as measured in kWh.

So, if you discover that your device is using 1,280W (the consumption level of the Antminer S9 SE, for example), then running the device for an hour uses 1,280Wh (watt-hours), or 1.28kWh. Multiply that by 730 hours in a typical month, and we end up with 934.4kWh.

So now all this information can be combined into a single equation: power (watts) * time (hours) = energy (kWh). This energy value can then be converted into local electrical cost with this equation: energy (kWh) * price ($) per energy (kWh) = total energy cost ($).

So, if your cryptocurrency mining hardware draws an instantaneous electrical power value of 1,280 watts, and your electricity price per kWh is $0.10, this is how you would estimate your monthly electrical bill:

1,280 watts * 730 hours = 934.4kWh

934.4kWh * $0.10 per kWh = $93.44/month in electricity costs

Some electrical utilities also charge a demand fee, capacity charge, or maximum power (kW) consumption charge, ranging from a few dollars to upwards of $15 per kW. The fee is generally charged to particular customer classes, such as commercial and industrial (though if you build a large enough mining operation at home, you may end up changing your class!).

The charge is calculated based on the 15-minute period during the month that had the highest electric power consumption. In other words, you multiply the demand charge by the highest kW level you reach at any point during the month.

Say that you have a mining operation that at some point during the month reaches 5kW, and your utility has an $8 demand charge. In this case, you'd be charged $40. (You may reach this peak for only 15 minutes, or consume that much power over the entire month; regardless, the demand charge is the same.)

Total network hash rate

You're also going to need to know the network hash rate for the cryptocurrency you plan to mine. The always-useful BitInfoCharts site provides hash rates (and much, much more) for many of the most popular cryptocurrency networks (see https://bitinfocharts.com). If you can't find it there, you may find it on the cryptocurrency's own website, at a pool mining site, or through an online search.

Again, your revenues will be in proportion to the amount of the network's hash rate that you provide. Provide 1 percent of the hash rate, and, over time, you're likely to earn 1 percent of the network's mining rewards. (We're using 1 percent as an example, of course; you're unlikely to be able to provide such a large proportion of the hash rate, even for smaller, less popular cryptocurrencies.)

Nothing lasts forever, though. Typically, over the life of a cryptocurrency (assuming it's successful and lasts), the network hash rate steadily increases. More miners enter the market, and the equipment being added becomes more efficient.

Only in a handful of instances over the past decade of the Bitcoin network's existence, for example, has hash rate dropped and block difficulty gone down. (This has happened after the value of Bitcoin has dropped significantly, dragging down market sentiment with it.) So, as the network hash rate goes up, your equipment's proportion of the hash rate goes down, of course (unless you add more equipment). And as your proportion of the hash rate goes down, so, too, does the proportion of the rewards you earn. In other words, a mining rig that provides a constant hash rate toward the network will produce a diminishing return as measured in the asset being mined as both the network hash rate and mining competition increases.

In terms of your local fiat currency, however, that may still be fine. If the proportion of the cryptocurrency that you earn goes down, while the value of the cryptocurrency, say, doubles, you're still ahead of the game.

Information about your pool

If you're working with a pool, you need information about that pool. (In fact, you may want to run the calculations for both pool mining and solo mining.)

You need to know several things: the pool's total hash rate, how often the pool mines a block, and how much reward is paid to the miners each time the pool mines a block (that is, the block subsidies and transaction fees, minus the fees charged by the pool). You can find this information at the pool's website, of course. See Chapter 7 for more information on pools and links to various pools.

Block earnings

Our calculations require some information about the blocks you intend to mine. We need to know two things: how often the network adds a block to the block-chain, and what the winning miner earns when the block is added — the block subsidy, if any, and the transaction fees, if the miner earns those. (Different networks pay miners in different ways.)

The rate at which each cryptocurrency adds blocks to the blockchain, as well as the amount of the rewards paid for each block, varies by cryptocurrency. This data also varies in time due to transaction-fee and hash-power fluctuations. Fees may vary from block to block and more generally over time, and if hash power has increased since the last block-difficulty adjustment, blocks will be found more frequently. Again, you may be able to find this information on BitInfoCharts (`https://bitinfo charts.com`) or a similar site, on the cryptocurrency's own website, or through an online search. For the Bitcoin network, you can find the average blocks found by each major pool over a week's time at `https://coin.dance/blocks/thisweek`.

Cryptocurrency conversion rate

Cryptocurrency market values measured in local fiat currencies fluctuate widely in price over any given day, and even more over extended periods. The following sites offer some good resources for checking the exchange rate of the cryptocurrencies you want to mine.

>> **CoinMarketCap:** `https://coinmarketcap.com`

>> **CoinCap:** `https://coincap.io`

>> **Messari:** `https://messari.io/onchainfx`

>> **CoinGecko:** `www.coingecko.com/en`

>> **BitInfoCharts:** `https://bitinfocharts.com/index_v.html`

>> **CryptoCompare:** `www.cryptocompare.com`

>> **Coinlib:** `https://coinlib.io`

Calculating Your ROI

After you know the factors that contribute to a mining operation's profitability and return on investment (ROI), you can now run the numbers and see what is likely to happen with your projected mining operation. Will you make money? Or is it a losing proposition?

We end up with two numbers: your absolute gain (or loss), and a percentage ROI number. ROI is typically calculated by the following formula:

Profit divided by Total Investment multiplied by 100 = ROI (%)

If your calculated ROI is a positive percentage, the venture was a net benefit to you. If the percentage is less than zero, you would have been better off staying in bed.

To start, figure out how much cryptocurrency you're going to mine (the value of the block subsidies and transaction fees that you will earn). Oh, and you need to calculate monthly numbers: your income (or loss) and ROI on a monthly basis.

Your block earnings

To estimate your earnings, we begin right at the top, with how much a miner earns each time a block is mined, and how often that happens. You'll earn only a fraction of this, but it's our starting point. We begin by calculating under the assumption that you are solo mining — running your equipment directly connected to the cryptocurrency network rather than through a pool. Then we look again at the calculation assuming that you're going to work with a pool.

Calculating for solo mining

We use mining Monero (XMR) in the fall of 2019 as an example. Each time a block is added to the Monero blockchain, the winning miner earns a block subsidy of about 2.6XMR. The miner also earns transaction fees. These fees fluctuate, of course, but at the time of writing, a good sample average is 0.00277, for a total of 2.60277XMR. At the time of writing, each Monero coin is worth $153, so the total block earnings are around $398.22.

Now, the Monero blockchain adds a block roughly every two minutes (you can find all these Monero stats at `https://bitinfocharts.com/`). So around 720 new blocks are added to the blockchain every day, which comes out to an average of about 21,900 per month.

In 2019, those 21,900 blocks mined each month were therefore worth about 57,000XMR ($5,960,559.33) to the miners (21,900 blocks x 2.60277XMR x $104.57).

Okay, now you need to know how much of that reward you're going to grab. First, we assume that you are solo mining, rather than working with a pool. The first thing you need to figure out is what proportion of the blocks you'll mine. You need to divide your hash-rate contribution by the total Monero network hash rate, to find the fraction of the network hash rate that you'll provide.

The Monero network has, at the time of this writing, a hash rate of around 325 MH/s (megahashes per second; millions of hashes per second). Assume that you have a fairly nice GPU that will output 1.95 kH/s (kilohashes per second; thousand hashes per second) — that's how many hashes an AMD RX VEGA 64 GPU will output, for example.

Make sure that you're using the same units, of course. Depending on the cryptocurrency you're working with, your equipment may be rated in GH/s (gigahashes per second, or a billion hashes per second), while the network hash rate may be expressed in, say TH/s (terahashes per second) or even PH/s (petahashes per second) . . . 1 trillion hashes per second or 1 quadrillion hashes per second, respectively. Or even EH/s (exahashes per second; a quintillion hashes per second). So, of course, you'll need to convert one side to match the other before running this calculation.

You need to divide your mining equipment's hash rate (1.95 kH/s) by the network hash rate (325 MH/s), but you can't simply divide 1.95 by 325, because the first number is stated in thousands and the latter is in millions. The numbers, fully expressed, are

1,950 hashes per second (the equipment hash rate)

325,000,000 hashes per second (the network hash rate)

So you divide 1,950 by 325,000,000 to arrive at 0.000006. That's the fraction of the network hash rate that the equipment will contribute. To see it expressed as a percentage, multiply by 100 (0.0006%).

Okay, so you know that each month during 2019, Monero miners

>> Mined approximately 21,900 blocks

>> Earned approximately 57,000XMR in block subsidies and transaction fees

At that time, this was worth around $5,960,559.33, so

>> 0.0006% of 21,900 was 0.1314 blocks

>> 0.0006% of 57,000XMR was 0.342XMR, or $35.76 at the exchange rate of $104.57.

So, on average, you could expect to earn $93.08 each month with this particular piece of equipment. Of course, you can't mine a fraction of a block, so when the numbers show that you mine, on average, 0.1314 block a month, what this really means is that, on average, you'd mine a block every 7.6 months or so, during 2019. Data today would be slightly different, of course.

Depending on various factors — the popularity of the cryptocurrency you want to mine, the amount of money you're willing to invest in equipment, and so on — you may find that the calculations are telling you that you'll mine a fraction of a block each month. What does that mean? What does it mean, for example, if it tells you that you'll mine 0.01 block each month? It means that, on average, you'll mine a block every 100 months! You may mine and discover a block the very first day, or you may have to wait years before you mine a block!

On average, over time — a hundred years, for example, considering all factors remain stable — you could expect to mine a block every 100 months or so (every 8.33 years). What this is telling you is that your numbers don't work! Your percentage of the hash rate simply isn't enough to mine solo, at least not with the equipment you have or are planning to use. You would need to increase your hash rate — by buying better equipment, or more of it — or you may try pool mining, which provides an effective mechanism for accruing steady mining rewards. (See Chapter 7 for more information on working with pools.) See the next section for how to calculate the pool mining numbers.

Calculating for pool mining

If you're mining through a pool, rather than solo mining, you approach the calculation a little differently. You need to know the total hash rate of the pool, how often the pool mines a block on average, and how much all the miners are paid each time a block is mined. From this, you can calculate your earnings.

We use a different example this time. Assume that you are mining Bitcoin with a Bitmain Antminer S9 with a 14 TH/s hash rate. (The Antminer S9 actually comes in a few different batch versions, with different hash rates, but we'll use the current highest, 14 TH/s.) You choose to point your mining hardware toward the Slush Pool, which typically mines 10 to 12 blocks per day with a pool hash rate of 5.0 EH/s (5 million TH/s).

We start by calculating your pool contribution percentage. Divide your hash rate by the total pool hash rate, and multiply by 100.

14 / 5,000,000 = 0.0000028

0.0000027 * 100 = 0.00028%

Thus, your hash rate, from your S9, is roughly 0.00028 percent of the Slush Pool's hash rate. So now, to find your estimated earnings for your contribution to the pool, you would take that percentage and multiply it by the average block rewards (the block subsidy and transaction fees).

Now, Slush Pool takes the entire block earnings, both block subsidy and transaction fees, subtracts 2 percent as a pool fee, and pays out the other 98 percent to its miners. At present, the block subsidy for Bitcoin is 6.25 Bitcoin (sometime in 2024, probably in May, this will decrease to 3.125). Transaction fees fluctuate from block to block and day to day, but currently average somewhere around 0.1 to 0.5BTC. Say the average block earns Slush Pool 12.9BTC, of which 98 percent (12.642) is paid out to the miners.

Say that Slush Pool mines 11 blocks a day. That's 139.062BTC being paid out to miners each day. But wait, you're calculating monthly numbers, so multiply that by 30.42 (to get a really average month!); 139.062 x 30.42 is 4,230.26604BTC paid out to miners each month, a considerable sum.

As you saw a moment ago, you are contributing 0.00028 percent of Slush Pool's hash rate; 0.00028 percent of 4,230.26604BTC is 0.01184474491BTC. How much is that in dollars? Well, that depends, of course. At the time of this writing, 1BTC = $11,220.20. (By the time you read this, it could be very different). Thus, 0.01142172BTC is, at the moment, worth $132.90.

So, in this scenario, you would earn $132.90 from a month of mining with an S9 toward the Slush Pool.

TECHNICAL STUFF

In our calculations, we assume a cleanly proportional sharing of the mining rewards. As we point out in Chapter 7, pool rewards are a little more complicated than this. Different pools calculate rewards in different ways, but Slush Pool uses the *scoring hash rate* method (see https://slushpool.com/help/reward-system), which can increase or lower your proportion based not only on the total number of hashes you contributed, but also how consistently your equipment was hashing. (Inconsistency may lead to earning a lower proportion. In theory, if you keep your mining equipment running 24/7, you may actually earn a little more than your percentage.)

So, now you know how much money you'll make each month, in your local fiat currency (and whether solo or pool mining). Next, you need to know how much it's going to cost to run the mine.

Your expenses

This step's a little simpler. You need to know how much you're spending in order to run your mining operation over a month. Add up these numbers:

>> Maintenance costs per month

>> Facility costs per month

>> Electricity costs per month

You may also amortize your equipment. Consider how long you are likely to use your equipment — how long it will remain viable considering increasing network hash rates and the increasing efficiency of new ASICs. You may, for example, divide the cost of your equipment by 36 and apply the value to your monthly expenses, allowing three years of use. Or perhaps you may allow for four years and divide by 48 months.

Calculating ROI

You're almost there, and the next step is so simple, you may have already jumped ahead. You know how much you'll earn each month (*Earnings*), and how much it's going to cost to run the operation (*Expenses*). So now you can calculate the profit and ROI like this:

Earnings − Expenses = Profit/Loss

If, for example, you're mining enough blocks each month to make $1,200 once the cryptocurrency is converted to dollars (or whatever fiat currency you work with), and you're spending $800 to run the operation, then

$1,200 − $800 = $400 profit

As for a percentage ROI, we calculate it like this:

(Profit or Loss/Expenses) * 100 = % ROI

So, with the previous example,

($400/$800) * 100 = 50% ROI

Of course, if you're losing money, the calculation looks a little different. Say that your expenses are still $800, but you're only earning $600 and thus losing $200 a month. Now the calculation looks like this:

(−$200/$800) * 100 = −25% ROI

For example, if you invested $1,000 into cryptocurrency mining over a certain period and your total revenue from the venture was $1,200, your profit would be $200 from a total investment of $1,000. The ROI formula for this exercise would work out to be 20 percent: ($200/$1,000) * 100 = 20%. But if your $1,000 investment only produced $800 in total revenue, your net profit would be −$200. Thus, your ROI calculation would work out to be negative 20 percent, and you should not have made that investment!

(−$200/$1,000) * 100 = −20%

Knowing the unknowns

Many variables exist in the cryptocurrency mining arena, and only some of them are within your control. As Donald Rumsfeld, one-time U.S. Secretary of State for Defense, famously stated, "There are known knowns — things we know that we know. There are known unknowns — things that we now know we don't know. But there are also unknown unknowns — things we do not know we don't know."

In this chapter, we help you figure out the known knowns: the cost of equipment and electricity, your hash rate, the network hash rate, and so on.

But you also need to be aware of the known unknowns. We don't know when the overall network hash rate will rise, or by how much, or whether it may fall. But we do know this is a possibility, and that it will affect the profitability of the mining operation. We don't know how much the value of the cryptocurrency we're mining will fluctuate, but we do know this is a possibility, and we know it will affect profitability, both up and down.

Unfortunately, you can't do much about the known unknowns. At least, we can't help you with them. These are things you'll have to guess at, perhaps based on your belief regarding what is likely to happen with the cryptocurrency you're mining, and you'll have to accept the risks that the unknown unknowns pose. That's the miner's life!

Our calculations are based on static metrics. Over time, your proportion of the network hash rate may well drop — though at times it could go up.

Projecting cryptocurrency mining returns into the future is a tricky exercise that contains many assumptions and different variables that will greatly skew the results of your projections. Some of these variables include network hash rate, which varies wildly from day to day — though it generally increases over time (at least for a successful cryptocurrency), which would reduce your returns as measured in that cryptocurrency. And there is also the cryptocurrency exchange rate, which also fluctuates frequently and can significantly alter your estimated returns.

As for the unknown unknowns, the things we don't even know are possible? Well, there really aren't that many in this realm — at least, we think that's the case, but of course, how would we know that for sure!?

Online profitability calculators

Cryptocurrency mining profitability is a difficult subject to grasp and even harder to accurately project. This chapter explains how you make these calculations. Luckily for us, many sites provide easy-to-use tools in which you input your mining equipment's data and get an estimated value for your cryptocurrency rewards, based on current network conditions and the different fluctuating variables.

These calculators also provide useful information when considering which cryptocurrency mining hardware to buy or use. There are weaknesses, though, because the calculators can't predict the future. (They know neither the known unknowns nor the unknown unknowns.) For example, they may overestimate the amount of cryptocurrency mining returns by basing the calculation on constant network hash rate, rather than allowing for increasing network hash rate and block difficulty. They may also underestimate the fiat-currency value of the mined cryptocurrency by not taking into account future increases in value (or overestimate by not considering drops in value). Still, these tools offer a great way to run the calculations, as long as you're aware of their weaknesses. You can see an example of one of these calculators in Figure 11-7.

Here are a few popular web-based cryptocurrency mining projection sites.

>> **CoinWarz:** This site will project cryptocurrency returns on a large variety of cryptocurrencies based on an expansive list of hash algorithms. It also has tools that will allow you to enter the data we looked at in this chapter to estimate and project how your mining hardware's specifications will perform on any given cryptocurrency (www.coinwarz.com/calculators).

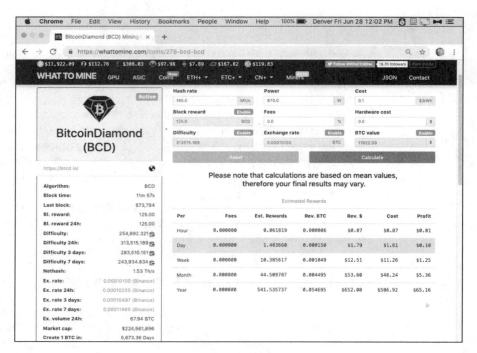

FIGURE 11-7:
A cryptocurrency
calculator at
WhatToMine.com.

>> **WhatToMine:** The WhatToMine site also works with a wide range of crypto-currencies, allowing you to estimate mining rewards for a large swath of hardware as well. They allow GPU, CPU, and ASIC hardware categories so that you can test out many different scenarios and hardware setups to discover what's right for you (`https://whattomine.com/calculators`).

>> **Braiins Insights:** The mining insights found here can provides a useful estimator that specializes in SHA-256 hashing for the Bitcoin network (`https://insights.braiins.com/en/cost-to-mine/`).

>> **Hashrate Index:** Another great tool for miners to use is the Hashrate Index calculator to try to estimate the mining ecosystem (`https://hashrateindex.com/tools/calculator`).

Historical estimates

You may find it useful to run a real-world model to see how your mining equip-ment would have performed historically. That is, you use historical data for the cryptocurrency you want to mine, combined with your equipment performance and costs, to see how much you would have earned or lost over a particular period.

You can do this fairly easily using the average network hash rate data from your selected cryptocurrency on a historical basis. You could enter your equipment's hash rate, and the varying hash rates for the cryptocurrency network over time, into a spreadsheet like this:

Date	Network TH/s	My TH/s	My Hash %
7/4/18	35728406.94	14	0.0000391845%
7/5/18	36528296.65	14	0.0000383265%
7/6/18	42660784.4	14	0.0000328170%
7/7/18	41594264.79	14	0.0000336585%
7/8/18	42127524.6	14	0.0000332324%
7/9/18	36261666.74	14	0.0000386083%
7/10/18	39727855.48	14	0.0000352398%
7/11/18	35995036.84	14	0.0000388943%
7/12/18	37594816.26	14	0.0000372392%
7/13/18	38128076.06	14	0.0000367183%
7/14/18	35461777.04	14	0.0000394791%
7/15/18	35461777.04	14	0.0000394791%

Ideally you'll want to find data you can download, of course. For Bitcoin, you can find this information at www.blockchain.com/charts/hash-rate. (Look for the little CSV button within the Export Data drop-down list that lets you download the data for the period you selected on your chart.) You can find the data for many other popular cryptocurrencies at https://bitinfocharts.com, though that service doesn't provide a download at present. Perhaps it will by the time you read this, but if not, it shouldn't take too long to type the values into your spreadsheet for, say, every five or ten days over a year. Or you may be able to find downloadable data for the particular cryptocurrency you are interested in from some other site.

So this spreadsheet takes your mining equipment's average hash rate for that network's hash algorithm (in the *My TH/s* column) and divides by that day's (or week's or whatever period you choose) network hash rate (*Network TH/s*) to show you the rolling percentage of the network hash rate that your equipment would have been mining. (Figure 11-8 shows an example of an estimated network hash rate percentage over time for a Bitmain Antminer S9.)

You can now multiply your rolling percentage value over time by the network mining rewards during that same period to arrive at an estimated value for your equipment's mining rewards. (Again, you can find this information for many cryptocurrencies at https://bitinfocharts.com.) For the Bitcoin network, the block subsidy is 6.25BTC per block, with around 0.08BTC additional earnings in transaction fees (it fluctuates, but we'll use that for a rough average), for a total of 6.33BTC. On average, 144 blocks are mined each day, resulting in roughly 911BTC earned by miners each day.

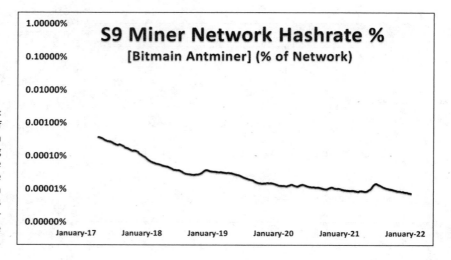

FIGURE 11-8: An example of the Bitcoin network rolling hash rate percentage calculation of an Antminer S9 14 TH/s miner over the entire network.

For example, say that you calculate on any given day that your SHA-256 mining hardware would have been 1 percent of the total Bitcoin network hash rate on that day. (Again, this is just for the sake of an example; 1 percent of network hash rate is a monstrous amount!) Take the mining rewards for that day, which for the Bitcoin network would be valued at around 911 Bitcoin, and multiply your 1 percent mining percentage by the daily network reward to arrive at your estimated earnings for the day, roughly 9.11BTC.

WARNING

Cryptocurrency mining reward projections and mining rewards as measured in your local fiat currency, even with the handy tools found online, are very fickle and can vary wildly in either the positive or negative directions. If the cryptocurrency you intend to mine becomes more difficult to mine, your projections will be inaccurately high. If the local fiat exchange rate of your chosen cryptocurrency goes up in value, your projections will be inaccurately low.

REMEMBER

As Nobel prize-winning physicist Niels Bohr said, "It's very hard to make predictions, especially about the future." There is no way to accurately predict your mining future, and these reward calculators depend on input variables that will inevitably change. Do not invest more into cryptocurrency mining than you are willing to lose! Mining is often one of the best ways to steadily acquire cryptocurrency over long periods of time, but it can also be a losing venture. Tread lightly, and as always, do your homework.

Chapter **12**

Reducing Negatives and Gaining an Edge

The cryptocurrency mining business has upsides and quite a bit of opportunity for rewards. However, a handful of obstacles and negative aspects are involved with mining as well as plenty of room for error. Some of these difficulties can be overcome and even used to your advantage to maximize your benefits from mining.

The impediments of profitable cryptocurrency mining include electrical costs, thermal heat discharge, an ever-changing cryptocurrency landscape, block difficulty increases, and fierce mining competition. We discuss strategies for tackling and mitigating these obstacles in this chapter, so you can maintain a competitive advantage in the cryptocurrency mining industry.

The cryptocurrency mining space is an incredibly competitive and fast-changing environment that forces miners to craft creative strategies to maximize returns and minimize cost and losses. You can pursue a few routes to help improve — or maintain — your mining, such as upgrading your mining hardware to the latest and greatest equipment, reducing electricity costs, using otherwise wasted heat, and staying up to date on current events. Strategies like this can help fully capitalize on your mining deployments and help maximize your cryptocurrency mining gains.

Profitability through Efficiency

In the cryptocurrency mining arena, every bit counts (pun intended). Profit margins are often slim, especially during market downturns in the exchange rate between the cryptocurrency and your fiat currency (for example, when the value of the cryptocurrency drops). This makes it especially important to squeeze every last benefit from the scarce and expensive cryptocurrency resources you're committing to mining.

Upgrading aging equipment

As block difficulty and total cryptocurrency network hash rate increase steadily over time, your proportion of the mining rewards will diminish, which (depending on the value of the cryptocurrency in your fiat currency) may also mean your overall profitability will drop. In other words, your mining equipment will eventually become unprofitable.

You can help mitigate aging equipment by upgrading your mining gear as it nears its end of life. The average useful life span of modern cryptocurrency-specific ASIC mining hardware is generally between four and five years. By upgrading to newer, more efficient mining hardware, you can maintain your cryptocurrency mining competitive advantage.

Mining different cryptocurrencies

Upgrading equipment often can be expensive and wasteful, however, so another route is to find alternative cryptocurrencies for your ASIC or GPU mining hardware to mine.

We cover the various types of cryptocurrency hashing algorithms and the different cryptocurrencies that use them in Chapter 8. Even if you're mining using an ASIC, the ASIC will work with other cryptocurrencies that use the same algorithm.

If your mining hardware becomes unprofitable mining the cryptocurrency you originally set out to mine, you may find that you can still generate rewards on other proof-of-work blockchains that use the same algorithm. Perhaps a new cryptocurrency has come on the scene since you began, or perhaps a cryptocurrency that you looked at and disregarded earlier has become more profitable. So keep your eyes and ears open and don't think you're stuck with your cryptocurrency mining choice forever.

Using exhaust heat

The intense computational processes involved in mining proof-of-work cryptocurrencies produce quite a bit of typically wasted heat exhaust. This is especially the case for application specific integrated circuits (ASICs) and for large-scale GPU mining rigs, as they are essentially electric space heaters converting electricity into heat while they steadily mine cryptocurrency.

A way to stack value and increase margins when mining cryptocurrency is to not waste this heat exhaust and instead utilize it for your own benefit. According to the U.S. Energy Information Association (EIA), the estimated winter heating bills of the average American household range from around $600 to $1,600, depending on home size, fuel source, and local climate. Figure 12-1 shows the past few winters of EIA data by fuel type as well as an average value from all sources. (The data is from www.eia.gov/todayinenergy/detail.php?id=37232.)

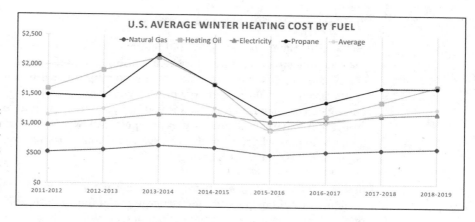

FIGURE 12-1:
EIA data on average winter heating costs from propane, heating oil, electricity, and natural gas.

If you live in a colder climate and are running a mining operation at home, the equipment is going to pump heat out, reducing the level of heating you need for your home, and thus in effect reducing the cost of your mining operation. (Take this into consideration when running your calculations; see Chapter 10.)

CREATIVE USES FOR HEAT DISCHARGE

Crafty cryptocurrency miners have put the heat discharge from mining equipment to good use in other ways. Some have used it to heat greenhouses or other grow facilities during the winter. Other enterprising miners have also created heat exchangers and used their mining heat exhaust to warm bodies of water, such as outdoor pools or hot tubs. Miners have also submerged mining equipment in mineral oil and other engineered fluids, which act as a dielectric, electrically insulating liquid to help dissipate the heat for reuse and to dampen the noise from the mining equipment. Admittedly, some of these more intricate methods of heat management would take quite a bit of skill and planning to properly deploy, but they are possible and have allowed creative miners to put their equipment's excess heat waste to good use.

Reducing electricity bills

As discussed in Chapter 10, electrical expenses for proof-of-work mining equipment make up the largest portion of operational expenditures for cryptocurrency mines. So reducing your electrical bills is obviously a good thing! It may be enough to push you into — or keep you in — profitability. The following sections discuss a few ways to save.

Utility rate structures

One way to reduce your electrical bill that may be available to you is to sign up for a special rate structure from your electric utility. Many electric utilities offer Time of Day rates, peak demand rates, or other such rates (rates that sometimes provide pretty decent discounts on energy prices). For example, if you sign up for Time of Day rates, you may find that even if you run your equipment 24 hours a day, you still end up paying less. You may pay 50 percent lower rates during the nonpeak hours, which may be most of the day, so even if you're paying twice that rate during peak hours, you're still saving.

Research your local utility provider's rates (or tariffs) to see whether any rate structures would help reduce your energy cost. (You can probably find the information you need on their website.) Commercial electrical rate structures normally provide cheaper bulk electric rates, but are not available for homes, a factor to take into consideration when trying to decide whether you need a home-based or industrial mining facility.

You should also shop around, if possible. Some states, such as Texas, have deregulated electrical markets that allow the consumer to choose from a variety of retail electrical providers (REPs). If you're in such an area, you really need to check around and find the best deal; you'll want to know how much electricity you're going to be using before you start shopping, of course.

Another option is to relocate your mining equipment to the service territory of an electrical utility that has more affordable electricity or a variety of rate structures that can benefit you. You may be surprised at how much electricity costs vary around the country. Figure 12-2 shows average electricity prices per kWh throughout the United States (www.eia.gov/electricity/monthly). As you can see, mining profitably in Hawaii is likely to be pretty tough (it's hot, too, so you have additional cooling costs). A state like Wyoming may be good, though. Not only does it have electricity costs near the bottom of the rankings, but it's one of the coolest states, too; one of the coldest states in the summer and in the top ten coldest states in the winter.

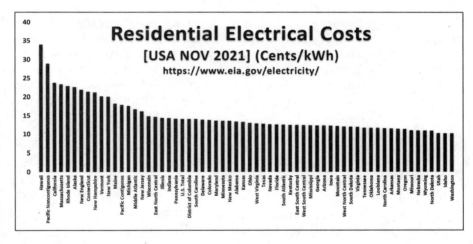

FIGURE 12-2: Average residential electricity cost per kWh by state compiled from EIA data produced in November 2021.

Alternative energy sources

Beyond researching alternative rate structures or transferring to a different retail electrical utility provider, you may have other options for securing more affordable electricity for your cryptocurrency mine. Cryptocurrency miners have sought out sources of excess electrical energy that would otherwise be wasted, such as areas with excess hydroelectricity or flared natural gas.

Perhaps these options are not practical for your mine. However, another option would be to explore alternative energy sources (renewable energy), ideally ones with zero fuel cost. Renewable energy technology is rapidly developing, and costs are dropping dramatically, to the point where, in many contexts, renewable energy is now cheaper than fossil fuel energy.

According to a team of researchers from MIT, solar panels now cost just 1 percent of the 1980 price. ("Solar is cost-competitive with natural gas and coal in most geographies in the United States," the team said. "We've already reached that threshold.") The researchers also expect prices to continue dropping, perhaps 40 percent over the next five years.

Wind and solar would be excellent auxiliary sources to reduce electrical grid consumption and would increase margins on cryptocurrency mining (though, of course, you need to factor in the capital costs; free energy is great, but you'll have the upfront equipment and installation costs).

Installing a wind tower at a residence or commercial facility may not be feasible, perhaps, but solar panels are more affordable and much easier to install, and they can be used in many situations, especially in a home application. Some electric utilities and most solar installation companies offer turnkey solutions that require little effort on the part of the consumer and may not even require upfront investment. If you went this route, you'd also have the benefit of trained, licensed professionals specifying your system and installing it. Solutions like this would allow for increased mining returns and less electrical consumption from the grid to help reduce your electrical bills, and thus increase your mining margins. And even if you stop mining, you will still be getting free energy to use or sell back to the utility.

Knowledge Is Power

TIP

The best method of checking the pulse of the burgeoning cryptocurrency mining industry is to stay up to date using online resources, such as social media and specific online forums covering the topic. Due to the infancy of this space, many news sources in the space can be misleading, downright inaccurate, or even propagate bought-and-paid-for content without a sponsored label. A recent study found that many of the top cryptocurrency news sites were posting sponsored content — essentially ads — under the guise of news.

This kind of misinformation makes it important to stay plugged into the community and various other peer-based resources: don't trust, verify. Check out the following list of resources that we like to pursue to stay up with current events.

>> **Bitcoin Talk:** Use Bitcoin Talk to inquire into almost any cryptocurrency topic, including (but definitely not limited to) mining. Despite the name, it's not just for Bitcoin anymore. You'll find many different cryptocurrencies being discussed. For example, it is where most popular alternative cryptocurrencies were announced prior to launch (https://bitcointalk.org).

- » **Bitcoin subreddit:** The Bitcoin subreddit provides a great forum for lots of breaking news and current events, and provides a window into the current sentiment in the community. It's not all serious stuff, though; you'll find plenty of memes, jokes, and other nonmining content, so do surf lightly (www.reddit.com/r/Bitcoin).

- » **BitcoinBeginners subreddit:** The BitcoinBeginners subreddit is an even better resource for recent entrants into the ecosystem, providing plenty of great information for newbies (www.reddit.com/r/BitcoinBeginners).

- » **CoinDesk:** CoinDesk is a decent news source in an industry riddled with faulty cryptocurrency news outlets. It also provides exchange-rate data from a variety of different cryptocurrencies (www.coindesk.com).

- » **CoinJournal:** CoinJournal is also a good source for cryptocurrency-related news, but clearly separates press releases from news articles so users can differentiate public relations from journalism (https://coinjournal.net).

- » **Bitcoin Magazine:** *Bitcoin Magazine* has long been a reliable news outlet in the cryptocurrency space. Although print releases of the magazine stopped years ago, it still provides good and consistent news coverage on its website (https://bitcoinmagazine.com).

- » **Merkle Report:** The Merkle Report curates a wide variety of relevant content from various news sources in the cryptocurrency space. It offers a good one-stop shop for news across the industry (www.merklereport.com).

- » **Messari:** Messari has a ton of cryptocurrency-focused data, research, and news from across the industry. It also offers a periodic daily newsletter to stay up to date on current trends (https://messari.io).

- » **Block Digest:** Block Digest is an excellent source of news in the form of a weekly podcast that features various community members discussing and digesting news and headlines from the Bitcoin space (www.youtube.com/c/blockdigest).

- » **Stack Exchange:** The Bitcoin Stack Exchange has a large trove of questions answered by other cryptocurrency enthusiasts. Anyone can post a question or an answer. If you are looking for specific insight, chances are someone has already answered the question you may have (https://bitcoin.stackexchange.com).

Why current events are important

Cryptocurrencies and blockchains act as an immutable record of data, indisputable information that is accessible to anyone with the tools and knowledge to look for it. This isn't the case with off-chain data, such as current events and news in the space, which is why it is very important to stay up to date on accurate information from reliable sources if you intend to mine cryptocurrency.

REMEMBER

Current events affect what's going on in the mining space. They can affect the value of the cryptocurrency, and thus, in response to fluctuation in the value, the network hash rate, your percentage of the network hash rate, the amount of blocks you'll mine, and ultimately your loss or profit.

There is plethora of news sources in the cryptocurrency mining space, but not all can be trusted. Some peddle misinformation with the intent of misleading you. Staying up to date on the latest and greatest in the mining industry is crucial to your continued success in the space. Reliable content from sources such as those listed in the preceding section is the best defense against spin and distortion from those that would lead you astray. Without information, you may find yourself mining a cryptocurrency without much future value, or on the uneconomical side of a blockchain fork.

The "fork wars"

You may have heard of the concept of *forking* a cryptocurrency. Understanding blockchain forks is critically important to maintaining your mining competitive advantage. Forks can provide a great little bonus — free money! But make the wrong decisions when a fork occurs, and you could end up losing money. If you're not paying attention and pick the wrong side of the cryptocurrency fork, you may find yourself mining the side of a fork that is not economical.

Also, some forks are pitched as upgrades by their participants, but tread lightly: You may find yourself being duped by bad actors and cheap imitations that simply copied the code and branding of the original cryptocurrency blockchain. This is another reason why being up to date on information and news in the cryptocurrency mining space is so vital to the long-term viability of your venture.

TECHNICAL
STUFF

The term *fork* is used in the software-development business to describe a situation in which a line of development splits into two lines, and the two different lines proceed independently of each other. Think of it as a fork in a road. You're driving along a road and arrive at a fork; you can take the left fork or the right fork, but whichever you take, you're now on a different road.

Software forks are especially common in the open-source community. Here's an example of a successful open-source fork (most are not successful, by the way): OpenBSD, an open-source operating system, is a fork of NetBSD that forked off from the original NetBSD development in 1995. NetBSD had already been in development for several years before that. After the fork, OpenBSD and NetBSD were two separate software systems, with different features, different software developers working on each one, and so on.

Now, in the cryptocurrency world, the term *fork* has an additional meaning. Certainly the software itself can be forked; a developer takes a copy of existing cryptocurrency software and begins modifying it and running a new cryptocurrency. For example, Ixcoin was an exact copy of the Bitcoin code that was launched in the early days of Bitcoin (in 2011). The founder took a copy of the Bitcoin code, set it up, and created a brand-new blockchain (that ran in exactly the same way as Bitcoin). It's still running, though not much activity occurs in the Ixcoin markets. In other cases, copies of Bitcoin have been downloaded, modified, and then set up as new cryptocurrency networks with new features, even using different algorithms. In fact, this has happened dozens of times.

TIP

However, *forking* can mean something else, something, from our perspective, far more important. Forking in the cryptocurrency space is what occurs when a node or group of nodes in a cryptocurrency system break away from consensus of the original blockchain. *Consensus* is the rule set that the nodes on the network comply with, so they ensure that all copies of the blockchain remain in sync and all agree on the transactions added to the blockchain. When nodes fork and fall out of consensus on the blockchain, an entire new chain of blocks is created; thus two different blockchains, two different networks, move forward from the fork point. They both have the same transaction history — the same blocks up until the fork point. But after the fork, there is no longer only one blockchain, one cryptocurrency, and one network; now, two blockchains, two cryptocurrencies, and two separate networks exist.

Some people in the cryptocurrency field refer to this situation — the hard forking of both the code and the blockchain — as forking, and the other kind of fork — taking the code and starting a brand-new blockchain — as *cloning.* Many of the blockchains in existence today are clones of the Bitcoin code, some with only slight modifications. In the case of Ixcoin, it began as a clone of the Bitcoin blockchain, but later the Ixcoin code and blockchain forked, producing another cryptocurrency named IOCoin. (At one point, an IOCoin was worth as much as $7.26; today, it's worth around 11 cents. It's sometimes suggested that IOCoin's lack of success is partly due to the fact that nobody knows how to spell or pronounce it!) By the way, here's a link to a great chart showing how many different cryptocurrencies have evolved — through forks and clones — from Bitcoin: https://mapofcoins.com/bitcoin.

Anyway, when we use the term *fork* or *forking* from now on in this discussion, we're referring to the forking of the blockchain, typically in conjunction with modifications to the software. That's the issue you need to understand if you're going to mine.

Here's what happens. A schism occurs in the developer community for a particular blockchain. One group wants to do something to the code that another group doesn't approve of. At some point, the disagreement reaches a point at which some of the developers are so dissatisfied that they break away. (The term *civil war* is sometimes used to describe the level of conflict in the community that leads up to a fork!)

For example, the cryptocurrency's code may be modified in some way, and some of the developers say, in essence, "No, we want the code to remain the way it was!" That's the situation with Ethereum Classic, by the way. Ethereum was forked in July 2016 (in response to the theft of around $50 million worth of ether, the blockchain was forked to restore the lost money). Some in the community felt this fork should not have been created, and thus continued using the original Ethereum code and blockchain. So then there were two networks, two blockchains, and thus two different cryptocurrencies.

In most cryptocurrency forks, the forked network is given a new name and ticker symbol. The Ethereum fork was a very unusual situation, though; the network that had forked away from the original network *kept the original name and the ticker symbol* (ETH)! The people who wanted to continue with the original blockchain and software, in a minority, were forced to come up with a new name (Ethereum Classic) and ticker symbol (ETC).

Thus Ethereum is a fork of what used to be known as Ethereum, but is now known as Ethereum Classic. The Ethereum fork is also unusual in that it's generally a minority that breaks away — that forks — from the original cryptocurrency. In Ethereum's case, the *majority* forked from the original code and blockchain, while a minority continued running the original software, network, and cryptocurrency.

Here's another example, but of the opposite situation: Bitcoin and Bitcoin Cash. In August 2017, a small group of Bitcoin developers forked the code in order to increase the blockchain's block-size limit. The majority continued developing on, and operating nodes with, the original code, and the minority developed the new, forked code and managed the new network and blockchain. The forked code was also renamed Bitcoin Cash (BCH).

Technically, forking is really cheap and easy; remember, most cryptocurrencies are open source, which means anyone can go to the code repository (usually on GitHub; here's the Bitcoin repository, for example: `https://github.com/bitcoin/bitcoin`), download the code, tweak it (change the consensus rules, for example), and relaunch as a new cryptocurrency. Because it's so cheap and easy to do this, hundreds, maybe thousands, of new cryptocurrencies have been created from forks of existing cryptocurrencies, and forks created from forks.

Many of the most popular cryptocurrency networks over the years have had small groups of their users change the rules of consensus and fork off, taking minority portions of their networks (the nodes and miners) with them. At the time of this writing, around 74-plus Bitcoin network forks — including Bitcoin Cash (BCH) and Bitcoin SV (BSV) — now exist as their own coins on separate, active, albeit less secure, cryptocurrency systems.

Other popular blockchains that have been forked many times include Ethereum (Ethereum Classic, Ether Gold, Ethereum Zero), Litecoin (Litecoin Cash, Super Litecoin), and Monero (Monero Original, Monero Classic, MoneroV). It is relatively inexpensive for developers to fork a cryptocurrency system and easy to mimic a blockchain with slight changes in the codebase and branding, so it's likely we'll continue to see forking into the future, and you need to be aware of that. (Litecoin, by the way, was itself a clone of the Bitcoin code — with significant modifications — though not a fork of the Bitcoin blockchain.)

WARNING

Each of the newly created minority-forked blockchains have a few things in common: a reduced node count, fewer developers, lower hash rate, and reduced blockchain security. We recommend treading lightly when dealing with forked blockchains and, in most cases, avoiding them completely. Some forks may not have *replay protection* enabled, which could lead to a loss of funds, and other forks drastically lose exchange rate value over time as measured in both local fiat currency and the original blockchain's cryptocurrency.

REPLAY PROTECTION

Replay protection is a technical safeguard that developers can implement prior to or during blockchain forks. Replay protection makes the transaction on the new forked blockchain invalid on the first blockchain, preventing duplicated transactions on both sides of the fork, and thus preventing nodes and users from spending or misspending funds after the fork. This replay protection helps to prevent what is referred to as a replay attack. A *replay attack* is a node mimicking the valid transaction message on one side of the forked blockchain and replaying it onto the second chain. This type of attack could potentially lead to a theft or accidental loss of funds on one side of the fork or the other. Without replay protection, it is also very easy for unsuspecting cryptocurrency users to lose funds accidentally or have them stolen in some other way.

Your forking decisions

If you are mining a cryptocurrency and it forks, you have two primary decisions to make:

>> Which fork do you continue mining?

>> What do you do with your new currency?

Imagine you're mining a coin called DummyCoin. And assume that instead of selling your mined DummyCoin as soon as you receive it, you have been keeping DummyCoin, so you have an address (maybe a few addresses) in the DummyCoin blockchain that are storing your mining revenues.

You realize that a fork war is going on in the developer community (because you have been paying attention to the community news and conversations), and one day, in fact, the cryptocurrency splits. Now there are two networks, two block-chains, and two cryptocurrencies (DummyCoin and DummerCoin).

The nice thing is that you now not only have coins in the DummyCoin blockchain, but you have the same number of DummerCoins in the DummerCoin blockchain. Remember, both cryptocurrencies use the same blockchain up until the split point. Thus, the founders of DummerCoin took a copy of the DummyCoin blockchain and began building on that, so all the original transactions from DummyCoin are now in the DummerCoin blockchain, too. The transactions — and your coins — are in *both* blockchains!

Now, this sounds great. You've just doubled your money, right? Well, not quite. First, there are situations in which the forked cryptocurrency fails quickly and badly, and you may not even be able to get to the new coins in DummerCoin. But say that in this case, DummerCoin does enjoy a modicum of success, and you are able to safely manage your DummerCoins in the new blockchain.

What do you mine?

Let's get back to those two decisions you have to make. The first decision is, what are you going to mine?: DummyCoin or DummerCoin? The original cryptocurrency or the forked cryptocurrency? In most cases, forked cryptocurrencies don't fare as well as the original cryptocurrency, from the perspective of the coin's market value. But deciding which to mine is a more complicated subject than that.

ANOTHER PROBLEM WITH CUSTODIAL WALLETS

Many people in the cryptocurrency arena disapprove of *custodial wallets* (wallets managed for you by another party). The belief is that you need to control your own private keys. Exchanges, for example, get hacked and have money stolen, and in some cases custodians have ripped off their clients. Well, here's another reason. There have been occasions in which exchanges have decided to not support forks of a cryptocurrency that they have on their platform. So, you have a wallet on an exchange managing DummyCoin. The cryptocurrency forks, so you now own both DummyCoin and DummerCoin. But the exchange does not set up a wallet that will allow you to manage the DummerCoin, so you may own it, but you can't get to it! (There have been lawsuits related to this very issue.) Not your keys, not your DummyCoin or DummerCoin.

You may find that the new cryptocurrency has a lower value, but is still worth mining because your equipment's hash rate is a larger percentage of the new network's hash rate than the previous network's hash rate. In other words, you'll be able to win more blocks on the new network than the old. On the other hand, what if the value of the new cryptocurrency declines precipitously? Perhaps, you may decide to mine the new cryptocurrency and sell the coins as soon as you receive them. But whatever you decide — to stick with the original network or move to the new one — it's a tricky decision, and it greatly depends on your values and your assessment of what is likely to happen to the forked cryptocurrency. Which is why you need to be plugged into the cryptocurrency's community, to get a feel for the community sentiment.

TIP

Here's a general rule: The side of the fork that has the most community support, that the most nodes are supporting, and that most of the hashing power is supporting, is the side that is most likely to survive, most likely to remain stable, and most likely to thrive. But these factors can also switch back and forth. As miners see an opportunity — a lower overall network hash rate on one side of the fork — they may switch their hashing power (many, perhaps most, miners are mainly motivated by profit, after all); as miners switch, network hash rate goes up, returns decrease, and some miners may leave, and so on. We generated a chart at the wonderful BitInfoCharts site that shows this phenomenon (see `https://bitinfocharts.com/comparison/hashrate-btc-bch.html`). In Figure 12-3, you can see the Bitcoin network hash rate (top line) in comparison with the Bitcoin Cash network hash rate when it first forked. As the Bitcoin Cash hash rate went up, the Bitcoin hash rate went down. Miners switched back and forth, and on a couple of occasions, the fork's network hash rate was actually higher than the original network's hash rate.

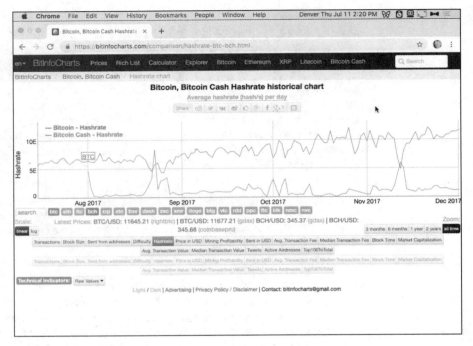

FIGURE 12-3:
A BitInfoCharts.
com chart
showing how
miners switched
their hash rate
back and forth
between the two
sides of the
Bitcoin and
Bitcoin Cash fork
during the Bitcoin
blocksize debate.

Cryptocurrency miners are opportunistic and motivated by profits (of course!). Thus, during times when Bitcoin Cash was slightly more profitable to mine than Bitcoin, portions of the SHA-256 hash rate moved to the Bitcoin Cash network, and vice versa. Bitcoin Cash profitability didn't last, however, and today Bitcoin Cash has around 1 percent of the hash rate that Bitcoin does. See `https://fork. lol` for real-time comparisons on hash rate, value, and miner rewards between these two forks.

There's another twist in the Bitcoin Cash story. Originally, Bitcoin Cash had more pledged support, as far as hash rate goes, than Bitcoin. Large companies that were providing a very significant portion of the network hash rate supported the idea of a fork, but many people did not. The majority of network nodes did not switch to the forked network, and most of the miners' hashing did not ultimately switch either, as you can see from Figure 12-3.

What should you do with your new cryptocurrency?

Assuming you can get to your DummerCoin, the cryptocurrency in the new blockchain, what do you do with it? First, consider if (and how) it has value. How can there be one cryptocurrency with a real-world value, a currency that can be converted into goods or fiat currency, and all of a sudden there are two, and both have value?

Well, it all depends on whether people want to buy the new cryptocurrency. There may well be a futures market before the fork actually occurs, in which the market will set a value for the new coin. Such markets will generally value *both* sides of the upcoming fork, providing some idea of what the market is thinking, and perhaps help you decide which currency is most likely to survive and thrive. The currency with the highest future value is being voted for, in effect, by investors and the cryptocurrency community. But, regardless, once the fork occurs, you then have coins that can be sold, if someone out there is willing to buy. Sometimes they are (and sometimes they aren't).

There's no reason to believe, however, that both coins will have the same value. One side of the fork will typically be more successful than the other, and value may slip from one side to another as the market (the multitudes of investors) make their choices. If people really like DummerCoin, then DummerCoin may rise in value, while DummyCoin drops a little.

In the case of Ethereum, for example, the forked side became far more valuable than the original side. (Remember, Ethereum Classic was the original software, network, and blockchain, while Ethereum was the fork.) At the time of this writing, Ethereum Classic is worth just 1/50 of Ethereum; so the fork is worth more. On the other hand, Bitcoin Cash, a fork of Bitcoin, is currently worth merely 1/90 of the Bitcoin price; in other words, the fork is worth far less.

WARNING

If one side of the fork is clearly supported by a minority, or thought by the community to be somehow technically inferior, then it's likely that many owners will sell, either dumping their old coin for the newly forked cryptocurrency, or vice versa. One coin will crash while the other will skyrocket.

So there's no clear answer. In general, it does seem likely that the new cryptocurrency will be more valuable in the first few days of its life and drop off as enthusiasm wanes. That seems to have happened frequently, but there's no hard-and-fast rule that says this will happen.

In general, forks die

Forking a cryptocurrency is a risky business. It's likely that most forks will die or at least fade away to insignificance. Clearly, some don't, however. Ethereum is still around, bigger than the original blockchain. Bitcoin Cash may not be worth anywhere near as much as Bitcoin, or as much as it was when it forked, but it is still alive (in fact, it has also forked, and is likely to fork again *ad infinitum*), and on the day we wrote these words, more than one billion U.S. dollars' worth of Bitcoin Cash were bought and sold. It's very hard to predict these things, which is why keeping up with community sentiment is so important as well as understanding the fundamentals.

Here Today, Gone Tomorrow

You need to keep an eye on trends, within both the cryptocurrency you are mining and the alternatives. It's a simple fact that cryptocurrencies are very volatile. A hugely productive cryptocurrency today may be worthless tomorrow.

Zcash (ZEC) is a great example. When Zcash launched in 2016, it was very popular, greatly hyped by the community, and the first few hours of trading were crazy. As miners mined blocks and were rewarded with Zcash coins, and those coins came onto the market, they were snapped up. In Figure 12-4, you can see a chart we created at CoinMarketCap.com (see `https://coinmarketcap.com/currencies/zcash`), showing the first few days of Zcash's life, priced in both U.S. dollars and Bitcoin.

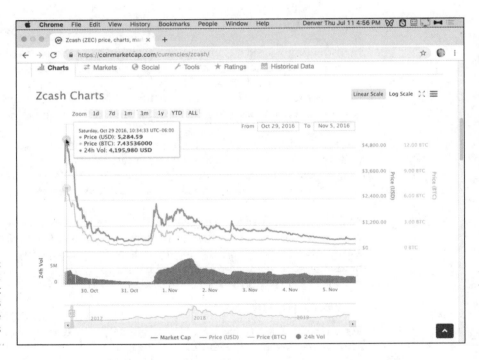

FIGURE 12-4:
A CoinMarketCap.com chart showing Zcash's wild pricing ride the first few days of its life.

Within hours of launch, it was trading at around $5,200 a coin and was worth more than 7 Bitcoin. Six days later, it was worth less than $600 and around three quarters of a Bitcoin. (Today? Less than $100 and around 0.0025BTC!)

Another classic example is Auroracoin (AUR). There was huge hype around this coin; it was, in theory, supposed to be an Icelandic Bitcoin, and even to act as an alternative to the Icelandic króna. Every Icelandic citizen was supposed to receive some (in the end, around 11 or 12 percent of the population did receive Auroracoin). AUR launched on the markets with a value of around $3 USD, reached almost $100 within a week, and then began dropping. Today, it's worth about 11 cents (about $65 worth traded on the world's Auroracoin markets today!)

Cryptocurrencies come and go. What's worth mining today may be a total waste of time tomorrow. So stay informed, monitor the community, and keep your eyes peeled for opportunities.

Evaluating Your Mining Resources

You need to know the value of the equipment, resources, and time you plan to dedicate to cryptocurrency mining. Having a good grasp on this information makes you better prepared to gain and maintain an edge while mining. In Chapter 11 we discuss the various types of mining profitability tools found online, which are great resources to use when estimating your mining income.

However, some aspects of cryptocurrency mining systems may make those predictions slightly inaccurate as you project further into the future. These aspects include block difficulty levels, mining competition, and ultimately, diminishing return of cryptocurrency rewards.

Increasing mining competition

As blockchains become more popular and mining equipment more capable, cryptocurrency mining trends toward a tougher, more competitive environment. As more miners spin up equipment pointed to your chosen cryptocurrency's proof-of-work algorithm, this leads to the same scheduled amount of predetermined coin issuance being split between more miners and hash rate.

Increasing block difficulty

Over time, as more miners and more effective mining equipment connect to a blockchain, the block difficulty will automatically increase to ensure block issuance time interval stability — that is, that the same amount of cryptocurrency is issued, on the correct schedule, regardless of how much computing power is being used to mine it.

Over the Bitcoin network's history, block difficulty has trended upward. There have only been nine months in the Bitcoin network's decade-long life where the block difficulty finished at a value lower than it started with; in other words, block difficulty reduction is a fairly rare occurrence on the Bitcoin network, and on other successful cryptocurrency networks. The increase in competition will lead to blocks being harder to find. Thus, your mining equipment, with a constant hash rate, will be less effective at finding blocks or contributing to a pool.

Diminishing returns due to halving events

With the increase of competition, hash rate, and block difficulty, your mined cryptocurrency rewards, as measured in the cryptocurrency you are mining, will be reduced.

There is also the block subsidy halving cycle to be aware of. On the Bitcoin network, every 210,000 blocks (or roughly every four years), the amount of Bitcoin issued to miners is cut in half. On May 11, 2020, the Bitcoin block subsidy halved, from 12.5 Bitcoin per block awarded to the winning miner, to 6.25. Sometime in the middle of 2024, the Bitcoin block subsidy will be halved, from the current 6.25 Bitcoin per block awarded to the winning miner, to 3.125. (The miner's reward comprises the block subsidy — the new coins issued — and the transaction fees.)

These issuance halving events will further affect the amount of cryptocurrency your equipment will earn. This trend of diminishing mined cryptocurrency returns is something to be very wary of when considering if mining is right for you. Of course, if the value of the cryptocurrency goes up (when measured in terms of dollars or whatever local fiat currency you are working with), there's still potential for profit. If, for example, the value of Bitcoin triples before the halving event, well, you're still ahead of the game. However, if the value of the cryptocurrency drops *and* the block subsidy halves, well, you really are in trouble.

These halving events are not unique to the Bitcoin network. Many other cryptocurrencies reduce the block subsidies periodically, so this concept affects a wide range of cryptocurrencies.

The BitInfoCharts.com website offers a historical perspective on how much reward a miner would have earned with a tera hash per second (TH/s) of SHA-256 mining capability per day as measured in present-day U.S. dollars, using the present-day exchange rate. This graph from `https://bitinfocharts.com/comparison/bitcoin-mining_profitability.html` provides a good perspective on diminishing mining rewards over time (see Figure 12-5). It takes into account the block subsidies and the halving episodes (the BTC icons on the chart show a description of important events when you let the mouse pointer sit on them for a moment, including halving events).

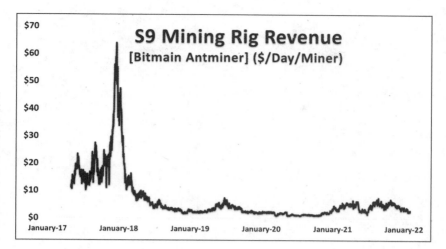

FIGURE 12-5:
A revenue chart showing the Bitcoin mining profitability of a single Antminer S9 14 TH/s, in U.S. dollars per day, from when the miner was shipped to time of writing.

The chart still gives a good estimation of how computing power has in effect been devalued over time. That is, it takes far more computing power to get the same result. Back at the beginning of 2019, an S9 mining on the Bitcoin network would have earned you over $60 a day. Now, you'd earn less than $5 a day.

These earnings tell a different story when measured in Bitcoin, however. Note, by the way, that the chart in Figure 12–6 is a *logarithmic* chart; the dramatic reduction would appear even more so in a linear chart.

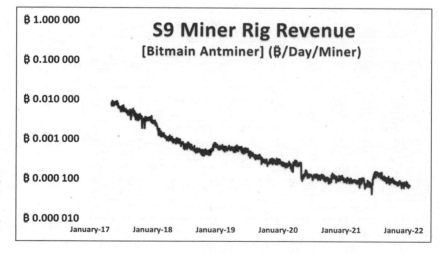

FIGURE 12-6:
The logarithmic chart showing the Bitcoin mining profitability of 14 TH/s, in Bitcoin per day, from 2017 to time of writing.

Chapter **13**

Running Your Cryptocurrency Business

O nce you're in business — you've determined what cryptocurrency to mine, deployed mining equipment, and have collected rewards back to your cryptocurrency wallet — the next issue to deal with is what you're going to do with your cryptocurrency earnings.

In fact, you have a variety of things to consider. You need to watch the market conditions for the cryptocurrency you're mining and others that you may consider switching to. You also need to understand the tax liabilities incurred during your mining adventure — both keeping your cryptocurrency and selling your earnings will have implications. (As Ben Franklin said, nothing's certain but death and taxes!) We also discuss scaling up your mining deployments and upgrading your equipment when it becomes obsolete or unprofitable.

What to Do with Your Mined Cryptocurrency

You can do various things with your mined cryptocurrency. With cryptocurrency being a scarce, electronic, decentralized digital asset that is borderless, sovereign, censorship resistant, and portable, you have many ways to use it.

Convert your cryptocurrency

The most obvious thing, of course, is to sell your mined cryptocurrency, most likely through an exchange, for your local fiat currency. After all, your business has expenses, most notably the cost of the equipment and electricity, and these bills have to be paid somehow. You may also want to recover the initial expense of setting up your cryptocurrency mining operation, and in most cases, you won't be paying bills directly with cryptocurrency.

You can often buy mining equipment with cryptocurrency — most commonly Bitcoin — as we discuss later in this chapter, but few utilities accept cryptocurrency, and if you've just begun mining, you probably bought your equipment with dollars. We discuss how to pay bills with cryptocurrency in the upcoming section, "Buying equipment and paying bills."

You should consider a number of things when converting your cryptocurrency:

>> **Would you be better off holding the cryptocurrency?** That's a subject we come back to in the section, "Hodling your cryptocurrency," later in this chapter.

>> **Are you mining a very volatile cryptocurrency?** If so, you may want to dump it as soon as you mine it, converting it into fiat currency or another cryptocurrency, one that you feel is more likely to increase in value, or at least hold value.

>> **What are the tax liabilities for converting your mined cryptocurrency into fiat currency?** (In fact, you'll encounter tax liabilities if you don't, too!) We cover this subject later in this chapter in the section, "Tax and Your Mining Business."

Buying equipment and paying bills

You may want to just pay bills and make purchases directly using your cryptocurrency. You *can* often buy mining equipment using cryptocurrency. Newegg, for example, one of North America's largest electronics retailers, accepts Bitcoin, and companies that build mining equipment or otherwise cater to the mining or cryptocurrency markets typically also accept cryptocurrency.

However, they typically accept only a small range of cryptocurrencies — generally Bitcoin, though sometimes also a few other popular cryptocurrencies. While gateways exist, such as CoinGate (https://coingate.com), that help ecommerce stores integrate far more cryptocurrencies (CoinGate currently accepts around 70), in general, most stores accept only Bitcoin and one or two others.

Here's a short list of places you can spend your Bitcoin (some also accept other cryptocurrencies), but many more are out there.

>> **AT&T:** www.att.com

>> **DISH:** https://my.dish.com

>> **Microsoft:** www.microsoft.com

>> **Newegg:** www.newegg.com

>> **Overstock:** www.overstock.com

>> **Virgin Galactic:** www.virgin.com

Coinmap (https://coinmap.org) can also help you locate many other local retailers where you can spend Bitcoin.

Paying with crypto when you can't pay with crypto

Various services allow you to spend cryptocurrency with retailers and service providers that don't accept cryptocurrency. For example, Amazon doesn't accept cryptocurrency. However, services such as Moon (https://paywithmoon.com) and Purse (https://purse.io) let you buy at Amazon using cryptocurrency.

For example, Moon lets you use Bitcoin, Bitcoin Cash, ether, and Litecoin to make purchases on Amazon. But, of course, all you are doing is converting your cryptocurrency and making a purchase in the same process; Moon acts as an exchange and payment service, taking your cryptocurrency, exchanging it for dollars, and then paying Amazon for you.

Those two companies work specifically with Amazon, but various others have sprung up recently that offer a Bitcoin or cryptocurrency-based bill-pay service in easy-to-use applications. The concept is straightforward: you make a purchase; the company then pays the retailer using dollars or other local fiat currency; you then pay the company in cryptocurrency. Some of these companies even provide a credit card. Coinbase, for example, perhaps the largest U.S.-based cryptocurrency exchange, provides a Visa card (see Figure 13-1). Use it anywhere you can use a Visa card, and Coinbase pays the bill and deducts the equivalent value of cryptocurrency from your Coinbase account.

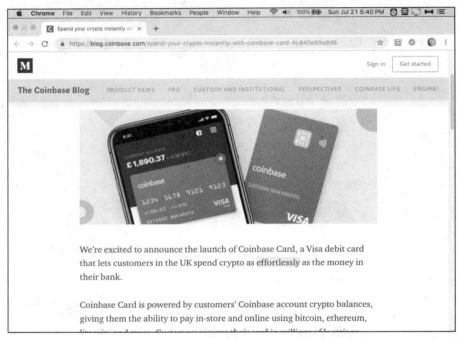

FIGURE 13-1: Coinbase, a large exchange, lets you spend your cryptocurrency using a credit card.

Source: www.coinbase.com/card

Here are a few other companies you can check out.

>> **Bitrefill** (www.bitrefill.com): Gift cards and mobile-phone refills; 1,650 businesses in 170 countries.

>> **Gyft** (www.gyft.com): Buy gift cards with Bitcoin.

>> **Living Room of Satoshi** (www.livingroomofsatoshi.com): An Australian company that lets users pay credit cards and BPay online banking bills with Bitcoin.

>> **Piixpay** (www.piixpay.com): An Estonian bill pay company, operating in 120 countries, including the United States.

>> **Paid by Coins** (https://paidbycoins.com): Another Aussie company working with BPay, but that also allows users to purchase Australian gift cards.

Expand or upgrade your mining operation

Later in this chapter (see the section, "Scaling Up?"), we discuss the subject of expanding and upgrading your business. Cryptocurrency mining hardware is often sold directly from manufacturers in local fiat currency, but they may accept only Bitcoin or other cryptocurrencies. Some also accept wire transfers, and if you have ever gone through that painstaking process, you will understand why Bitcoin and cryptocurrencies are such an innovation. So, of course, you might also buy your expansion or upgrade equipment directly using cryptocurrency. Again, such purchases are business expenses; you won't be paying tax on the mining income you use to buy more equipment.

But don't forget the tax

Your mine is a business. You spend money with the intention of making money — that is, making more money than you spend. That's what profit is, and it's taxable!

Consider that your purchases are part of your taxation picture. If you use your cryptocurrency to make business purchases — to pay utility bills, buy new mining equipment, pay rent for a mining facility, and so on — those expenses are tax deductible. (Exactly *how* you deduct them is complicated, but we get to that later in this chapter — see the section, "Tax and Your Mining Business.")

However, if you use your cryptocurrency to make personal purchases — groceries, your apartment rent or mortgage, nights on the town, and so on — then those expenses are *not* deductible. That is, they become taxable to you personally. They are regarded as payments to you personally, from your business.

Hodling your cryptocurrency

You can choose to do nothing but keep possession of your mined cryptocurrency rewards as an investment, with the expectation that eventually their value will increase. This is often known within the cryptocurrency community as *hodling*. Why? Because way back when, in the distant cryptocurrency past (that is, 2013), someone in a Bitcoin forum mistyped a message. Intending to say that he was planning to hold on to his Bitcoin, with the solid belief that its price would rise, he instead wrote, "I AM HODLING!" The message poster claimed he was drinking whisky at the time that he posted this message. (You can see it here if you're interested. It is somewhat entertaining, and hey, you're seeing a bit of Bitcoin history live: https://bitcointalk.org/index.php?topic=375643.0.)

LAW-ABIDING TAXPAYER, OR CRYPTO ANARCHIST?

There's a strong crypto anarchist thread running through the cryptocurrency community. What's a *crypto anarchist,* you ask? The term was likely first coined (if you excuse the pun!) by Tim May, in his 1988 *Crypto Anarchist Manifesto.* He explained that cryptography was "on the verge of providing the ability for individuals and groups to communicate and interact with each other in a totally anonymous manner. . . . Interactions over networks will be untraceable. . . . These developments will alter completely the nature of government regulation, the ability to tax and control economic interactions. . . ."

Crypto anarchists believe in the use of cryptography to protect personal, economic, and political freedoms. These freedoms have to be protected from the state, crypto anarchists believe. And, quite frankly, many don't believe in paying taxes. We're going to assume in this chapter that that's not you. We're also going to assume that you want to stay on the right side of the state, at least as far as paying taxes goes.

Anyway, the terms *hodl* and *hodling* have now become part of the cryptocurrency culture. The principle is simple. If you are convinced the cryptocurrency will rise in value, why would you sell? If you're so sure it will go up, then hodl!

In fact, this choice is very popular, and the long-term scarcity of many cryptocurrencies and the community's expectation that the value will go up often makes this a self-fulfilling prophecy. (But not always. Many of the smaller cryptocurrencies have dropped to zero.)

We're not going to tell you whether to hodl or sell. Both choices come with risk. Many people have lost huge sums of money investing in cryptocurrencies. But many multimillionaires have been made, too.

In fact, with the exception of a catastrophic one-year crash, from mid-December 2017 to late December 2018, Bitcoin has been an incredible investment. Had you purchased in August 2017, and held your Bitcoin for four years until the time of this writing (January 2022), your investment would have increased more than eightfold. Investors who have held since May or June of 2016 have seen the value increase around 85 times (see Figure 13-2.) Still, past performance is no guarantee of future results, as they say in the investment business! And Bitcoin is the world's primary cryptocurrency; others are often much less successful in value appreciation. Always do your research on the viability and history of your cryptocurrency before you decide to hodl for any significant amount of time.

FIGURE 13-2:
This A graph of various types of network value estimations for the Bitcoin network over the past nine years.

Source: https://charts.woobull.com/bitcoin-valuations

So, should you sell, or should you hodl? Keep an eye on the market and make your own decision!

Invest your cryptocurrency

Some ventures can be invested in via Bitcoin or other cryptocurrencies. Many early Bitcoin miners have invested in cryptocurrency-related businesses using their mining profits. For example, Kraken, a major cryptocurrency exchange, was mostly bootstrapped by early Bitcoin investors.

Does this make sense? Perhaps. But also consider that when you invest your cryptocurrency into a stock, real estate, or other business opportunity, you are betting that the return on the investment will be greater than the return on simply hodling that cryptocurrency. That hasn't always been true.

On the other hand, you may consider investing mining profits into other businesses as a form of investment diversification, spreading your overall financial risk by holding different types of investments with different risks and benefits.

Donate your cryptocurrency to charity

Many organizations accept cryptocurrency donations to help support their charitable efforts. There may also be tax benefits associated with donating assets, such as cryptocurrency, to charity. Following are just a few noteworthy efforts you could donate to that accept cryptocurrency donations.

>> **American Red Cross:** www.redcross.org/donations/ways-to-donate/corporate-supporters.html

>> **BitGive:** www.bitgivefoundation.org/donate

>> **Electronic Frontier Foundation:** https://supporters.eff.org/donate

>> **Free Software Foundation:** https://my.fsf.org/donate

>> **Internet Archive:** https://archive.org/donate

>> **Tor Project:** https://donate.torproject.org

>> **United Way:** www.unitedway.org/get-involved/ways-to-give/donate-bitcoin

>> **The Water Project:** https://thewaterproject.org/donate-crypto

>> **WikiLeaks:** https://shop.wikileaks.org/donate

>> **Wikipedia:** https://donate.wikimedia.org/wiki/Ways_to_Give#Cryptocurrency

Gift your cryptocurrency

One use of your freshly mined cryptocurrency that is sure to get friends, family, and other individuals interested in finding out more about blockchains and cryptocurrencies is to have them try it out for themselves. Gifting them some of your cryptocurrency is a great educational tool as it requires them to set up a wallet and to witness a transaction. There is no direct tax benefit to you, the person giving away the cryptocurrency (except that you won't pay tax on any gains you've made by hodling).

But, on the other hand, the person receiving the gift doesn't have to declare it to the Internal Revenue Service or to pay tax on it, so many people use gifts to pass on wealth to their children. There is something known as the *gift tax* — above a certain (truly huge) level, the giver has to pay tax on the money given. But in the United States in 2019, that's anything over $15,000. That is, no tax is due on the first $15,000 gifted during the year. And, in fact, there's an $11.7 million lifetime exclusion in addition to the $15,000 a year.

Talk to your tax advisor if you're making enough mining money to consider this. (But before you do, read *The Millionaire Next Door* [Taylor Trade Publishing]. Author William Danko will probably convince you *not* to give money to your kids; it really hurts them. Sorry, kids!)

Determining When to Sell

Cryptocurrency miners may believe in the longevity of the blockchain system they decide to mine and decide to part ways with their coins only when it's absolutely needed to cover expenses or due to market conditions, such as exchange rate downturns.

On the other hand, miners sometimes take a different approach and sell very frequently to quickly realize any profits generated from mining. They may feel that as long as a profit is there to be taken, it should be taken, because the cryptocurrency price could drop at any moment.

There isn't a right or wrong answer (well, until you look back with hindsight, of course!), and individual miners must make these types of decisions themselves. If or when you do decide to sell, however, a handful of helpful resources can assist you to determine the right timing and the right amount to part with. Important ramifications also come with selling, including tax liabilities and custodial exchange rates and associated fees, which we discuss later in the chapter (see the section, "Tax and Your Mining Business").

Cryptocurrency market indicators

Market indicators may help you get a feel for where your cryptocurrency's market is headed. No market metric is a 100 percent predictor, but they are still good resources to use when trying to figure out what's going on in the market cycle. Here are a few examples of metrics related to Bitcoin.

>> **Mayer Multiple:** The Mayer Multiple, created by Trace Mayer, tracks the current price of Bitcoin in U.S. dollars, divided by the 200-day moving average price (a *moving average* is one that filters out short-term fluctuations). For example, if the price today is $12,000, and the price over the previous 200 days has been on average $6,000, then the Mayer Multiple is 2. This indicator gives a good relative signal as to when the market has spiked up in price or, inversely, crashed. Higher multiples are warning signs; lower multiples are suggestions that it may be a good time to buy (https://stats.buybitcoin worldwide.com/mayermultiple/).

» **NVT ratio:** The *network value to transactions ratio* (NVTr) tracks the dollar value of on-chain cryptocurrency transactions to the relative total network value. It is calculated by dividing the daily average market capitalization (or total market value) in dollars by the amount of daily on-chain transactions in dollars. In other words, it's a measure of how much transaction activity is going on with the cryptocurrency (see Figure 13-3).

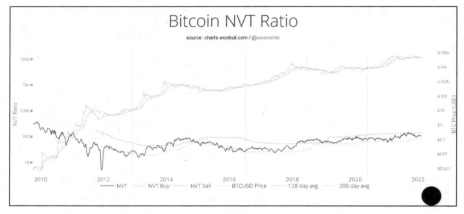

FIGURE 13-3:
The Woobull NVT
Ratio chart, an
indication of
activity in the
Bitcoin market.

Source: http://charts.woobull.com/bitcoin-nvt-ratio

» **NVT signal:** The NVT signal is very similar to the NVT ratio. However, instead of taking the market value and dividing it by the daily on-chain transaction total, it is the 90-day average market value divided by the daily on-chain transaction value (http://charts.woobull.com/bitcoin-nvt-signal).

» **Realized market capitalization:** A popular metric in the cryptocurrency space is the market capitalization, which is calculated by multiplying the current market price of a cryptocurrency by the total amount of the cryptocurrency in circulation. The realized market capitalization, however, is calculated by adding up the market value of each coin at the time it was last spent as a transaction on the blockchain. This page has a great explanation of how the RMT metric works; look for the link to the actual chart lower on the page: https://coinmetrics.io/realized-capitalization.

» **MVRV ratio:** The MVRV ratio, or *Market Value Realized Value ratio,* is calculated by taking the market value or capitalization and dividing it by the realized market value or capitalization. This indicator can help put the market value in perspective to detect over- and undervaluations (http://charts.woobull.com/bitcoin-mvrv-ratio).

Two of the sites we mention in the preceding list — Woodbull Charts (`http://charts.woobull.com`) and Coin Metrics (`https://coinmetrics.io`) — have really interesting and potentially useful metrics. Dig around a little and see what you find!

The charts we mention are all for Bitcoin. How about other cryptocurrencies, though? You may still be able to find such metrics for other cryptocurrencies. Coinmetrics, for example, provides them for literally dozens of cryptocurrencies. The chart shown in Figure 13-4 shows an NVT measurement for both BTC (Bitcoin) and VTC (vertcoin). Notice the option boxes at the bottom of the screen? You can add (or remove) cryptocurrencies to (or from) the chart by clicking these boxes, and you can find more choices in the More box at the top left of these three rows. (You can't retrieve all metrics for all cryptocurrencies.)

FIGURE 13-4:
A Coinmetrics NVT chart, showing data for two different cryptocurrencies.

Lots of cryptocurrency data and statistics websites can be very useful, helping you put each cryptocurrency in perspective. Here are a few.

>> **Bitcoin Visuals:** `https://bitcoinvisuals.com`

>> **Bitcoinity:** `https://data.bitcoinity.org/markets/volume`

>> **BitInfoCharts:** `https://bitinfocharts.com/cryptocurrency-charts.html`

>> **Coin Dance:** `https://coin.dance`

>> **Coin Metrics:** `https://charts.coinmetrics.io/network-data`

>> **CoinDesk:** `www.coindesk.com/data`

>> **Crypto51:** `www.crypto51.app`

>> **How Many Confs:** `https://howmanyconfs.com`

Unfortunately, many of the smaller cryptocurrencies are simply not popular enough for folks to do this type of in-depth study or real-time graphical analysis. Still, watching metrics for other cryptocurrencies can at least give you a feel for the overall market sentiment for cryptocurrencies in general, and often cryptocurrencies do move up or down together.

Where to sell: Cryptocurrency exchanges

If you intend to cash out and exchange your cryptocurrency earnings for local fiat, you should consider cryptocurrency marketplaces and exchanges. Some exchanges have a good track record, some exchanges are risky, and others are outright frauds. Some exchanges ban individuals from certain jurisdictions to avoid complying with laws associated with citizens of certain countries.

Exchanges collect trading fees, which depend on the exchange and the trade being performed, and different exchanges also have different market rates. In other words, selling your cryptocurrency on some exchanges will be more profitable (meaning you'll get more dollars for your crypto) than on others. How do you tell which is best? Here are a few resources that can help:

>> https://data.bitcoinity.org/markets/books/USD provides cool charts comparing ten different exchanges.

>> https://en.bitcoin.it/wiki/Comparison_of_exchanges provides a comparison between a couple of dozen exchanges.

Dollar Cost Averaging

Dollar cost averaging, or DCA, is a very common investment strategy that is intended to reduce exposure to volatility that comes from making large, high-cost purchases of an asset. The idea is that you avoid the harm caused by a sudden decline in value of the asset immediately after making a large purchase. Instead, you spread your purchase over a long time period. (Find out more on DCA here: www.investopedia.com/terms/d/dollarcostaveraging.asp.)

Many miners like the DCA concept, because in effect, that's what mining is: buying a little of the cryptocurrency each month, rather than buying a large lump sum. For example, you may invest $10,000 in mining gear and then mine month by month, instead of taking that $10,000 and buying your favorite cryptocurrency all at once.

Dollar cost averaging your purchases

Assume that you intend to invest $1,200 dollars into an asset such as Bitcoin this year (or stocks, bonds, whatever). You could make that purchase all at once in an attempt to time the buy at a low price, for a relative discount on your trade. However, if you were to dollar cost average that purchase over the course of a year, you would buy periodically — say, once a month. Thus, instead of spending $1,200 right now, you'd spend $100 per month over the entire year.

In bear markets, with a downtrend in price, this strategy is effective as it does not expose your investment to all of the reductions in price. In fact, each time you buy, you'll be getting the asset at a lower price. However, in bull markets, where the price is trending up, the DCA method would result in lower quantities of the asset being acquired, at overall higher prices.

The best thing to do, of course, is to invest everything at once into the asset at the point at which it's at its lowest price; but how do you do that? That's called market timing, and it's essentially impossible. You may be lucky and pick the market just right, but you won't be able to do that consistently.

So DCA is a way to spread risk. It's also a way for you to avoid FOMO (Fear Of Missing Out) investing. Instead of jumping into a market and grabbing a big stake, because you've seen the price jump up recently — because you're scared you're going to miss a huge opportunity — DCA provides a more disciplined mode of investing, almost set and forget. (Well, you have to remember to make the purchase each month.) On the other hand, some exchanges — such as Coinbase — let you set up automatic periodic purchases.

In fact, it may be argued that what we are really discussing here is known as *automatic investing*, which is similar to DCA but subtly different. We use the term *dollar cost averaging*, because that's the term people commonly use in the cryptocurrency arena (and, actually, in other areas of investing).

DCA works really well in markets that trend down for extended periods and then back up. DCA reduces your losses as the market declines (every time you buy an asset, the asset costs less than the previous time) and increases your profits when the market recovers (because you will have purchased much of the asset at a lower price than an original lump-sum purchase).

Here's an example. Say that you purchased a single Bitcoin on December 9, 2017. You would have spent around $13,680 (depending on the time of day, of course). During the month of July 2019, your Bitcoin would be worth $10,011. You've lost. But say, instead, you dollar cost averaged. Instead of spending $13,680 all at once, you invested $684 on that date and each of the following 19 months. Your Bitcoin would be worth about $18,072.

Of course, the opposite is true during a long period of price appreciation. Each time you buy, you'll get less Bitcoin than the time before. Had you just invested the lump sum, you'd be much better off. But again, how do you time the market? You pretty much can't!

The Dollar Cost Averaging Bitcoin website (at https://dcabtc.com) can show you the effects of DCA in the Bitcoin market. You enter a periodic investment sum, an interval (daily, weekly, biweekly, or monthly), and how many years you want to go back in time for a starting point, and the system calculates how much you would have invested, how much your Bitcoin would now be worth, and the profit you would have made.

What does this have to do with cryptocurrency mining? This book is about mining cryptocurrency, not buying it! Well, in effect, cryptocurrency mining is a form of dollar cost averaging cryptocurrency assets (or, as co-author Tyler Bain likes to call it, *electricity cost averaging*). If you are mining toward a pool, the rewards are steady and predictable. You spend money — for equipment, maintenance, and electricity — and every day or week, you gain more cryptocurrency. Your investment grows slowly over time, just like a DCA strategy.

Cost averaging your exits

For miners and hodlers alike who want to sell their cryptocurrency gains, the DCA approach can also be used to methodically time your exits. The same theory applies: If you intend to sell $1,200 worth of Bitcoin or other cryptocurrencies over a one-year period, instead of making this sale all at once, you can plan to sell $100 dollars of cryptocurrency every month to reduce your exposure to volatility.

However, the inverse is true for DCA sales versus purchases: If the market is trending downward, your DCA strategy will result in less local fiat currency acquired, but if the cryptocurrency market is trending upwards, the DCA method will yield more fiat currency gains. This method of timing is very effective if costs from the mining venture need to be covered.

Custodial exchange risk

Over the history of Bitcoin and other cryptocurrencies, there are many examples of exchanges that have been hacked, lost funds, or closed down due to insolvency, theft by management, or other mismanagement issues. Because of this, it is best to exercise extreme caution and due diligence when selecting an exchange to use.

It is important to not leave funds on exchanges any longer than absolutely necessary, to avoid exchange risk. As cryptographer (and potential Satoshi Nakamoto) Nick Szabo once said, "Trusted third parties are security holes." Remember, there is a rich history of exchange users losing access to their cryptocurrency funds on exchanges. The mantra in the cryptocurrency space is, "Not your keys, not your cryptocurrency." Let someone else manage your private keys for you, and you are risking that the manager (the custodian) steals from you or does not protect the keys properly.

Tax and Your Mining Business

Taxation for cryptocurrency is a complicated subject. At the time of writing, buying and selling crypto in the United States is taxable because the IRS identifies crypto as property, not currency. (We're discussing this issue from the perspective of taxation in the United States. However, some of the basic ideas we discuss here are likely to be valid in other countries, too.) However, quite a bit of tax relief is available to businesses that is not available to individuals, and for this reason, many miners elect to mine via a business entity.

Thus, the following is very general information. We recommend that you talk to a tax advisor who has experience with cryptocurrency.

But you're mining, not investing

Mining is very different from investing. Here's how we see it (but remember, don't trust us! You need to talk to a tax accountant who understands cryptocurrency and current tax legislation in that area!).

Your mining operation is a business. You put money into it, and out pops cryptocurrency (you hope). The profit you get out is immediately taxable. You'll want to account for everything in dollars. (The IRS doesn't have tax forms or tables that run calculations in cryptocurrency!)

Like any business, you have to track expenses: what you spend to buy your equipment, what you pay for electricity, the cost of rent (if your mining operation is in your home, you can deduct part of the cost of your home proportionate to the amount of space taken up by the equipment), and so on. Anything you spend to run your business is a deductible expense. Some of your expenses — sums spent on the mining equipment that has a multi-year life — may be depreciable. That is, instead of deducting the full price of the equipment in the year you spend the money, you may have to deduct a portion over several years. Again, a question for a tax accountant. (The rules are complicated.)

You also have to track your income — that is, the money, valued in dollars, you earn when you receive your cryptocurrency rewards. In other words, for reporting and tax calculation purposes, you have to convert the value of the cryptocurrency, at the time at which you receive it at your blockchain address, into dollars.

Even if you hodl this cryptocurrency, you'll owe tax on it. Think of it this way. Gold is an asset, and if you buy it and hold it, as long as you hold it, you don't owe tax on any appreciation in value. But do some work for someone and get paid with a gold coin, and you've just earned taxable income. It's the same with cryptocurrency. If you earn cryptocurrency from a mining operation, you owe tax on the gain you make after deducting mining expenses. Indeed, the Internal Revenue Service has ruled that mining gains are regarded as "gross income" (see Q-8 in www.irs.gov/pub/irs-drop/n-14-21.pdf).

How do you figure out the gain? You take your total cryptocurrency income for the year, valued in dollars at the time you earned the income, and then you deduct all your business expenses. What's left over is your profit, and your business owes tax on that profit.

What are you living on? Are you taking some of your cryptocurrency gains and converting them to dollars, so you can pay rent and buy groceries? Or even using the cryptocurrency to pay personal (nonbusiness) expenses directly?

Well, depending on your business form (a sole proprietorship, an LLC — limited liability corporation — a C Corporation, or whatever), the money you give yourself or spend on yourself will be regarded as payroll or distribution. It will be a deduction for your business, but taxable to you.

Okay, this can get complicated, and our goal is not to teach Taxation 101. Some forms of business structure — such as the sole proprietorship or LLC — treat you and your business as a single entity for taxation purposes. So if you give yourself money or spend money on yourself, it's not a deduction to your business because your business is you. You simply don't use those expenditures when calculating your deductions.

It gets complicated

Did we mention it gets complicated? Did we say that a lot of this is unclear right now? Perhaps we mentioned you should talk to a crypto-knowledgeable tax accountant?

What happens if you hodl? Say that you mine DummiesCoin, and it's worth, say, $1,000 at the point it's mined. But you don't sell it, you *hodl* it — keep possession of your mined cryptocurrency rewards as an investment, with the expectation that eventually the value will increase, as we discuss earlier in this chapter. So, by the end of the year, the value is $2,000. Do you regard $1,000 as the taxable income, or $2,000?

Well, most likely (see what your accountant says!), you'll file your taxes using $1,000 as the income from that block that you mined. But you'll now have an asset on the books with a basis of $1,000. In effect, you have purchased that Dummies-Coin for the $1,000 original price (that you paid tax on). Say that a year later, you sell the coin for $3,000; you'll owe tax on the difference between the $1,000 you "paid" for it, and the $3,000 you sold it for. You'll owe tax on $2,000.

You really need to track your cryptocurrency *basis* — that is, the original cost to you if you purchased it, or, if you mined it, the dollar value at the time it was mined. You also need to track the value when you disposed of the cryptocurrency; this is the amount you received in dollars when converting it to dollars, or the dollar value of the product or service you purchased when you made a purchase with cryptocurrency. All this can get, well, complicated. You need help, and we can provide a little for you with the following resources, a selection of systems for tracking the numbers and tax firms that specialize in cryptocurrency accounting.

>> **BitcoinTaxes:** https://bitcoin.tax

>> **Crypto Tax Girl:** https://cryptotaxgirl.com

>> **CryptoFolio:** https://cryptfolio.com/tax

>> **CryptoTrader.Tax:** https://cryptotrader.tax

>> **TokenTax:** https://tokentax.co

>> **ZenLedger:** www.zenledger.io

Scaling Up?

If you're making money in cryptocurrency mining, and if the current rewards and profits are significant, it is very tempting to scale up your mining operation. But think long and hard before you do so. This is a very volatile business, with a boom and bust nature. What may look like good market conditions showing an opportunity to expand may quickly turn around, resulting in a loss of critical funds that could have helped cover your operation's cost when the market turns down. In other words, sometimes it's nice to have a little financial padding to help you through the bumps, rather than investing every penny up to the limit.

We discuss some things to contemplate when considering whether to expand your mining operation.

Do not overextend

It is important to not overextend if you plan on scaling up your mine. If you grow your mining operation too quickly, you can evaporate any savings you have in local fiat currency, which would force you to liquidate mining returns to cover mining costs.

In Chapter 6, we cover the cryptocurrency mining death spiral. We discuss how cryptocurrency systems themselves are immune to the mining death spiral because of regularly scheduled block difficulty adjustments that ensure block rate production is kept steady over the long term.

Individual miners, however, are still exposed to the mining death spiral. If the exchange market prices of cryptocurrencies fall significantly enough over the short term, your mine may very well lose profitability, forcing you to shut down if you cannot afford your mining expenses. Overextend your mining operation, and you won't be able to continue to hodl your cryptocurrency rewards.

If you do intend to grow your mine, make sure you have plenty of funding to cover normal expenses in the case of a cryptocurrency market downturn. The best financial experts recommend that small businesses keep about three to six months of operating expenses on hand to cover expenditures in case of unforeseen market conditions.

However, in Bitcoin and cryptocurrency markets, the longest downturns have lasted up to 36 months! In extreme cases such as these, even the most profitable mining businesses are forced to rethink their operation and potentially make drastic changes.

Milestones to meet before you reinvest

Successful businesses, including cryptocurrency mining ventures, have set financial goals and long-range plans to make sure they will survive ongoing market conditions. Some miners measure their returns in the underlying cryptocurrency they are mining, while others measure it in their local fiat currency. There is some confusion in this area among many miners. Many don't like to think in terms of fiat currency. This harks back to the crypto anarchist roots of cryptocurrency, the idea that fiat currency is bad because it comes from the state, and that it will ultimately be replaced by cryptocurrency created and managed by the masses. This is a big mistake!

Any asset only has value *in comparison with something else!* You might say, "I own ten DummyCoin," and we can ask, "Well, what's it worth?" What would you answer? "It's worth ten DummyCoin"? That just doesn't make any sense, any more than asking someone how much an orange is worth and being told it's worth one orange!

"What's it worth?" means "What can you get for it?" How many pizzas could you buy with it, how many oranges could you get, could you buy a car with it? Or, to make things much, much, simpler: How many dollars is it worth?

So nothing has a value in isolation. You can compare it to apples, or oranges, or gold, or fiat. But one way or the other, cryptocurrency has some kind of value, which can be measured in units of some other thing, not in terms of itself.

Sure, you could convert your mining rewards into the number of oranges it could buy, but what's the point? Why not just use the most common medium of exchange in your country: your country's fiat currency!

If you measure your results purely in how many coins you mine, you have no real idea whether your mining operation makes sense. Even if your goal is to accumulate a particular cryptocurrency that you just *know* is going to be worth, one day, ten times what it costs you to mine it, you still need to understand the numbers in terms of fiat currency. After all, if you don't, you have no idea if you are spending more money to mine the cryptocurrency than you would spend to buy it.

So the most important metric you are watching should be profit or loss, based on fiat currency. Without knowing whether or not you are making money, it's hard to make any rational decisions about expansion.

On the other hand, perhaps this is just a hobby or cool experiment for you, and your goal is to find out about, and become proficient at, cryptocurrency mining and the cryptocurrency space in general. Or maybe it's an ideological statement; you *are* a crypto anarchist, or crypto libertarian, and want to see cryptocurrency succeed, and thus want to be involved. That's fine. Your goals may be different in that case.

Or maybe you're not so ideological, but you still believe in the future of the currency you mine, and cryptocurrency in general, and want to help support and secure the blockchain (if only because it holds some of your wealth!).

Some miners believe in what the cryptocurrency community is trying to accomplish, and thus are willing to mine at a fiat-loss for a short period, knowing they are supporting the blockchain and still accumulating cryptocurrency (which, they believe, will increase in value).

And, well, let's be honest here. There are also miners who are mining so that the cryptocurrency they earn is anonymous. If you purchase cryptocurrency from an exchange in the United States, the exchange has a record of that transaction and who you are. If you solo mine a cryptocurrency, nobody but you has a record of who you are. (This isn't true of pool mining.)

So there may be other reasons to continue mining, other metrics to consider. But from a *business* standpoint, you must know if you are making money or losing money, and how much either way. If you don't, you can't make a rational decision regarding expansion. (And even if you are mining for some other purpose, you can't fully understand your operation until you look at the numbers in terms of fiat. Or oranges if you prefer, but fiat will be much easier.)

Decide your goals prior to setting out on your mining adventure, and check back on them periodically. How *much* profit is sufficient, in relation to the investment you are making in time and money, for example?

And what would the effect of expansion be? Consider, for example, that doubling a small cryptomine will cost money for the equipment, but won't take much more of your time. You'll have to spend time to set up all the equipment, of course (though that should be much faster the second time), but it won't take much more of your time to watch over your additional equipment and keep it running. So, as far as your time input goes, there is a huge economy of scale in cryptomining. That is, as your mine gets larger, the amount of time contributed to earn each dollar declines dramatically.

Planning your expansion

Mining equipment has improved dramatically over the last decade. Hash rate output per rig has skyrocketed into the many trillions of hashes per second, and hashing efficiency has also increased, drastically reducing power consumption and doing more proof of work for less electrical cost.

This translates into easier deployment of staggering amounts of computational power. If you are planning to expand your cryptocurrency mining operation, you can do it with much less equipment and overhead compared to even a couple of years ago. Also, if your cryptocurrency mine is on the older side — say, two to five years (about the lifespan of an ASIC mining rig) — you may be able to simply replace your aging mining rigs with new state-of-the-art equipment and drastically increase your overall hashing capability.

But all this gear is expensive. "Is it worth expanding?" is a question that can only be answered by very careful calculations. Cryptocurrency mining is, after all, the consummate numbers game. It's all about dollars to buy equipment, the cost of the electricity to run it, the number of hashes the equipment outputs, the number of hashes the entire network outputs, the block time, and on and on. Mining for a while will give you a baseline to work with, but spending hours with a spreadsheet (or online calculations discussed in Chapter 11) is the only way you can predict what an expansion may do for you, and even then, it is only a *prediction*.

But remember, if you'd like to grow your operation from its current hobbyist deployment, you can take various different routes (which we discuss in Chapter 9), such as colocation hosting facilities, hash-rate marketplaces (in which thousands of people with hashing power sell that power to thousands of people who want to mine without the hassle of setting up equipment), or even cloud-mining companies, in which individuals buy hash power from the company itself.

REMEMBER

When expanding, be careful to not overextend, to plan thoughtful objectives and goals, and to maintain adequate cash reserves to cover multiple months of mining expenditures in case of market downturns or times of increased volatility.

5

The Part of Tens

Chapter **14**

Ten (or So) Tips for When the Market Dips

B ecause the cryptocurrency space is so immature, incredible volatility in the exchange rate of Bitcoin and other cryptocurrencies has occurred, along with rapid appreciations in asset prices and huge crashes.

There are two basic arguments for why this volatility happens. The skeptic will say that cryptocurrencies have no inherent value, any more than tulips have an inherent value that justified the Tulipmania of early 17th century Holland, during which tulip bulbs reached astronomical prices. (Tulip bulbs were selling for as much as 1,000 pounds of cheese, or 12 fattened sheep.) No, wait, the skeptic would argue that tulip bulbs had more inherent value than cryptocurrencies, because you can grow flowers from them. That's why the market is volatile, the skeptic says; it's because it's a market built on sand.

The believer, though, will shrug this off — and point out that gold has very little inherent value, either, yet has been used as a store of value for thousands of years. The believer will argue that this volatility is a normal process for new assets during which early price discovery occurs. The world has only been working with this asset for a decade or so. In fact, most of the world has not heard of it, and even among educated people in advanced nations, they have only been aware of cryptocurrency for a couple of years, and mostly don't understand it. Thus, it's no surprise that prices will bounce around as the world comes to grips with this new asset class.

Either way, cryptocurrency markets are volatile. Over the last decade, the overall trend, at least for the major cryptocurrencies, has been up, with intermittent dramatic drops. So you need to assume this volatility will continue for some time. In this chapter, we discuss various things to consider and how to best prepare for market movements and downturns.

Have a Plan, Hedge Your Mine

TIP

Always have a plan for market downturns. While things are going well, consider what you would do in the event of a mild downturn, a painful downturn, or a seriously catastrophic downturn.

You have a few options:

>> Put your head down and keep pushing forward. In other words, just keep moving and hope the market recovers (if you have the funds to do so).

>> Sell your hashing. Use a hash marketplace to sell your mining power to another party. That is, let someone else take the risk. (If you can find a viable market, of course. You'll need to run the numbers, as with any mining operation.)

>> Switch to another, currently more lucrative, cryptocurrency.

>> Hedge your operational expenditures.

>> Stop mining for a while and watch the market.

>> Cut your losses and leave the market entirely. Sell off your equipment to recover some of your capital costs, but understand that in a market downturn, your equipment will be worth less (and now it's used, and perhaps older generation gear).

If you have plenty of excess capital stored to cover operating expenses during a downturn, moving forward may be a valid strategy, depending on how much you're losing. Another would be to plan on shutting down your equipment during such periods, a subject we discuss at more length in the "Stop Mining" section, later in this chapter.

How Long Can You Last?

When mining cryptocurrencies, you'll need plenty of liquid capital, such as local fiat currency reserved to cover mining expenses during market downturns and dips (if you decide to continue mining that cryptocurrency, that is). Small businesses are often advised to keep anywhere from three to six months of equivalent operating expenditures on hand in case of unforeseen market changes, and that — or more — may also apply to cryptocurrency mining.

In the cryptocurrency space, exchange rate downturns can last a long time. If the market does take a dip to below previous exchange rates for an extended period of time, to the degree that you're no longer making money, you want to be prepared with plenty of operating reserves to cover expenses over the duration of the downturn. If you're actually losing money, you may want to stop mining or perhaps switch to another cryptocurrency (if you can buy the cryptocurrency for less than you are spending on operating costs, what's the point of mining?). But many cryptocurrency miners are in it for the cryptocurrency; their goal is to build up their cryptocurrency reserves. They may sell some of it to cover their costs, but overall they regard owning cryptocurrency as a valuable investment for the future.

So what if your operation is break even, if you are making enough money, in local fiat currency, to pay your costs but nothing more? You can continue mining, but you're not making fiat currency, and you're not accumulating cryptocurrency. That's a situation in which you may want to have reserves to allow you to cover your operating costs while you continue accumulating cryptocurrency.

In fact, such downturns can end up being very profitable in the long term. The cost of the cryptocurrency goes down as miners drop out. As the value of the cryptocurrency drops, miners leave the network, overall network hash rate goes down, and your proportion of the hash rate goes up, meaning you mine more of the underlying cryptocurrency for the same operating cost. So you'll earn more cryptocurrency at a lower cost. You may not be making money right now, but when the market comes back, you'll be glad you continued mining!

REMEMBER

The length of time you can withstand a market downturn will be determined by the amount of capital you have saved. You've presumably paid for your equipment up front, but you'll have daily expenses (predominantly electricity). Perhaps you're paying for the equipment monthly, too — you paid on a credit card or got a loan. Those are monthly expenses, but not directly associated with the cost of mining; you owe that money whether you mine or not.

So these calculations can get complicated very quickly because of the many variables at play. In effect, you are comparing four financial scenarios: continuing to mine, stop mining temporarily, stop mining altogether (and sell off your equipment), or switch to another cryptocurrency.

REMEMBER

It's not all about costs. If you continue to mine, you'll still have *some* income; it just won't be as much as it was before the drop. What you're trying to do is calculate your *burn rate* (that is, how much of your reserves you spend each month), and your *runway* (how many months it will take to burn through your reserves). Your burn rate can be calculated like this:

Your Reserves / [Total Monthly Expenses – Mining Revenue] = runway time

Say that you have $5,000 in reserve. Your expenses are $1,000 a month, but at present, even with the market drop, you're still making $300 a month in mining rewards. Thus,

$5,000 / [$1,000 - $300] = $5,000 / $700 = 7.14 months

We can make this more complicated . . . and will. First, although you'll be able to estimate expenses pretty closely (you'll likely be using the same amount of electricity each month, for example), you don't know what your mining income over this time will actually be. It will fluctuate; it could go lower, it could go up a little . . . it's a guess.

Next, if you have recurring capital expenses (you're paying off a loan you took out to buy equipment), that bill is due every month whether you mine or not. Or maybe you purchased your equipment outright, but you've been calculating profitability by amortizing the cost over several years. Well, that equipment has already been paid for; it is, from a cash-flow standpoint, a sunk cost. It would not be appropriate to include these costs in a calculation of burn rate or runway. These are cash-flow calculations; how much money is going out, and how much is coming in, each month, are the only things that count.

Beyond all the calculations, though, there's a big question. Why, if you're losing money, would you continue mining? That's a question we deal with in the upcoming "Switch to Another Cryptocurrency" and "Stop Mining!" sections.

WARNING

These projections are just that, projections. They may not be right, and most likely won't be. However, making these estimations is better than not having a plan or idea at all. Market volatility can cause monthly revenue to fluctuate and drastically alter your calculation's assumptions and conclusions. This is something you should watch closely.

Learn from Market History

But will the market come back? As financial advisors say, "Past performance is no guarantee of future results." And, in fact, this is the case for many alternative cryptocurrencies, for which the market has dropped and never come back!

But we're in a new financial world, and if you believe that cryptocurrency is here to stay, then you have to believe that some cryptocurrencies will continue to increase in value over the long term. Sure, the world probably doesn't need the 2,000-plus cryptocurrencies that exist today, but some cryptocurrencies will increase in value in the short term, even if they eventually die off, and others will be around for the long haul.

So it's interesting to have a picture of the market and what has happened to cryptocurrencies thus far in their decade-long life, if only to gain some peace-of-mind when the market drops.

Bitcoin, the most popular, most talked about, most valuable cryptocurrency, has a history of slow increases in value, followed by periods of exuberance in which the value increases rapidly, followed by a sudden drop, followed by months of slow decline . . . and then the value starts going up again and the cycle repeats. But overall, the value keeps rising. Take a look at Figure 14-1, a chart from CoinMarketCap.com, showing the price of Bitcoin from April 2013 until the end of 2016. Then look at the data from April 2013 until the present day in Figure 14-2. The period up until 2016 barely registers as a blip on the chart now, but in any case, we can see the same basic pattern. We had a big drop at the end of 2017, a long, slow decline during 2018, followed by an upswing until April 2021, another drop until July, followed by another peak in November, yet another drop . . . and now we seem to be in another upward trend. Go to CoinMarketCap.com and play with this chart. It's interesting to zoom in on the early days to see the same pattern at the very low prices that Bitcoin had back in those days.

Another interesting way to look at the data is by considering the All Time Highs, and how long the market has gone between All Time Highs; that is, the length of time between market historic highs, and from the current time to the last All Time High (ATH).

BuyBitcoinWorldwide.com used to provide an easily interpreted chart showing the various times since ATH over Bitcoin's history, though it has recently replaced it with a color-coded chart that seems to us to be difficult to understand. Perhaps they'll bring back the old chart sometime (see `https://stats.buybitcoinworld wide.com/days-since-high`). You can also find a table of times since ATH for various cryptocurrencies at `www.coingecko.com/en/coins/ath` (or search the web for "time since all time high" to find various different representations of this concept).

FIGURE 14-1:
A CoinMarketCap.
com chart
showing the price
of Bitcoin from
April 2013 until
the end of 2016.

FIGURE 14-2:
A CoinMarketCap.
com chart
showing the price
of Bitcoin from
April 2013 until
August 2019.

At the time of writing, it has been more than 150 days since the ATH of $67,567 on November 7, 2021. The previous time since ATH had been 189 days, from April 12, 2021, until October 18, 2021, when the cost of Bitcoin broke through the previous price of $63,503.

When we wrote the previous edition of this book, we had experienced 600 days since the previous ATH (of $19,497 on December 15, 2017), and it wouldn't be until November 29, 2020, that the price broke through again, a total of 1,063 days. But even that almost three-year period was by no means the record. Back in February 2017, the price of Bitcoin recovered to the high value previously set 1,170 days earlier. (Over the next ten months, it would increase in value from around $1,000 to almost $20,000 . . . and then drop again.)

Just because it's been a while since the last time the price of a cryptocurrency was at an all-time high doesn't mean a miner can't make money mining that cryptocurrency, of course. In fact, although it's been 600 days since the last ATH, it's also been around 160 days of a general upward trend in the price of Bitcoin. Profitability of mining is not related to what the price used to be; it's related to the current mining conditions — the network hash rate, your proportion of the hash rate, the price of electricity, and so on (see Chapter 11).

But perhaps what these concepts do is to put the current value of cryptocurrencies into context for you. We're seeing a market that bounces up and down (see the section "Consider Market Volatility," later in this chapter), but it's on an upward trend, at least for some of the major cryptocurrencies. Some miners are so sure of this that they even run the calculations in Chapter 11 based on the previous All Time High, under the assumption that currency will reach that level — and more — again.

We don't recommend you do this, or at least if you do, you also run the numbers based on current value. (Otherwise, you won't know if it's cheaper to simply buy the cryptocurrency rather than mine it.)

Don't Panic! (Keep Calm and Carry On?)

Market volatility is a natural occurrence in the Bitcoin and cryptocurrency space, so it's important not to fear these occasions. Understand them, prepare for them, expect them, but if you're going to panic, then mining may not be for you.

It is easier to not panic if you have an underlying understanding and belief in the cryptocurrency you're mining. If instead you are motivated only by immediate, short-term profit (as measured in your local fiat currency), these market downturns can lead to significant fear and distress. If you believe cryptocurrency is a fad, your mining experience will be very stressful; you'll constantly be waiting for the final crash. If you believe cryptocurrency is a revolutionary technology that's here to stay, you'll have a very different perspective. You have to accept that downturns happen and are part of the cryptocurrency landscape. You might then "Keep Calm and Carry On," as the British World War II saying goes . . . or, to use the cryptocurrency equivalent, "Hodl on!"

Many miners and cryptocurrency enthusiasts have learned to avoid panic and to actually embrace these market downturns as an opportunity to acquire more of the underlying asset that they mine. Remember, as the price of an asset drops, miners leave the network, the network hash rate goes down, your proportion of the hash rate goes up, and you may end up mining more of the asset at a lower price (in terms of mining expenses).

This is an example of individuals acting on asymmetrical information that the market may not be correctly pricing during the act of price discovery. *Price discovery* is defined by Wikipedia as the process of determining an asset's value through natural interactions in the marketplace of buyers and sellers. (See `https://en.wikipedia.org/wiki/Price_discovery`.) Information asymmetry may occur when some actors in a market do not have the full picture or make actions based on fear or misinformation.

As actor (and Seinfeld executive producer) Larry David once said, "I tend to stay with the panic, I embrace the panic."

Don't get discouraged, and keep in mind that eventually your hard work may pay off. Keep in mind what Winston Churchill has widely been reported to have said, "If you're going through hell, keep going." (Okay, so he never actually said it, but any quote can be given 50 percent more gravitas by claiming it came from the lips of Winston Churchill.)

On the other hand, if you're going through hell, maybe you should get out! (See, perhaps Churchill was smart *not to* say this.)

Buy the Dip

Many people in the Bitcoin and cryptocurrency sphere are ardent supporters of their blockchain of choice and strongly believe in the long-term prospects of the cryptocurrency in particular and cryptocurrency technology in general. As such, they may view market downturns and dips as a chance to be able to acquire more of the coin that they hold and believe in, at steep discounts.

Buying the Dip is another example of individuals acting on asymmetrical information that the market may not be correctly pricing the cryptocurrency during the act of price discovery (or at least, a belief that the market information is not correct and the asset is underpriced). There's also the idea of dollar cost averaging, which we discuss in Chapter 13. Market downturns and dips offer an opportunity to lower your average dollar cost of the cryptocurrency you are mining. Why? Because although your expenses will be stable, you will mine more of the cryptocurrency. As miners leave the market, network hash rate goes down, your proportion of the network hash rate goes up, and statistically you win a larger share of the total block rewards.

Look for the Advantages

There's a silver lining in every cryptocurrency mining cloud (perhaps). While the mining outlook may appear bleak, there are still advantages that occur during extreme market-price downturns.

First, a significant market drop results in a lower network hash rate, as other miners shut down unprofitable equipment or leave the network entirely.

This lower hash rate leads to less competition, and thus more rewards for the miners that remain, as measured in the underlying cryptocurrency asset. You may even find that even though the dollar value of a coin is less, because you are mining more you are staying even or perhaps ahead.

There are also often significant discounts on slightly used hardware that hit the secondhand markets, as the miners leaving the network sell off their equipment. You may find that market downturns are great times to upgrade your mining equipment to newer, more efficient, and more profitable gear, helping you to maintain profitability during the dip and come roaring back when the market recovers. Buyer beware though, as some of this equipment can be heavily used, near its end of life, and not currently profitable given the various market variables.

TIP

Always do your research prior to buying second-hand equipment and use the profitability calculators we cover in Chapter 11 to ensure that the equipment you purchase is in fact a good buy. Ideally, buy on terms that allow you to return the equipment if it does not function correctly. (Many markets, such as Amazon and Newegg, provide such a guarantee; personal sales, of course, generally won't.)

Anticipate the Market Recovery

Market recovery in the Bitcoin and cryptocurrency space isn't ever a guarantee and nothing is certain. (Hey, maybe the skeptics are right, and it is a fad! On the other hand, that's what the skeptics said about the Internet.)

However, over the course of Bitcoin's roughly 13-year existence (as of this writing), the market has recovered from plunges an astounding nine times.

It's a good idea to plan for both market crashes and market recoveries. Many miners can continue mining during these downturns, in anticipation of the recovery, if they planned properly for the dip. So plan accordingly, stockpile resources to help cover mining costs, and reduce expenditures to ensure that your mining operation is as lean and economically efficient as possible.

During the downturn, keep an eye on useful cryptocurrency metrics and statistics for on-chain activity, such as network hash rate, block difficulty, and daily transactions, as well as market data, such as trading volume and exchange rate.

These metrics indicate market sentiment and may signal a pending market recovery. For example, during the dramatic market downturn for the Bitcoin network in 2018, the average daily hash rate bottomed out at just above 31 EH/s in December 2018 (see Chapter 5), the block difficulty dropped to 5,106,422,924,659 (see Chapter 6), and right around that same time the exchange rate started recovering from the relative bottom of $3,200 per BTC.

In other words, many market indicators may signal market recovery is coming, before the price actually begins rising. Although many of these indices are intertwined, and there is a large debate in the community as to whether hash rate lags, or leads, price, it is without question that there is some kind of correlation and it is still useful to study and understand these metrics to get an idea of what may be coming soon.

Learn From Your First Dip

There is no better source of knowledge and insight than experience. That's true of all life experiences, including cryptocurrency market corrections. Learn from your first mining dip, which may occur quicker than you think!

Watch the markets closely. (We know you will.) It can be a painful and stressful experience, and there's nothing better than pain and stress to make human beings pay attention!

Take note of the many variables in the space and how they shift during a market dip, variables such as exchange rate, network hash rate, equipment costs (hardware, such as ASICs, may drop in price), social engagement, and so on.

What do we mean by social engagement? Pay attention to the amount of activity on social networks related to the cryptocurrency. If activity seems to be gradually dropping, maybe interest in the cryptocurrency is waning, for example. Several tools attempt to measure social engagement. For example, see `www.theblock crypto.com/data/alternative-crypto-metrics/social` and `https://lunar crush.com/markets`.

Watch what's going on with your cryptocurrency at all times. After a while. you'll get a feel for how things work. Take the lessons learned from this experience and use them to plan for your mine in anticipation of the next market correction. It's a bit like jumping out of an airplane; it gets a lot less stressful after you've done it a few times.

Consider Market Volatility

A volatile market is one in which the price of the item being tracked bounces around a lot. That's pretty imprecise, though, so, we can get more specific. Volatility can be measured; there are degrees of volatility. *Volatility* is defined as the amount of variation of a market exchange rate over a certain period of time, as measured by the standard deviation of logarithmic returns. *Standard deviation* is a measurement of the degree of variation of a set of data values (in this case, of course, the data values are the daily prices of the cryptocurrency).

Volatility may be stated as a percentage of the average market exchange rate over a particular period, though it may also be seen as a dimensionless unit; the higher the number, the higher the level of volatility. Volatility in cryptocurrency markets is a measure of the steep increases and declines in market exchange price. (Volatility measures the amount of change, not the direction.) The higher the volatility value, the more the price of the cryptocurrency is varying from the average over that period . . . the more the value is bouncing up and down.

So volatility has to have a time range; we might measure BTC-to-USD volatility over 30 days, for example, or over 60 days, or longer. In other words, volatility on any particular day is shown in comparison to the average price over that 30- or 60-day period.

Getting a feel for volatility is tough, as it is a difficult metric to grasp. In rough, layman terms, the more the value of the currency bounces around during the period being measured, the higher the percentage of volatility.

You can't tell from a volatility chart what the price was at a particular point in time; the volatility percentage doesn't directly indicate the price at that point. For example, when the price of Bitcoin fell 50 percent during the market downturn in December 2018 (from about $6,000 to around $3,000), volatility spiked to around 40 percent.

Over the past decade, Bitcoin volatility has trended down as the market valuation has increased (the more value and liquidity in the market, the harder it is to move the price significantly with large market orders).

The following resources can help you get a feel for the volatility of Bitcoin and various other cryptocurrencies:

» **Bitcoin Volatility Index** (www.buybitcoinworldwide.com/volatility-index): The Bitcoin Volatility Index is not just for Bitcoin. This volatility index provides percentage-based Bitcoin *and* Litecoin over 30, 60, 120, 252 days, measured against the U.S. dollar (see Figure 14-3). You also get Bitcoin and Litecoin price charts.

» **Satochi.co Bitcoin Volatility Index** (www.satochi.co): The Satochi.co Bitcoin volatility index tracks daily, 30-, and 60-day volatility estimates against the USD. It also has volatility comparisons for gold, Ethereum, and many other currencies.

» **Woobull Bitcoin Volatility** (http://charts.woobull.com/bitcoin-volatility): Woobull Bitcoin Volatility is a useful chart tracking 60-day Bitcoin volatility over the past decade, compared to dollars and euros. You can even add USD/EUR volatility, Bitcoin price, and a 200-day average Bitcoin price over the same period of time.

» **Woobull Bitcoin Volatility Comparisons** (http://charts.woobull.com/bitcoin-volatility-vs-other-assets/): This Bitcoin volatility chart allows you to compare 60-day Bitcoin volatility estimates against oil, U.S. stocks, gold, U.S. real estate, and other noteworthy assets.

So, why do we care about market volatility? What does it tell us, and how can we use it? Many miners like to keep an eye on the volatility of the cryptocurrency they are mining, and compare to earlier levels, to give them an idea of what may be coming. Volatility can help put current price fluctuations in historical context. To some degree, this may be a "peace-of-mind" thing, in which looking back in time and seeing high volatility says to the miner, "Don't worry, we've been through this before!" If you see high volatility, that means something is going on in the market, and you may want to keep an eye on things, especially if the level of volatility is much greater than the market has seen before.

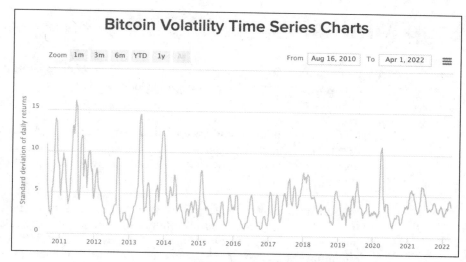

FIGURE 14-3:
The Bitcoin
Volatility Index.
You can see how
Bitcoin's volatility
has dropped over
the years.

Source: www.buybitcoinworldwide.com/volatility-index

Of course, volatility needs to be seen in the context of the cryptocurrency's price movements. So a cryptocurrency can be volatile while on an overall upward trend, or an overall downward trend . . . or simply bouncing around a level price.

Switch to Another Cryptocurrency

If your mining equipment becomes unprofitable during market downturns, one option for cryptocurrency miners is to search for profitability on an alternative cryptocurrency that uses the same algorithm as your ASICs. If you are mining with a GPU mining rig, you have a wider variety of blockchains as possible options to switch to because they are more flexible and not hash-algorithm specific.

Refer to Chapter 8 for a list of popular cryptocurrencies by hash algorithm if you are looking for alternatives to work with your equipment, or for a more exhaustive list of coins by algorithm use an online resource like https://cryptorival.com/algorithms. You may find that your equipment, while unprofitable on your cryptocurrency of choice is still viable on other blockchains.

TIP

This is something that comes under the "plan ahead" category, too. It's a good idea to know what your options are, so you can move quickly, if necessary. As with any entry into a new cryptocurrency network, though, you'll want to run the numbers carefully to make sure it makes sense.

Stop Mining!

If the market drops, crashes even, you may not want to continue mining if the only way you can do so is to spend all of your cryptocurrency rewards from mining to keep going.

If you're spending more to keep mining than the mining rewards you earn bring in, you're losing money. That shortfall has to be made up somehow, either by selling some of the cryptocurrency you're holding or by investing more fiat currency.

If you cannot sustain your mining expenses with cash reserves or the rewards from your mining equipment, it simply doesn't make sense to continue mining under extreme market circumstances. If you can purchase the cryptocurrency you are mining at a discount via the market, compared to the cost of acquisition from your mining deployment, there is significant incentive to shut down. There comes a point when you should stop mining!

There are really three financial scenarios in cryptocurrency mining:

>> **Your expenses are less than your mining rewards.** You are profitable; you're spending less than the income you are making, and can decide whether to sell the cryptocurrency to pay expenses (withdrawing your profit), or hold the cryptocurrency in the hopes that it will increase in value. (In effect, you've just converted it to an investment by holding it; remember, though, you owe taxes on that profit; see Chapter 13.)

>> **Your expenses are more or less equal to your mining rewards.** You're in balance. You haven't made any money — if you sell the cryptocurrency you can cover your costs, but not more. But if you hold the cryptocurrency in the hopes that the price goes up, you are, in effect, investing in the cryptocurrency. (And no taxes are due now, because you haven't made money, but maybe will be in the future if the cryptocurrency goes up in value and you sell it.) You are spending money on electricity and other monthly costs, and in exchange getting an equal amount of cryptocurrency.

>> **Your expenses exceed your mining rewards.** You're losing money. (You may have a tax write-off, reducing your tax bill, if you have other business income to write it off against.) In fact, you're better off taking the money you spend each month and buying the cryptocurrency on the open markets.

Consider that last scenario. Say that it costs you $1,000 in monthly expenses (not including equipment amortization) to mine 100 DummyCoins.

Now assume you can go to an exchange — Kraken, or Poloniex, or Coinbase, or whatever — and sell those 100 DummyCoins at an exchange rate of 8:1; $8 for 1 DummyCoin. You've just made $800, $200 less than your expenses. Or, another way to look at it is that you spent $1,000 to buy 100 DummyCoins; you paid $10 a coin, $2 more than the market rate. The coin's market value has to increase in value 25 percent (from $8 to $10) before you ever break even on what is now an investment.

Okay, now say you turned off mining for a month; you would have saved $1,000. If you really believe in the cryptocurrency you've been mining, that it will increase in value, you could take that $1,000 to an exchange and buy 125 DummyCoin; or you could buy 100 DummyCoin for $800, and keep the other $200 in the bank.

Scenario 1 makes sense; if you're turning a profit, that's good business (assuming the profit is better than alternative uses of your time and money). Scenario 2 makes sense, too, if you believe in the value of the cryptocurrency and its growth opportunity and view it as an investment. (And you don't mind the time and hassle of running your mining business.)

But Scenario 3? There is no point in continuing to mine if it's cheaper to spend the same amount of money at an exchange to get more of the cryptocurrency or get the same amount of the cryptocurrency for less money! (Except for reasons such as ideology and fresh coins.)

REMEMBER

If your goal in mining is to make money short term, mining at a loss doesn't make sense. If your goal is to acquire more cryptocurrency, it still doesn't make sense. It is illogical to continue mining for coins if you can purchase them for less than it costs to mine.

These are simple calculations

The calculations necessary are not complicated. You should know

>> **Your monthly expenses:** How much you're paying for electricity primarily (for both the equipment and, if necessary, air conditioning), rent, if you are paying rent for a mining facility, maintenance on the equipment, and so on. You should be keeping records of these expenses (for tax reasons — they are deductions! — and for business-management purposes).

>> **Your revenues:** If you are pool mining, your pool reports will show you how much you are earning. If you are solo mining, your mining software will show rewards you have received.

>> **The exchange rate for the cryptocurrency you are mining and the dollar value of your cryptocurrency revenues:** You can go to an exchange or a cryptocurrency pricing site (such as CoinMarketCap.com) to find the present value of your mining rewards. You can then simply subtract your dollar expenses from your dollar revenues to arrive at your profit or loss.

This is not complicated stuff; it's something you could quickly do each day to keep track of your mining profitability *for that day*. Set up a spreadsheet, and these calculations could be done in a couple of minutes each evening. Add a chart, and you'll see where your profitability is headed; Up or Down. Some miners may actually use this information to determine, on a daily basis, if it's worth mining the next day or not.

After you set up a spreadsheet to do these calculations, you can also do what-if calculations by changing field values. What if the value of the cryptocurrency drops 20 percent or 30 percent? You can play with the spreadsheet and get a feel for it.

WARNING

There are some costs that you might track for taxation purposes, but should not be included in these profitability calculations. One would be a portion of your rent. If your mining operation takes up 10 percent of the space in your house, you can deduct 10 percent of your rent or mortgage and other household expenses against your income before paying tax (talk to a tax accountant!). But if you stop mining, you're still paying these expenses, so don't include them in your profitability calculations.

Another expense would be amortization of your mining equipment. For tax calculations, you may subtract a portion of your mining equipment's cost each year (talk to a tax accountant!). But you don't want to use these costs in your profit or loss calculations. What you are concerned about in these "mine or don't mine" calculations are monthly costs moving forward. "If I continue mining next month, how much money will I spend next month to do so."

You can also use the mining estimation tools we cover in Chapter 11. This is particularly helpful if you have a variety of different rigs you're mining with; say, an S7, an S9, and something much more efficient like a new S19. Your numbers, based on overall expenses and overall mining rewards, may show that you're profitable, but if you were to look at each individual mining rig, you might find that it would make economic sense to shut down the S7 because that mining ASIC could be mining at a loss. With equipment of different efficiencies it's possible to be profitable overall, with one rig in effect subsidizing the other rigs while they mine at a loss.

However, going offline would reduce only electrical costs, and some of your other expenses (such as hosting costs, Internet-access fees, and other fixed costs) may not be affected, furthering your loss of capital and limiting the loss-reduction that occurs by having your miners offline.

REMEMBER

Market downturns typically result in significant portions of the network hash rate being taken offline, as miners shut down inefficient equipment due to lack of profit. Ideally, if it is break even or slightly profitable and you can afford to, it is best to continue mining during these types of market conditions as the amount of cryptocurrency rewards (measured in Bitcoin or other cryptocurrencies) you can mine will increase as system hash rate decreases and your percentage of the network increases.

Stop or go?

So do you stop, or do you continue? It's a more complicated question for many miners, because for them it's not all about short-term profit.

Note that the most successful miners mined at a time when there was no real market exchange rate, so they were mining at a total loss . . . until it wasn't. The price of Bitcoin went from essentially nothing to thousands of dollars, and the mining paid off. Many of the most profitable mining periods (measured in BTC) through Bitcoin's decade-long history would have shown "unprofitability" when calculated in dollars.

There are also ideological reasons to continue. Many miners believe in the future of cryptocurrency, see it as a way for the masses to protect themselves against the devaluation of their local fiat currency and against the Big Brother state. They want to secure, protect, and build their blockchain into the future, so it's not all about money.

There is, of course, the belief in the future value of the cryptocurrency. If you're sure its value is going up, you'll be willing to mine at a loss short term. Also, as we have seen historically, this has often been the case, at least for Bitcoin and some other popular cryptocurrencies. However, as they say in the investing business, past performance is no guarantee of future returns (did we mention that?).

Then there's the *fresh coins* issue. In the cryptocurrency world, fresh does not mean recent; we're not talking about recently mined coins. Rather, fresh means unsullied in some way — coins that cannot be traced back to the original owner and coins that cannot have been involved in something bad in the past, such as a hack or other nefarious usage.

For example, say that a hacker steals cryptocurrency and sends it to his own address in the blockchain. Over time, those coins get moved around, from blockchain address to blockchain address, until they end up associated with one of your addresses. Remember, all transactions are traceable within the blockchain. The cryptocurrency associated with your address is now most definitely not "fresh coins."

Many miners value their privacy and anonymity, and like the idea of totally anonymous coins. (Remember the crypto-anarchist origins of cryptocurrency.) Thus, some miners believe that there's a premium on fresh coins. We've even seen the figure of 20 percent bandied about — that is, that if a traceable cryptocurrency coin is worth $1,000, then a fresh coin should be worth $1,200. (Some currencies, such as Monero, have no fresh-coin premium, because they have anonymized blockchain, so there's no difference between new and old coins.)

In effect, mining allows you to "buy" cryptocurrency in a more private manner than buying it at an exchange. The exchange generally knows who you are and can thus associate the purchased cryptocurrency with you. If you are solo mining, then your mined cryptocurrency is fresh, with no identifying information. (The same generally isn't true with pool mining, of course.)

Many miners have continued mining during unprofitable times on a number of occasions and not regretted it. They've considered the long-term value proposition and made money when the market recovered, even though short term, the numbers didn't look good. So there's no easy answer to the "Should I shut down?" question. It depends on many conditions and variables and also your personal belief (or lack of belief) in the market.

However, consider what Adam Smith said in *The Wealth of Nations*, 250 years ago: "It is the maxim of every prudent master of a family, never to attempt to make at home what it will cost him more to make than to buy." Sometimes it makes more sense to buy than to mine!

» **Smart scaling and mining deployments**

» **Ensuring your mine remains profitable long term**

» **Timing your entries and exits**

» **Mining alternative cryptocurrencies**

Chapter **15**

Ten Ways to Boost Your Return on Investment

I n the cryptocurrency mining space, revenue is important, and profit is critical. You do not want to spin your computational hash cycles for zero gain, and you want your investment of time, mining hardware, electricity, and other expenses to pay off. We have compiled a list of ten things that will help you become profitable and receive a return on investment (ROI) in your cryptocurrency mining adventure.

Doing Your Homework

Doing plenty of research and study prior to jumping into the cryptocurrency mining space in any capacity is crucial. It's a complicated arena, with plenty of room for error, and cryptocurrency mining is not a quick walk in the park. We discuss the ROI calculations and math exercises required to see projections of mining returns in Chapter 11; study those carefully.

If the mining gear you plan to acquire and deploy is not profitable or the market is in the midst of a large downturn, you may be much better off simply buying the underlying cryptocurrency asset you intend to mine from an exchange. We cover a few reputable exchanges to use in Chapter 13.

Setting up hardware and software can be complicated, too, in particular if you decide to build a GPU mining rig from the ground up! Before you start, study.

REMEMBER

There is no rush! It's better to take your time and get everything right than to jump in without being fully prepared and lose money. Better in fact, if your research leads you to *not* mine cryptocurrency, than if you do little research, jump right in, and fail. If the cryptocurrency markets survive and is no short-term fad, you have plenty of time to get in and mine. And if they don't? Well, you haven't lost anything, have you? (We think they'll survive!)

Timing Your Entry

There are good and bad times for cryptocurrency mining. For example, during the Bitcoin and cryptocurrency market boom in 2017, mining hardware was practically sold out from many of the original mining equipment manufacturers. Much of the most efficient and cost-effective (profitable) cryptocurrency mining equipment was being resold on second-hand marketplaces at prices above the brand-new-from-a-manufacturer price, virtually eliminating any projected gains of mining with that gear.

And, of course, the market declined dramatically starting in late December 2017, and still, at the time of writing, has not fully recovered. (It's still around three to four times its post-December 2017 low, though.)

While December 2017 would have appeared, to many outsiders, to be a great time to get into cryptocurrency mining, the conditions were actually quite poor, and hardware speculators were extracting as much out of the market as they possibly could.

Often, in the Bitcoin and cryptocurrency space as with many traditional markets, the best time to enter into the fray may be when the perceived outlook is the worst. During these market downturns, Bitcoin and other cryptocurrencies may trade at a reduced rate, and profitable mining hardware may hit second-hand marketplaces at steep discounts, (You may be able to acquire hardware directly from manufacturers during this time as well.)

Baron Rothschild, an 18th-century member of the infamous banking family, reportedly said that you should "Buy when there's blood in the streets, even if the blood is your own." What he meant is that it's a good time to buy when a market is crashing; you'll buy the assets cheaply, and they'll recover eventually.

The timing of your entrance into the cryptocurrency mining space may very well determine your success. However, you may not want to wait too long, as the old cryptocurrency adage goes: "The best time to mine (or buy) cryptocurrency was ten years ago, the second-best time is now."

Playing the Markets

Many cryptocurrency miners increase their profits by actively trading on exchanges, even buying on one exchange and selling on another, exploiting the differences in prices between exchanges in a form of arbitrage.

However, this subject is totally different from cryptocurrency mining, of course, requiring different skill sets, knowledge, and strategies.

In many cryptocurrency markets, trading provides needed liquidity, and traders help absorb some of the volatility. Keep in mind that tax liabilities are likely incurred from actively trading (see Chapter 13). However, a few smart trades a year can multiply profits significantly, and if you do have a tax liability, that may be a good thing. (It shows you have made gains on your trades!)

Once the conversion has been made from mined cryptocurrency to local fiat currency, the mining ROI calculations for those mined cryptocurrency rewards are locked in.

WARNING

While quickly trading for fiat-based returns is an effective strategy for some miners to boost their ROI, it isn't recommended for everyone. Tread and trade lightly. Obviously, we don't teach trading strategies in this book, so you have another learning journey in front of you before you can trade safely.

Identifying Low Hash Rate Alternative Cryptocurrencies

If your ROI and profit calculations for the cryptocurrency you are mining show that you're losing money, you have another option beyond mining through the downturn or shutting down your mining equipment and taking the loss on hardware investments. You can switch cryptocurrencies.

Miners often study the mining profitability on other cryptocurrency blockchains to see whether they'd fare better mining a less popular cryptocurrency. Just because your current cryptocurrency market is in trouble, it doesn't mean all cryptocurrency mining is unprofitable at the same time. You may be able to find a more profitable cryptocurrency. In fact, it's often possible to find a smaller cryptocurrency that offers a better ROI than the larger, better known cryptocurrencies.

TIP

These smaller cryptocurrencies generally have a lower price per coin on the exchanges, but price per coin is not an indication of profitability. What counts is how much equipment and electricity you need to use to mine each dollar's worth of the coin.

Smaller cryptocurrencies also have lower network hash rates, which means you can contribute a larger percentage of the hash rate and gain a larger percentage of the mining rewards. So, the coins you mine are worth less, but you will likely mine more of them.

So keep an eye on other cryptocurrency markets, in particular the ones that you *can* mine. That is, if you're mining with ASICs, you don't need to watch all the other markets, just the other cryptocurrencies that work with the algorithm your ASIC was designed to mine. (See Chapter 8 as a starting point; we group cryptocurrencies by algorithm there.)

If you're mining with a GPU rig, your choices are broader. You will have the flexibility to mine many different cryptocurrencies, using many different algorithms, on low hash rate cryptocurrencies. You'll want to watch what's going on with these other cryptocurrency markets, and of course, before you jump, you'll need to run the numbers and see whether they work for you (see Chapter 11).

WARNING

Be careful, however, as many small market value and hash rate cryptocurrencies do not have the type of blockchain security that other cryptocurrencies boast. Smaller cryptocurrencies also tend to lose value over time, and may experience significant price fluctuations, so you'll want to be quick on your feet. Get in when it makes sense, get out when things start to go badly.

Mining the Start of a Chain

Mining a brand new cryptocurrency can sometimes be very profitable (and, like everything in cryptocurrency, sometimes not).

When a new cryptocurrency is launched, there is often a short period of euphoria, during which all the promises and hype of the launchers serve to pump up interest in the new currency. Typically, despite their propagators' best efforts, the new currency does not last, or at least does not remain valuable. However, some of these new blockchains may have significant value for the first few days after launch, possibly even months, as originally the coins on these cryptocurrencies are inherently scarce (assuming there isn't a large pre-mine associated with it), and traders may value them at a premium.

TECHNICAL
STUFF

A *pre-mine* is what those in the cryptocurrency space call a cryptocurrency blockchain that was launched with coins already in existence from nonmining activities, typically though a crowd sale, initial coin offering (ICO), or other early adopter distribution method. *Pre-mined* cryptocurrencies have been criticized by the mining community as being unfair and unfriendly to miners.

Extreme early mining profitability has been the case for a few different coins in the past, including Zcash, Grin, and many others. You can see the example of Zcash in the CoinMarketCap chart shown in Figure 15-1. In the first few hours of the cryptocurrency's life, it reached more than $5,000; within a couple of days, it was worth a tenth of that value.

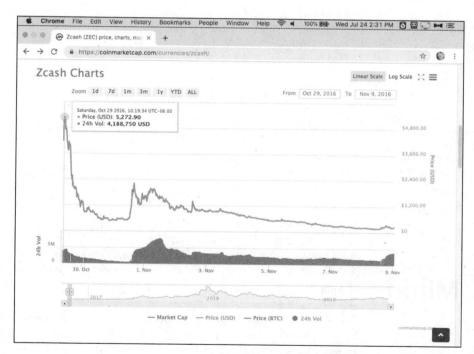

FIGURE 15-1:
This CoinMarketCap chart shows the first few days of Zcash trading.

Source: https://coinmarketcap.com/currencies/zcash

This kind of profile is very common. Here's a little experiment for you. Go to www.coinmarketcap.com and experiment with a few charts. Pick some of the smaller, less popular cryptocurrencies and look at their charts. Adjust the date range to the first week or two, or month or two perhaps, of the cryptocurrency's life, and you'll frequently see the same kind of profile. In Figure 15-2, for example, you can see the first two months of WAX's life. It started out around $4.60 to $5 a coin, but declined to around 50 cents within a couple of days.

Source: https://coinmarketcap.com/currencies/wax

FIGURE 15-2:
This CoinMarketCap chart shows the first two months of WAX trading.

Thus, mining a brand-new cryptocurrency can (sometimes) be very profitable if you're there right at the start. You can mine with GPUs, or even CPUs in some cases, as ASICs have not yet had the time to develop for their algorithm (unless, that is, the new cryptocurrency is using an existing, ASIC-developed, algorithm, of course).

Unfortunately for many newly created cryptocurrency systems, healthy network effects and other aspects of a successful cryptocurrency are difficult to create, so many tend to lose value against other assets and local fiat currency over longer periods of time, or even fairly quickly. (Refer to Figure 15-2; WAX started high, but dropped within a couple of days.) However, there may still be an opportunity in some of these systems for enterprising miners who may be able to direct their computational hash power toward the chain early and quickly exchange their rewards for other more proven systems as well as for local fiat currency. (You'll want to sell off your new coins within minutes or hours in some cases.)

Starting Small

REMEMBER

The best way to test out the waters in any business endeavor, and particularly in the cryptocurrency mining industry, is to start small. This is especially true for beginners new to the space; you have a lot to learn, so your first mine will be a big experiment.

Starting small also makes any losses less painful, of course. If you don't manage to create a profitable mine, your losses are limited. Starting small is a great way to build the skill sets and learn the lessons needed, discovering what works well and what may not. Once you have everything figured out, *then* you can scale up.

Scaling Choices

Rapidly expanding in the cryptocurrency space can lead to many unforeseen issues, such as increased burn rate and an evaporated runway. (Chapter 13 has more information on this.) However, you can scale your mining operation using other methods that may not involve getting large amounts of additional mining equipment online at your home, business, or other facility.

Some miners scale by replacing aging equipment, which in many cases, due to hardware efficiency gains, can result in significant increases in hash rate while maintaining similar, or even lower, energy expenditures, which would increase mining profits and possibly hasten ROI.

Other miners may choose to use hash-rate marketplaces to purchase mining capability from willing sellers. Another method to scale mining operations quickly is cloud mining where individuals can purchase large chunks of hash rate for their favorite cryptocurrency or algorithm from companies that specialize in managing mining equipment for miners.

Any of these options are decent choices for expansion, but some of them come with inherent third-party risk. See Chapter 9 for some pros and cons between the different mining deployment options. Do the profitability calculations we cover in Chapter 11 and know the risks of growing too quickly before diving into large new deployments of cryptocurrency mining equipment.

Finding Cheap Electricity

Inexpensive electricity is very important for cryptocurrency mining endeavors, as we mention in Chapter 11, because electricity is often the largest operational expenditure involved in cryptocurrency mining. Reduce your electricity cost, and you increase your profit, of course. Every dollar saved in electricity is a dollar that goes directly to your "bottom line."

Some mining equipment may be profitable running in one place, but not in another, simply due to the difference in electricity costs between both locations. Some areas of the world have significant seasonal fluctuations in electricity prices, so there are even examples of nomadic cryptocurrency miners who move their operations periodically to take advantage of inexpensive and excess energy. Migratory miners!

Many enterprising miners have increased ROI by accessing energy resources that would otherwise go unused, with very little to no cost associated with them, in order to save significantly on electrical costs. These miners have resorted to capturing natural gas prior to being flared, excess hydroelectric capacity, wind, solar, or even geothermal energy.

Since mining equipment typically runs 24/7, it has electrical load characteristics, such as a high load factor, which some electrical utilities will provide discounts for.

TECHNICAL STUFF

An electrical *load factor* is a measure of electrical utilization rate over a given period of time. The equation for load factor is (Average Monthly Load in kW)/(Peak monthly load in kW) and is normally provided in percentages.

For example, if an S9 was running all month and didn't shut off (as mining equipment typically does) and its peak load was 1.6kW, the load factor would be 100%: [(1.6 kW/1.6 kW) * 100%].

If you are running the equipment only half the time during the month, the load factor would be 50%: [(0.8 kW/1.6 kW) * 100%].

So it's worth talking to your utility about the best rates they can provide, to see what rates would be tailored to the type of load pattern (a load factor that is close to 100%) that is inherent to most mining operations.

In some cases, it may even make sense for a miner to run mining rigs only during low-cost electricity periods during the day. But run the numbers carefully. Obviously it means you'll mine less cryptocurrency, and you need to understand the effect on profitability when taking into account the capital costs of your equipment; run just half the day, and you're doubling the time it takes to pay for that equipment.

For example, one miner we know recently switched to a new, hybrid residential/industrial rate that his electric utility introduced, which provides rates similar to industrial rates, saving him 20 to 40 percent on his energy costs compared to average residential rates in his area. This plan is a ToD (Time of Day plan) that saves money for people with high load factors — people who are running at a pretty steady, high load throughout the month.

If you're like most electricity consumers, you have no idea you had choices, right? You simply pay the bill they send you each month. But spend a little time digging through your utility's rate structure and spend some time talking to them, and you may be surprised what you find.

This really is a huge issue, in particular for miners who get beyond the hobbyist stage. Large, professional mines are all about finding cheap energy!

Cooling Efficiently

Mining equipment creates a lot of heat. We discuss this topic in Chapter 12, but you can mitigate this heat exhaust, or even use it to your advantage, to increase overall ROI.

Some miners spend a lot of money running expensive air-conditioning systems to cool cryptocurrency mining hardware to datacenter temperature levels. However, cryptocurrency mining hardware is equipped with large heat sinks and powerful fans and is typically rated for higher temperatures than sensitive data servers (such as web servers) being held in datacenters. This is a little scary for people who are used to the idea that computer equipment has to be cooled significantly. However, some miners really do play this game, running their equipment at higher temperatures. Many miners in Texas (not the coolest place in the world!) do not use cooling equipment and don't mind the rigs' intake air being just regular ambient temperature, which means a high temperature in that state. Tyler has his mining rigs running in 50 to 70° F air during the winter, and 70 to 90°F in the summer.

In fact, ASIC chips are often rated to run at high temperatures. For example, Bitmain recommends that its ASICs run in an ambient air temperature of 15 to 35°C or 59 to 95°F. (The company also claims in their documentation that the chips themselves can operate at temperatures as high as 127°C . . . 271°F! Don't touch them!)

Miners may also avoid high cooling costs by operating in cooler climates and by circulating outside air through and out, bringing the temperature down to the outside ambient temperature. In cold climates, mining equipment may be used to heat rooms in homes or businesses. Mining equipment can even be spread around a home, comfortably heating multiple rooms rather than baking one single room. The drawback is that the gear is often very noisy. Even in a basement, you may be able to hear it upstairs. Some miners, however, have used liquid cooling and a heat exchanger to cool their equipment, which also quietens it.

Consider that if you heat your house with your mining equipment, you're reducing the cost of heating your house. You normally won't see this in your profitability calculations (see Chapter 11), though you may want to add your personal-heating savings to the profit to find your true profit.

But you would not want to include this number when calculating your taxes. In general, you can most likely count this reduction in personal expenses as a nice little bonus that the Internal Revenue Service doesn't need to know about. (Of course, we don't provide tax advice, so talk to your tax advisor!)

Some miners have even used immersion cooling for their hardware, using mineral oil or other engineered fluids as a dielectric insulator to protect equipment from electrical faults and to easily dissipate heat. Mineral oil conducts thermal energy well but doesn't conduct electricity, so electrical mining equipment can be submerged into it and operate fine without failure. Miners then cool this fluid with thermal exchangers to dissipate the excess heat from the dielectric fluid.

Whichever strategy you end up using for cooling your mining equipment, reducing cooling costs as much as possible is an effective way to boost ROI.

Scoring Hardware Deals

TIP

Mining equipment hardware will be your largest capital investment. Being able to recognize and take advantage of savings on the original acquisition of the mining equipment is a great way to reduce your initial cost and ensure a quick ROI on that investment.

So you need to be a good shopper. Search online marketplaces, such as Craigslist, eBay, Amazon, NewEgg, and others to keep an eye out for discounted cryptocurrency mining hardware. Before buying a particular piece of equipment, do a quick search engine query and see whether you can find it cheaper. Have a really good understanding of what different types of equipment can and should cost.

WARNING

Use the equations and online tools covered in Chapter 11 to find out whether that hardware is indeed profitable before buying, but be careful, as even these calculations can be misleading. Second-hand hardware may not be feasible to run in the long term due to market conditions changing, such as cryptocurrency exchange price, block difficulty, and increased network hash rate. Often deals that appear too good to be true may very well be; they may be great today, but have a short operational life.

If you're on the hunt for the latest and greatest hardware, be prepared to pay a premium for the most efficient and highest hash rate mining devices. Run the numbers, and you'll sometimes see that you're better off using less efficient equipment that costs you less.

Also, sometimes it is best to buy new pieces of mining gear straight from the manufacturer to avoid unnecessary middleman price markups. Tread lightly with mining hardware acquisition, as it is likely to be the most significant contributor to your initial investment and the choices you make early on in your mining endeavor will greatly affect your ROI going forward.

Chapter **16**

Ten Types of Cryptocurrency Resources

A ton of helpful resources are online for aspiring cryptocurrency miners or those interested in learning more on the topic. We have split them into ten different categories, from resources that can help you track the price of cryptocurrencies to cryptocurrency whitepapers. Reviewing these resources can keep you busy for many happy hours!

Cryptocurrency Market Trackers

Following are sites that provide aggregated exchange rates and market capitalization for cryptocurrencies, a few of the more reliable sources in the industry. Note that in some cases exchanges have fed bad data to the tracking sites, but in general the data is good:

- » **CoinCap:** https://coincap.io
- » **CoinLore:** www.coinlore.com
- » **CoinMarketCap:** https://coinmarketcap.com
- » **CryptoCompare:** www.cryptocompare.com
- » **Messari:** https://messari.io/screener
- » **WorldCoinIndex:** www.worldcoinindex.com

Mining Profitability Estimation Tools

We discussed how to calculate cryptocurrency mining profitability in Chapter 11, and we also cover how to use mining profitability tools found online. Use these tools often when considering which cryptocurrency to mine and when thinking about expanding. Here is a quick list of some popular profitability tools:

- » **Braiins.com:** https://insights.braiins.com
- » **CoinWarz:** www.coinwarz.com/mining/calculators
- » **WhatToMine:** https://whattomine.com/calculators

Cryptocurrency Reddit Pages

Reddit is among one of the top social media sites for cryptocurrency communities to discuss and debate the trending topics of the day. In this section, we give you a list of some of the top cryptocurrency Reddit pages.

If you need a different one, just add your cryptocurrency's name or symbol to the end of the URL; some cryptocurrency Reddit forums use the name, some the symbol — for example, www.reddit.com/r/XRP and www.reddit.com/r/zcash. Due to conflicts, some can use neither and have to come up with something else (TRON uses www.reddit.com/r/TRXTrading, for example), so you may have to search.

>> **r/bitcoin:** www.reddit.com/r/Bitcoin

>> **r/bitcoincash:** www.reddit.com/r/Bitcoincash

>> **r/dashpay:** www.reddit.com/r/dashpay

>> **r/dogecoin:** www.reddit.com/r/dogecoin

>> **r/ethereum:** www.reddit.com/r/ethereum

>> **r/litecoin:** www.reddit.com/r/litecoin

>> **r/zec:** www.reddit.com/r/zec

Blockchain Explorers

Blockchain explorers provide an easy way to audit blockchains directly from your web browser. They can search for blocks, transactions, hashes, and addresses. In this section, we offer a list of useful Bitcoin and Ethereum blockchain explorers. For other cryptocurrencies, try a search engine query. Many smaller cryptocurrencies are not popular enough to have explorers, but some do. We include a few explorers for small blockchains you've perhaps never heard of at the bottom of the list.

>> **Bitcoin blockchain explorers**

- **Blockchain.com:** www.blockchain.com/explorer

- **Blockchair:** https://blockchair.com

- **Blockcypher:** https://live.blockcypher.com/btc

- **Blockstream Explorer:** https://blockstream.info

- **CryptoID:** https://btc.cryptoid.info/btc

- **mempool.space:** https://mempool.space

- **OXT:** https://oxt.me
- **TradeBlock:** https://tradeblock.com/bitcoin

» **Ethereum blockchain explorers**

- **etherchain.org:** www.etherchain.org
- **Etherscan:** https://etherscan.io

» **Other blockchain explorers**

- **Lykke:** https://blockchainexplorer.lykke.com
- **SolarCoin:** https://chainz.cryptoid.info/slr

Data Visualizations

While blockchain explorers are good resources for finding textual and numerical data for your favorite blockchains, some creative individuals have taken this concept a step further. There are many visually appealing data visualizations for the Bitcoin and cryptocurrency space. Here are some of our favorites:

» **The Bitcoin Big Bang:** https://info.elliptic.co/hubfs/big-bang/bigbang-v1.html

» **Bitcoin Blockchain Matrix:** www.doc.ic.ac.uk/~dmcginn/adjmat.html

» **Realtime Bitcoin Globe:** https://blocks.wizb.it

» **Bitcoin network graphs:** https://bitcoin.sipa.be

» **Bitcoin Transaction Visualization:** http://bitcoin.interaqt.nl

» **bitcointicker:** https://bitcointicker.co/networkstats

» **Bitnodes:** https://bitnodes.io

» **COIN360:** https://coin360.com

» **mempool.space:** https://mempool.space

» **OXT Landscapes:** https://oxt.me/landscapes

» **Statoshi.info:** https://statoshi.info

Cryptocurrency Data and Statistics

Cryptocurrency data, comparisons, and statistics websites can be very useful, helping you to compare between cryptocurrencies. Here are several good cryptocurrency data aggregators:

- **Bitcoin Cash Metrics:** https://markets.bitcoin.com/crypto/BCH
- **Bitcoin Visuals:** https://bitcoinvisuals.com
- **Bitcoinity:** https://data.bitcoinity.org/markets/volume
- **BitInfoCharts:** https://bitinfocharts.com/cryptocurrency-charts.html
- **Coin Dance:** https://coin.dance
- **CoinDesk:** www.coindesk.com/data
- **Coin Metrics:** https://charts.coinmetrics.io/network-data
- **Crypto51 PoW 51% Attack Cost:** www.crypto51.app
- **How Many Confirmations:** https://howmanyconfs.com

Cryptocurrency Wikis

Wikipedia has pages for most of the top cryptocurrencies, but these pages are often fairly short descriptions and not a deep dive resource that can cover every aspect of a typical cryptocurrency. Not to worry — some cryptocurrencies have their own (or multiple!) Wiki-style directories that define many of the terms and aspects associated with that cryptocurrency.

Some of the following Wikis also cover other cryptocurrencies. For example, BitcoinWiki has information on not only Bitcoin, but many other cryptocurrencies, too.

- **Bitcoin Wiki:** https://en.bitcoin.it
- **BitcoinWiki:** https://en.bitcoinwiki.org
- **WikiCryptoCoins:** https://wikicryptocoins.com/currency/Main_Page

- **The Ethereum Wiki:** `www.indexuniverse.eu/the-ethereum-wiki`
- **Ethereum Wiki:** `https://eth.wiki`
- **GitHub Ethereum Wiki:** `https://github.com/ethereum/wiki/wiki`
- **Litecoin Wiki:** `https://litecoin.info`

Cryptocurrency White Papers

The Bitcoin and cryptocurrency explosion that has occurred over the past decade all started out with Satoshi Nakamoto's release of his idea to the *Cypherpunk Mailing List* (archives found at `https://mailing-list-archive.cryptoanarchy.wiki`), some code, and an accompanying whitepaper.

Since then, many (countless?) whitepapers have been released, describing a wide variety of cryptocurrency and blockchain systems. We have compiled a short list of links to read some of the most popular cryptocurrency whitepapers over the past decade. You can search for others, of course, but many cryptocurrencies were launched without whitepapers (Litecoin and Dogecoin, for example).

- **Bitcoin:** `https://bitcoin.org/bitcoin.pdf`
- **Ethereum Original:** `https://web.archive.org/web/20140111180823/http://ethereum.org/ethereum.html`
- **Ethereum Updated:** `https://github.com/ethereum/wiki/wiki/White-Paper`
- **Monero:** `www.getmonero.org/library/Zero-to-Monero-1-0-0.pdf`
- **Zerocash:** `http://zerocash-project.org/media/pdf/zerocash-extended-20140518.pdf`

The Satoshi Nakamoto Institute

This site contains the entire known writings of Satoshi Nakamoto (whoever he/she/they is/are!; see Chapter 1), along with numerous other documents that "serve to contextualize Bitcoin into the broader story of cryptography and freedom." It's required reading and a great way for Bitcoin and cryptocurrency enthusiasts to go down the rabbit hole: `https://nakamotoinstitute.org/literature`.

A Cypherpunk's Manifesto

A Cypherpunk's Manifesto, written by Eric Hughes, is a foundational document that many cryptographers and cryptocurrency users have read over the years. It's an interesting introduction to the politics behind the origins of cryptocurrency: www.activism.net/cypherpunk/manifesto.html.

Bitcoin Guides and Walkthroughs

After 13 years of Bitcoin, if anyone claims they completely understand Bitcoin, they're either fooling you or fooling themselves. Bitcoin is a nice, humbling lesson in lifelong learning. Even as we type these words, we know we can't cover everything about Bitcoin, and we've likely missed many important details, but the following resources should help. As the common Bitcoin saying goes, "Stay Humble, Stack Sats."

There are more education resources available now than there ever have been for Bitcoin. It is easier than ever to become a basic Bitcoiner. Here are some of our favorite repositories of resources and learning tools:

>> **Peter's own eight-hour video course, Crypto Clear: Bitcoin and Cryptocurrency Made Simple:** www.cryptoofcourse.com

>> **21 Lectures:** www.21lectures.com

>> **Bitcoin EDU:** www.bitcoinedu.com

>> **Bitcoin for Everybody:** https://learn.saylor.org/course/view.php?id=468

>> **Bitcoin is Hope:** www.hope.com

>> **Bitcoin Lessons:** www.bitcoinlessons.org

>> **The Bitcoin Standard:** https://saifedean.com/eco21

>> **Bitcoin Support:** www.bitcoinsupport.com

>> **BTC Sessions:** www.youtube.com/c/BTCSessions

>> **CaseBitcoin:** www.casebitcoin.com

>> **Jameson Lopp:** www.lopp.net

>> **Learn Me a Bitcoin:** https://learnmeabitcoin.com/talks

>> **Teach Bitcoin:** https://teachbitcoin.io

Chapter **17**

Ten Criticisms of Cryptocurrencies and Mining

M any criticisms and complaints have been leveled at cryptocurrencies and, in particular, the Proof of Work mining that often underpins them. Many of these criticisms are valid, but these topics have a ton of nuances that deserve thorough explanation, discussion, and debate. In this chapter, we explain some of the most common criticisms as well as some of the counter arguments associated with them.

Energy Consumption

There has been much ado about Bitcoin's and other cryptocurrencies' network energy consumption that occurs as a result of Proof of Work mining. As you learn in this book, it takes truly massive amounts of electrical energy to mine the Bitcoin blockchain.

It is true that Proof of Work mining consumes a very large amount of electricity. However, the exact amount is in dispute and, in fact, very difficult to calculate precisely. Many frequently cited estimates are based on a single-sourced energy estimation that performs an estimation based on how much energy network miners could *afford* to expend. In other words, it is an economic calculation with many assumptions involved, including market price, miners' electricity costs, and miners' electricity consumption.

This type of economic energy estimate ignores many on-chain statistics that can more accurately calculate network energy consumption with physics based on chain data, such as blocks mined per day, total network hash rate, and average mining equipment efficiency.

Luckily, today there are now many different estimations of the Bitcoin network's Proof of Work energy consumption, from a variety of reputable sources that have calculated energy consumption using more realistic physics-based calculations. Table 17-1 lists a variety of estimates of Bitcoin's mining instantaneous power consumption in Gigawatts (GW), and yearly energy equivalents (in Terawatt-hours/year — TWh/year).

You can see these various estimations in the chart shown in Figure 17-1. The chart shows the various energy estimations in TWh/Year on a timeline, along with the Bitcoin network hash rate (EH/s) from 2017 to 2019 (as hash rate goes up, power consumption rises, of course).

To put these consumption figures in perspective, the United States typically uses 6.63 TWh/Year to decorate and celebrate the holiday season with Christmas lights (and those typically are only on for around a month).

TABLE 17-1 ## Estimates of Bitcoin's Mining Power Consumption

Source	URL	Instantaneous Power Consumption	Yearly Energy Equivalents
Alex de Vries (July 2019)	https://digiconomist.net/bitcoin-energy-consumption	8.34 GW	73.12 TWh/year
Coin Center (May 2019)	www.coincenter.org/evaluating-estimates-of-bitcoin-electricity-use	5 GW	44 TWh/year
CoinShares (June 2019)	https://coinshares.com/research/bitcoin-mining-network-june-2019	4.7 GW	41.17 TWh/year
EPRI (April 2018)	www.epri.com/research/products/3002013910	2.05 GW	18 TWh/year
Hass McCook (August 2018)	www.academia.edu/37178295/The_Cost_and_Sustainability_of_Bitcoin_August_2018_	12.08 GW	105.82 TWh/year
IEA (July 2019)	www.iea.org/commentaries/bitcoin-energy-use-mined-the-gap	6.62 GW	58 TWh/year
Marc Bevand (January 2018)	http://blog.zorinaq.com/bitcoin-electricity-consumption	2.1 GW	18.39 TWh/year
University of Cambridge, Judge Business School (June 2019)	https://ccaf.io/cbeci/index	6.36 GW	58.97 TWh/year

FIGURE 17-1: The various Bitcoin yearly energy estimates measured in Terawatt-hours per year, along with the Bitcoin network hash rate measured in Exahashes per second.

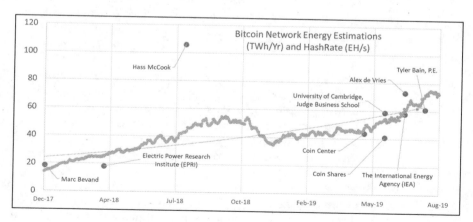

Perhaps a more appropriate comparison would be the amount of electrical energy annually dedicated to gold mining and recycling. Hass McCook, in the paper previously cited, estimates the amount of global energy used in this arena is the electrical equivalent of 196.03 TWh/Year, almost twice the energy (based on Haas' calculations) used by Bitcoin mining, even including the power used to create the mining equipment — considerably more if we take some of the other power estimates for Bitcoin. And, by the way, have you any idea of the huge environmental impact of gold mining? Do a search for *gold mining environmental impact* . . . the more environmentally minded among you might just give up gold jewelry! For example, gold mining creates huge amounts of toxic waste: 60 tons of toxic waste, including cyanide, arsenic, and mercury, for every ounce of gold mined by some measures!

Around 90 percent of the world's gold is used as an asset store of value and for jewelry, and much of the world's gold jewelry is itself regarded as a store of value, so the industrial uses of gold makes up a relatively small portion of its use. Thus, according to McCook's numbers, around 175 TWh/Year of energy is being used for these essentially nonproductive uses of gold. One might argue that shifting the investment role of gold over to Bitcoin (as some cryptocurrency proponents claim will happen eventually) may actually save energy! (And the environment.)

In a similar report from 2014, Hass McCook also estimates (see `www.coindesk.com/markets/2014/07/19/under-the-microscope-conclusions-on-the-costs-of-bitcoin`) the amount of yearly energy dedicated to paper currency printing and coin minting (11 TWh/Year) and the amount of yearly consumption of the banking system (650 TWh/Year). A new world of cryptocurrency (wait 25 years and see what happens!) may well reduce the amount of energy expended each year to manage the world's money supply. See Figure 17-2 for a graphical display of these various comparisons in estimated yearly electrical energy. The cryptocurrency mining yearly energy bar includes estimates of power consumed by the Bitcoin, Ethereum, Litecoin, DASH, and Zcash networks.

We also estimated the energy consumption levels for other popular Proof of Work cryptocurrencies, by comparing the network hash rates with the efficiency of the network's ASIC miners based on manufacturer-provided data. These include Bitcoin, Ethereum, DASH, Litecoin, and Zcash. Figure 17-3 shows the comparisons. Data includes instantaneous electrical power consumption, measured in Gigawatts, as well as yearly energy values, measured in Terawatt-hours per year.

While the levels of energy consumption for global Bitcoin mining may sound obscenely large, they only total around 0.2 percent of global electricity usage, and a few of the preceding studies also estimate that 60 to 75 percent of the electricity sourced for Bitcoin and cryptocurrency mining is from renewable resources.

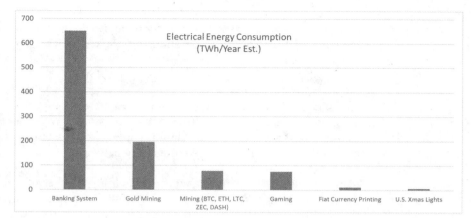

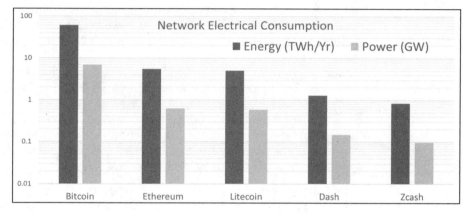

Wasted Processing

Another criticism often leveled is that Bitcoin or cryptocurrency mining is a waste of processing resources that could be better used elsewhere. This criticism has some validity. Vast amounts of processing power are being used to mine cryptocurrency rather than cure cancer or malaria or solve critical physics problems that could lead to new materials or energy supplies.

Of course, it all depends on what an individual considers waste. The definition of both waste and value lie in the eyes of the beholder.

Waste is typically defined as careless usage toward no purpose. Certainly, cryptocurrency mining *does* in fact have a purpose: to secure the various peer-to-peer blockchain networks against would-be attackers by making it too computationally expensive to manipulate the network. The Proof of Work mechanism rests in game theoretical mechanisms and economic theory that make it more rewarding for an attacker to work in cooperation with the network than to use their computational resources against it.

However, it still seems wasteful that as soon as a block has been added to the blockchain, the value of the computations that went into mining the block has gone, and no further value is provided (and remember, we're not talking about the computations provided by the winning miner; we have to count the vast amount of computing power provided by the entire network).

Many people cringe at the thought of this immense waste, and so, perhaps not surprisingly, there are examples of Proof of Work cryptocurrencies that have tried to solve the wasted-processing-power problem. After all, Proof of Work depends on a mathematical game. What if that game could, at the same time as it secures the blockchain, provide humanity with an additional benefit, the icing on the cake as it were? Here are a few examples of cryptocurrencies that have attempted to point their Proof of Work mechanisms toward philanthropic causes:

>> **Primecoin** (http://primecoin.io) is a cryptocurrency system that rewards miners for finding prime numbers. A *prime number* is a whole number that can only be divided evenly by itself or 1. Prime numbers have been a subject of mathematical study since the time of the ancient Greeks and are very valuable to mathematicians for, um, whatever they do with prime numbers. (Okay, a real example is encryption, which uses prime numbers; apparently, it's useful to have a library of these things. Quantum physicists like them, too.)

>> **Foldingcoin** (https://foldingcoin.net) is cryptocurrency that rewards miners for folding proteins based on the Stanford Folding@home distributed-computing project. Protein folding helps search for protein compounds that can help cure cancer, Alzheimers, and other diseases.

>> **Curecoin** (https://curecoin.net) is another cryptocurrency rewarding miners for folding proteins based on the Stanford Folding@home project.

>> **Gridcoin** (https://gridcoin.us) is another coin based on a different distributed computing project, but this time using the BOINC (no, it's not a joke) distributed-computing project. BOINC uses spare computing resources (and, through Gridcoin, computing power being employed for mining) to help with a variety of science-research projects that investigate diseases, study global warming, discover pulsars, and do many other things.

Unfortunately, these cryptocurrencies are all pretty small, with a total combined market capitalization of around $7 million, a drop in the bucket compared to Bitcoin's current $177 *billion*. But, there could be a day when the world's cryptocurrencies are mined using algorithms that both protect the blockchains *and* do additional good. As Sunny King, founder of Primecoin, puts it, "I would expect Proof of Work in cryptocurrency to gradually transition toward energy-multiuse, that is, providing both security and scientific computing values." On the other hand, the argument against this is that the Proof of Work algorithms of the major cryptocurrencies are pretty simple. Introducing more complicated algorithms may also introduce vulnerabilities and create more potential for attack.

One more thing: How much computing power do you suppose the world's gamers use? That's hard to accurately compute, but someone *has* tried to compute the energy use, and as a lot of mining is using similar equipment (GPU cards were designed for gaming!), the comparison is probably similar (that is, the relationship between energy consumption and computing power is similar, although gamers also have to power their displays). This guy, Evan Mills of the Lawrence Berkeley National Laboratory, and a member of the Intergovernmental Panel on Climate Change, came up with 75 TWh/Year.

Scalability, Transaction Speed, and Throughput

Bitcoin and other cryptocurrencies have often been criticized for having low transaction speed and throughput. This criticism is valid, as current on-chain transactions per second average between 2 and 8. The theoretical maximum for on-chain transactions on the Bitcoin network stands at around 14 transactions per second, which would equate to roughly 1.2 million transactions per day.

To put this amount in perspective, think about the credit card networks. Visa processes around 150 million transactions per day, a little more than 1,700 a second. That's an average, of course, so they must be able to handle plenty more than that during peak hours, and they claim to be able to handle 24,000 a second, though it's unclear if that is true. Regardless, these numbers are vastly higher than Bitcoin's capabilities.

Credit card systems are widely misunderstood; they appear instantaneous to the user — they seem to take just seconds to process while you're in the grocery checkout line — but in fact they actually take considerably longer. Take a look at your credit card statement, and you will find transactions taking a day, sometimes two — sometimes even longer — to post to your account. Then, of course, the transactions can be challenged, and sometimes reversed, often weeks later.

Your credit card transactions go through multiple steps, in fact, and this system is very complicated with multiple parties involved. A transaction begins with a payment processor, such as First Data (America's largest processor for brick-and-mortar stores), or an ecommerce payment processor, such as Stripe or PayPal; it gets passed to the credit card company's own network — VisaNet, for example, or, for MasterCard, BankNet — but it ultimately ends up at a bank, which handles the final clearance, running it through the SWIFT network (the Society for Worldwide Interbank Financial Telecommunication). The process frequently takes a day, but it can take as long as four business days to complete a credit card transaction, and in some cases, the transaction can be disputed for up to three months later.

These types of credit card charge backs and disputes are one reason some credit card companies do not allow Bitcoin or cryptocurrency payments via their credit card infrastructure, because credit card transactions can be disputed, reversed, and refunded while Bitcoin transactions cannot.

How about Bitcoin and other cryptocurrency transactions? As far as Bitcoin goes, a transaction is considered to be settled and essentially irreversible in a matter of six blocks, or so (roughly an hour). This may seem slow until you compare it to the one to three days for credit card transactions. We think Satoshi Nakamoto put this settlement time in perspective: "Paper cheques can bounce up to a week or two later. Credit card transactions can be contested up to 60 to 180 days later. Bitcoin transactions can be sufficiently irreversible in an hour or two." (For a comparison of relative blockchain transaction security and finality times for other cryptocurrencies, view the real time statistics on https://howmanyconfs.com.)

The on-chain transaction count for Bitcoin and other cryptocurrencies is somewhat skewed, however, as many transactions can occur off-chain. These off-chain transactions can occur via exchanges, custodial wallets, or more distributed second layer solutions, such as the Lightning Network. This protocol is built on top of the Bitcoin blockchain that uses Hash Time Locked Contracts (HTLCs) that allows for more transactions per second and quicker transaction finality. A single on-chain Bitcoin transaction can contain thousands (or more) lightning network transactions. (For more information on this complicated subject, check out the lightning network whitepaper at https://lightning.network/lightning-network-paper.pdf and the lightning network Bitcoin wiki at https://en.bitcoin.it/wiki/Lightning_Network.)

Another way that transaction speed can be higher than the simple Bitcoin transaction count is through the use of batched transactions. A pool or exchange can batch a single on-chain transaction that includes up to 100 to 250 output addresses, essentially increasing the transaction throughput while the blockchain counts only a single transaction.

However, the underlying criticism still remains: There is an on-chain throughput bottleneck, but this blockchain space scarcity is also critical to the network's decentralization. Each on-chain transaction is verified, validated, and stored on the entire peer-to-peer system of nodes, and efficient utilization of this scarce space and shared resource is critical to maintaining the distributed nature of cryptocurrency systems such as Bitcoin.

Coin Distribution Fairness

Cryptocurrencies such as Bitcoin are often criticized for unfair coin distribution. This criticism stems from the front-loaded block subsidy rewards. The Bitcoin network subsidy rewards programmatically decline over time, as shown in Chapter 8. As seen in Chapter 8, rewards are greater for early miners and steadily decline over time (the Bitcoin subsidy halves roughly every 4 years or 210,000 blocks). Many cryptocurrencies mimic this same type of distribution.

However, Proof of Work coin distribution is much fairer than Proof-of-Stake (POS) systems that reward large stake holders and also more fair than initial coin offerings (ICOs) that often steal investor funds with no measurable return. Cryptocurrencies that have significant *premines* rewarding early investors, or even our current paradigm of the fiat-based currency distribution system, in which certain large financial institutions control the flow of money through the economy, taking large bites out of it as it passes through their hands, are much less fair.

Market Bubbles and Volatility

Another common criticism of cryptocurrencies is that it's nothing more than an investment bubble. Skeptics often compare cryptocurrencies to other famous investment bubbles, such as the Dutch Tulipmania in the early 17th century, the South Sea Company (early 18th century), and the Internet, or Dotcom, bubble (from 1994 to 2000).

Peter has an interest in financial bubbles, having lived through and intimately experienced the Dotcom bubble. The summer before it began, 1993, he was writing the *Complete Idiot's Guide to the Internet* (he dates the start of the bubble to the dramatic growth in press coverage, and the millions of Americans jumping online, in the summer of 1994). By the time the bubble burst (the late summer and fall of 2000) he was running a VC-funded dotcom. Early in 2000, he read *The Internet Bubble* (Harperbusiness), a book predicting the coming crash, and circulated it among his dotcom's executive staff.

The authors of this book, Anthony Perkins and Michael Perkins, editors at Red Herring (a dotcom-business print magazine that ironically did not long survive the bubble bursting!), proposed that financial bubbles typically last six to seven years. The South Sea Company's stock price crashed about nine years after the company was founded (though it's hard to say exactly when the bubble began, of course). The Dotcom bubble burst six years after the Internet craze began.

Are cryptocurrencies, and Bitcoin in particular, in a "bubble"? That's hard to tell, but so far it's not looking that way. The Bitcoin software was first released in January 2009, so it's been around for more than 13 years now. (Of course, it doesn't mean the bubble itself began with the founding of Bitcoin; the Internet dates to the 1960s, but the Internet Bubble did not begin until the 1990s.)

It may be that because cryptocurrencies have relatively low market capitalizations compared to other traditional assets, such as gold or the U.S. dollar, they are subject to less liquidity, and thus more volatility. Any new asset, as it gains popularity and acceptance, has large fluctuations in market exchange rates. This is, in part, due to market price discovery and asymmetric information surrounding the cryptocurrency markets. Volatility and the perception of a bubble may not completely subside until Bitcoin and other cryptocurrencies gain relative market capitalization parity and exchange rate stability in comparison to other large capitalized assets.

For the moment, it looks very much like cryptocurrencies are not going away. In fact, more and more large companies, including financial powerhouses, are getting involved. There are good reasons why cryptocurrencies may be a technical advancement that can be beneficial and will stick around.

Also, consider this: While the South Sea Company crashed and eventually went out of business . . . while tulips in Holland eventually came down to a reasonable price and stayed there (though even today rare tulips command high market prices) . . . the Internet or Dotcom bubble destroyed thousands of companies, *but the Internet didn't go away!* The Internet is now thoroughly entrenched in modern life; it's inconceivable, barring global catastrophe, that it will go away. And many companies founded *before* the bubble burst are still with us. One of the very earliest, Amazon, is today one of the world's largest companies.

Centralization

Centralization of cryptocurrencies is often cited as a serious problem. Cryptocurrencies require decentralization to function safely and securely. Both mining and code development needs to be decentralized and distributed to ensure that no single party or group can dominate and manipulate the currency.

It's often claimed that mining is centralized in a few countries and dominated by a few pool entities, and even that the program code running the cryptocurrency networks is written and managed by relatively few people. This calls into question the distributed properties of these peer-to-peer cryptocurrency networks. While these criticisms are valid and worth intellectual pursuit, they are also somewhat misconstrued.

Bitcoin and most other cryptocurrencies are based on open-source software, to which anyone can review and contribute code improvements. While many code improvements can and do occur on these open, distributed cryptocurrency systems, and numerous individuals are involved in adding code changes, for those who would like to change the underlying principles and mechanisms of the Bitcoin code base for their own personal or business interests, we think Satoshi Nakamoto said it best: "The nature of Bitcoin is such that once version 0.1 was released, the core design was set in stone for the rest of its lifetime." In other words, the consensus rules are set from the start of the blockchain, from the genesis block. Change the consensus rules, and you become "out of consensus" with the rest of the chain and network; you "fork off" and become a different blockchain and network.

However, centralization is a real concern. These peer-to-peer systems were designed to center around CPU miners running their own fully validating node. However, since Bitcoin's inception, mining pools have been popularized, ASIC equipment has developed, and massive cryptocurrency mining farms have become commonplace. These developments have led to greater centralization of the ecosystem.

In Chapter 8, we discuss the decentralization scale, how centralization and decentralization are not simply two distinct things, but that systems can be centralized or decentralized to differing degrees. That applies here; Bitcoin and cryptocurrency mining centralization falls somewhere on that scale, at the time of writing arguably more toward the decentralized side of the scale. With proposed mining developments, such as BetterHash pool improvement and Stratum v2 (which are proposals to improve the integration mechanisms between pool users and pool operators), Bitcoin and other Proof of Work mined cryptocurrencies may move toward even greater decentralization.

Scams and Rip-offs

The cryptocurrency arena is rife with scams and rip-offs. Between hacked exchanges, nefarious mining equipment providers, and dishonest cloud mining companies, the history of Bitcoin is littered with many examples of companies and individuals taking advantage and scamming well-intentioned consumers out of their hard-earned value in Bitcoin, other cryptocurrencies, or local fiat currency.

There have also been countless scams involving initial coin offerings (ICOs) that have promised more than their propagators can deliver (or ever intended to deliver) and stole billions of dollars' worth of investors' money.

This is a serious problem for cryptocurrencies, as it helps to paint a picture of cryptocurrency as being dangerous and unreliable, and not something the average Joe would want to be involved with. This viewpoint, of course, retards growth in the cryptocurrency markets.

These criticisms are incredibly valid, and the only way to protect yourself from would-be bad actors, scams, and rip-offs in the Bitcoin and cryptocurrency space is to learn and understand what you are doing, do your research thoroughly, and as always don't trust, verify.

Hardware Price Inflation and Scarcity

Another issue with Bitcoin and cryptocurrency mining as of late is that hardware price inflation and scarcity has led to shortages for other uses of the equipment.

For example, as GPU mining was gaining popularity and profitability, demand for this form of computational hardware skyrocketed, prices soared, and availability dropped. This led to typical users of this type of computer equipment (predominantly PC gamers, as well as video producers and graphic designers) to have to pay higher prices for their equipment, if they could get it at all.

However, it can also be argued that the high demand for GPUs and ASICs led to innovation in the printed circuit board (PCB) arena, resulting in increased production, development, and manufacturing volume and the improvement of other chip applications, such as cells phones, laptops, and basically any other electronic devices that rely on PCB-based computer chips. The innovations that have been spearheaded by cryptocurrency mining ASICs have leaked into almost every other industrial computer-chip application.

Fire Hazards

There have been a few noteworthy examples of cryptocurrency hardware catching fire; it's not common, but it does sometimes happen. GPU rigs and ASICs run at very high temperatures, and if the equipment, which uses large amounts of electrical power, is not properly installed, configured, or maintained, it could very well be a fire risk.

For example, a fire in a cryptocurrency mine, operating out of an apartment in Vladivostok, Russia, destroyed eight apartments; 30 more were flooded when firefighters were dispatched to put out the blaze.

This just means you must do this right! You need a properly rated and installed power supply and electrical infrastructure; in fact, if electrical supply equipment is installed correctly by a qualified and certified electrician, this problem is almost nonexistent.

WARNING

Seek the advice of a local certified electrician in the installation of circuits or the inspection of existing wiring to be used for your cryptocurrency mining electrical equipment. Also, ensure fire alarms and proper fire extinguisher equipment is always nearby in the event of an electrical fault or an equipment fire. (Of course, this is good advice for *any* home or work location.)

Neighbor Complaints

Cryptocurrency mining equipment can be very loud, thanks to its high-frequency cooling fans. Neighbor complaints related to both small and large mining operations are common. (Go ahead, search your favorite search engine for *neighbors cryptocurrency mining noise,* and you'll find a bunch of headlines: "What's that noise? One of the world's largest Bitcoin facilities is too loud." "Bitcoin mining operator struggles to comply with city noise ordinance." "Buzz From Bitcoin Mining Upsets the Neighbors," and so on).

This criticism falls into the category of NIMBY (Not in My Back Yard). Not surprisingly, folks don't want their peace disturbed by what are essentially industrial processes near their homes. A few small towns have even lobbied their local governing boards to place a moratorium on cryptocurrency mining due to the noise and other concerns, such as power usage and local grid limitations, related to cryptocurrency mining.

What's the answer? For large facilities, probably the only reasonable answer is to locate far from homes! For small, home-based mining operations, it may be more difficult, especially if you are an apartment dweller. However, silencing mechanisms do exist for mining equipment, and some enterprising miners have deployed quiet installations (see Chapters 12 and 15).

Index

A

Accelerated Processing Unit (APU), *vs.* CPU cs. GPU *vs.* ASIC, 139

addresses
  for blockchain, 22–23, 26
  changing, 46–47
  for payouts, 114

Albanian Generals Problem. *See* Byzantine Generals Problem (Byzantine Fault)

algorithms
  cryptocurrencies and, 131–138
  mined without ASICs, 134–138
  requiring specialized ASICs, 133–134

Amazon, 251

AMD, 91, 189

American Red Cross (website), 256

Angry IP Scanner, 114, 181

antifragile, 144

anti-money laundering (AML), 25

Antminer Bitmain S9, 176, 222

Antonopolous, Aundreas, 61

AntPool (website), 104

Application Specific Integrated Circuits (ASICs)
  about, 36, 56, 101
  algorithms mined without, 134–138
  algorithms requiring specialized, 133–134
  vs. CPU *vs.* GPU *vs.* APU, 139
  dominance and efficiency of, 77–79
  manufacturer ratings, 206–207
  mining rigs, 175–183
  rig producers of, 164–165

applications, of Proof of Work (PoW) algorithms, 55–56

ASICs (Application Specific Integrated Circuits). *See* Application Specific Integrated Circuits (ASICs)

ASUS, 187–188

AT&T (website), 251

Auroracoin (AUR), 244–245

Australia, cryptocurrency in, 91

B

B250 Mining Expert, 187–188

bandwidth, 167

BCD, 138

Beenz, 10

BetterHash (website), 103

BFGMiner, 200

Big Three criteria, 102

bills, paying, 250–251

Binance Pool (website), 104

Bitcoin (BTC)
  about, 11–12
  block subsidy in, 31–32
  blockchain explorers, 305–306
  competing for, 48–50
  full node network (website), 43
  global legal status (website), 90
  mining pools for, 104
  network graphs (website), 306
  peer-to-peer protocol, 40
  presets, 51
  as a Proof of Work (PoW) cryptocurrency, 56
  resources for, 116
  software, 321
  website, 104
  white paper, 10–11, 308
  winning, 50–51

"Bitcoin: A Peer-to-Peer Electronic Cash System" (Nakamoto), 10–11

Bitcoin Blockchain Matrix (website), 306

Bitcoin Cash, 241–243

Bitcoin Cash Metrics (website), 307

Bitcoin Core (website), 41

Bitcoin EDU (website), 309

Bitcoin for Everybody (website), 309

Bitcoin is Hope (website), 309

Bitcoin Lessons (website), 309

Bitcoin Magazine, 235

Bitcoin Mining, 165

Bitcoin Mining Container, 165

Bitcoin subreddit, 235

About the Authors

Peter Kent: Peter has been explaining technology to ordinary people for decades, through his more than 60 books (including *SEO For Dummies* and *Complete Idiot's Guide to the Internet*), corporate consulting, online courses, seminars and workshops, and court testimony (as an expert witness in technology related litigation). He's the author of around 60 technology books, including *SEO For Dummies* (Wiley); *The Complete Idiot's Guide to the Internet* (Que); books on public key encryption and JavaScript; and books on e-commerce and web development. Since the '80s, Peter has been teaching and explaining technology to readers, consulting clients (including attorneys, judges, and juries — he serves as an expert witness in litigation related to Internet technology), and even the U.S. Congress (he worked with a research institute visiting legislative offices to help them understand the new world of cryptocurrency). He also created an eight-hour video course on working with cryptocurrency called *Crypto Clear: Blockchain and Cryptocurrency Made Simple* (see www.cryptoofcourse.com).

Tyler Bain: Tyler has been in the cryptocurrency mining trenches gaining experience in the ecosystem for several years. He's a professional engineer registered in the state of Colorado and studied engineering with an electrical specialty at the Colorado School of Mines in Golden, Colorado. He has consulted with cryptocurrency mining firms, currently works as an electrical engineer for a local utility cooperative, and is an avid cryptocurrency and Bitcoin miner. He is also an active member of the Institute of Electrical and Electronics Engineering and the Rocky Mountain Electrical League and has advised the Electric Power Research Institute. His passions include financial and transportation electrification, peer-to-peer systems, and the electrical grid.

Dedication

Peter: This one's for Monique; sorry the last dedication didn't come to pass!

Tyler: I would like to dedicate this book to Satoshi Nakamoto, without whom this book wouldn't exist, and also to the entire Bitcoin and cryptocurrency community: We are all Satoshi.

Author's Acknowledgments

Thanks to Steve Hayes at Wiley (for his patience!), Elizabeth Kuball (who cleaned up the manuscript and made it readable), and the rest of the Wiley team ("it takes a village" to produce a book!).

Publisher's Acknowledgments

Executive Editor: Steve Hayes
Project Editor: Elizabeth Kuball
Copy Editor: Elizabeth Kuball
Technical Editor: Mark Hemmings

Production Editor: Saikarthick Kumarasamy
Cover Photos: © Mark Agnor/Shutterstock